Love in the Drug War

Love in the Drug War

Selling Sex and Finding Jesus
on the Mexico-US Border

SARAH LUNA

University of Texas Press Austin

Chapter 2, "Rumors of Violence and Feelings of Vulnerability," was originally published as "Affective Atmospheres of Terror on the Mexico-U.S. Border: Rumors of Violence in Reynosa's Prostitution Zone" and is reproduced by permission of the American Anthropological Association from *Cultural Anthropology*, Volume 33, Issue 1, pp. 58–84, 2018. Not for sale or further reproduction.

♾ The paper used in this book meets the minimum requirements of
ANSI/NISO Z39.48-1992 (R1997) (Permanence of Paper).

Library of Congress Cataloging-in-Publication Data
Names: Luna, Sarah, author.
Title: Love in the drug war : selling sex and finding Jesus on the Mexico-US border / Sarah Luna.
Description: First edition. | Austin : University of Texas Press, 2020. | Includes bibliographical references and index.
Identifiers: LCCN 2019021669
    ISBN 978-1-4773-2049-5 (cloth)
    ISBN 978-1-4773-2050-1 (paperback)
    ISBN 978-1-4773-2051-8 (library e-book)
    ISBN 978-1-4773-2052-5 (non-library e-book)
Subjects: LCSH: Prostitution—Mexico—Reynosa (Tamaulipas) | Church work with prostitutes—Mexico—Reynosa (Tamaulipas) | Sex-oriented businesses—Mexico—Reynosa (Tamaulipas) | Religion and culture—Mexico—Reynosa (Tamaulipas) | Drug traffic—Social aspects—Mexico—Reynosa (Tamaulipas) | Reynosa (Tamaulipas, Mexico)—Social conditions.
Classification: LCC HQ151.R48 L85 2020 | DDC 306.740972/12—dc23
LC record available at https://lccn.loc.gov/2019021669

doi:10.7560/320495

Contents

Acknowledgments

Research and writing were supported by the National Science Foundation Graduate Research Fellowship; the Fulbright-Hays Doctoral Dissertation Abroad Fellowship; the University of Chicago Trustee's Fellowship; the University of Chicago Center for Latin American Studies Field Research Grant; the University of Chicago Lesbian and Gay Studies Project Graduate Research Grant; the Northeast Consortium Dissertation Year Visiting Diversity Fellowship in the Department of Anthropology at the University of Rochester; the James C. Hormel Dissertation Fellowship in Sexuality Studies at the University of Chicago; the Center for US-Mexican Studies Predoctoral Fellowship at the School of International Relations and Pacific Studies at the University of California, San Diego; a National Endowment for the Humanities seminar entitled "The Cross-Border Connection: Immigrants, Emigrants, and their Homelands"; the Women's, Gender and Sexuality Studies Program and the Friends of Women's Studies at the University of Houston; the Consortium for Faculty Diversity Fellowship in the Latin American Studies Program at Davidson College; the Five College Women's Studies Resarch Center Writing Retreat; and a Faculty Research Award at Tufts University.

I will not name any of you in order to protect your safety and privacy, but my deepest gratitude goes to the people in Reynosa who shared their lives with me. *Muchas gracias a toda la gente en Reynosa que participó en mi proyecto: mi familia reynosense y mi mejor amigo, un extraterrestre como yo. Gracias también a los archivistas, historiadores, y todos los que me ayudaran a hacer esta investigación. A las mujeres que conocí en la zona: muchísimas gracias por haber compartido parte de sus historias y parte de sus vidas conmigo. Ustedes son gran mujeres, de quien he aprendido mucho. En los momentos cuando me costó trabajo escribir, pensaba en la fuerza y la tenaci-*

dad de ustedes. I would also like to thank the missionaries, without whom I would have had much difficulty conducting my research in *la zona.* You have been nothing but kind and generous to me, and I am grateful not only for your help with this project but also for your friendships.

This book grew from a doctoral dissertation at the University of Chicago, where I was fortunate to have the intellectual engagement and fierce mentorship of Susan Gal, Julie Chu, Melissa W. Wright, Kesha Fikes, and Danilyn Rutherford. This work also benefited from engagement with John Kelly, Judy Farquar, Nancy Munn, Anne Chien, Carly Schuster, Laura-Zoë Humphreys, Abigail Rosenthal, Rocio Magaña, Jessica Cattelino, Molly Cunningham, Lisa Simeone, John Davey, George Paul Meiu, Mike Cepek, Gustavo Rivera, Jonathan Rosa, Mara Fortes, Sarah Tuohey, Gina Olson, Samantha Twigg Johnson, LaShandra Sullivan, Elayne Oliphant, Elise Kramer, J Baker, Jay Sosa, Malic White, Tal Liron, Bea Jauregui, Abigail Rosenthal, Lauren Berlant, Linda Zerilli, Kristen Schilt, Jennifer Cole, Monica Mercado, Larisa Reznik, Julia Kowalski, Tracey Rosen, and Michelle Lelièvre. Thank you especially to Hadas Weiss, whose feedback substantially helped the book during the last push.

When I was an undergraduate at the University of Texas at San Antonio, my professors there both inspired me to pursue graduate study in anthropology and provided me excellent mentorship through the process. Thank you especially to Ann Eisenberg, Laura Levi, James McDonald, Kolleen Guy, Kirsten Gardner, and Christine Caver.

Through predoctoral and postdoctoral fellowships as well as short teaching stints, I was fortunate for the mentorship, support, intellectual engagement, and friendship of a number of people. The faculty at the University of Rochester provided me with an excellent environment to write part of the dissertation that would become this book. Thank you to Robert Foster, Eleana Kim, John Osburg, Daniel Reichman Ayala Emmett, Thomas P. Gibson, Anthony T. Carter, and Rose Marie Ferreri. At the University of California, San Diego, my work was influenced by conversations and engagement with Alberto Diaz-Cayeros, Joseph Hankins, Maurice Magaña, Michael Lettieri, Danny Zborover, Kathy Kopinak, Suzanne Brenner, John Haviland, Karina Kordova, Jillian Hernandez, Nancy Postero, Veronica Pacheco, Rupert Stasch, and Greg Mallinger. At the University of Houston, I want to thank Elizabeth Gregory, Keith McNeal, Guillermo de los Reyes, Dina Alsowayel, Maria Gonzales, Trevor Boffone, Rachel Afi Quinn, Laura McGuire, Keith McNeal, Christina Sisk, Leandra Zarnow, Caryn Tamber-Rosenau, Natalie Harren, Beverly McPhail, Sylvia Mendoza, Ayanna Jolivet McCloud, and Kavita Singh. At Davidson College, I want to thank Melissa Gonzales, Matt Sampson, Devyn Spence Benson, Jane Mangan, Wendy Raymond, Katie Horowitz, Patrick Barron, Alison Bory, Sarah Waheed, Roman Utkin, Laura Sockol, and Patricio Boyer.

Thank you to my colleagues at Tufts University for providing an engaging and supportive environment in which to finish the book. Thank you to Sarah Pinto, Amahl Bishara, Alex Blanchette, Tatiana Chudakova, Zarin Machanda, Nick Seaver, Emilio Spadola, Cathy Stanton, Lynn Wiles, Jamie Gorman, Lauren Sullivan, Hilary Binda, Lilian Mengesha, Kamran Rastegar, Kris Manjapra, Joe Auner, Hilary Binda, and Kareem Khubchandandi.

I am grateful to my students at the University of Houston, Davidson College, and Tufts University who read drafts of this work.

Thank you also to Katie Anania, Tshepo Masango Chery, Charlotte Ashlock, Amanda Englert, Howard Campbell, Roger Waldinger, Maria Islas-Lopez, Susana Vargas Cervantes, Carolyn Chernoff, Emily Wentzell, Sergio Sanchez Diaz, Christopher Fraga, Anita Khashu, Rachel Carrales, Bob Lopez, Michael Schramm, Pascaline Mary, Jennifer Knowles, Chris Fitzgibbon, David Hardley, Michelle Hyun, Jeff Martinez, Emily Sarpa, Malic White, Torie McMillan, Ariel Mejia, Angela Campion, kate-hers RHEE, Laura Letinsky, Christian Larsen, Matthew Deggenaro, Heide Castañeda, Andres Montoya Montes, Lily Hoang, Jane Koh, Annie Lok, Lauren Klotzman, Matthew Swarts, Clemence Taillandier, Patricia Montoya, Allison Meyers, Juan Carlos Tello, Julia Barbosa Landois, Gregory Mitchell, David Valentine, Amy Sara Carroll, and Luis-Manuel Garia.

I am grateful to the anonymous readers from the University of Texas Press for the careful reading and constructive critique, as well as to my editor, Casey Kittrell, for all of his support in seeing this book to publication. Thank you to Laura Helper-Ferris for helping to bring this manuscript to its potential. I also want to extend gratitude to Cymene Howe and the *Cultural Anthropology* editorial collective as well as the anonymous reviewers for their work on what has become chapter 2 of this book.

My family has shown me love and support throughout this process. Special thanks go to my parents, Janie and David Luna, my grandmother, Shirley Luna, my little brother, Zachary Luna, and my Aunt Laura.

Thank you to my partner, Alexis Salas, who has been endlessly supportive for the thirteen years I have been working on this project, from graduate school coursework and fieldwork to dissertation to final book edits. This is the hardest thing I've ever done, and without you, it would have been more difficult and less joyful.

Introduction

I arrived to this city of Reynosa in February of 1974, and, like every woman who prostitutes herself, I came to earn more money.
LUCÍA, A FORMER SEX WORKER, IN A SHORT MEMOIR SHE WROTE FOR ME

Sometimes I foolishly think that I've sacrificed things to be here and live life with the men and women of BT [Boystown, the prostitution zone]. The real truth is I've gained more than I ever dreamed of by being here. I've never felt so invited into a genuine relationship with Jesus as I do here. It has nothing to do with Mexico or BT, and everything to do with finding the people that Jesus is with—the poor, the lonely, the forgotten, the hurting, the desperate . . . Be with them, and you'll find Jesus there.
STACY WHITE,[1] AN AMERICAN MISSIONARY, ON HER BLOG

La zona, which Americans called "Boystown," was a prostitution zone made up of several city blocks surrounded by cement walls in the city of Reynosa, in the state of Tamaulipas, on the Mexican side of the Mexico-US border. The entrance/exit was guarded by a police station that often, but not always, displayed the insignia of Reynosa's municipal government (figure 1). Seven Mexican border cities had established compound *zonas* on the outskirts of cities and enclosed them in walls to contain vice[2] and to separate prostitution zones from other tourist areas. Vice or *vicio* is a term linked to Catholic ideas about sinful habits. In Reynosa, it was most used commonly in reference to prostitution, drug use, and alcoholism. Most compound zonas formed in the 1950s and '60s when some border cities feared that prostitution in the city's center showed the "wrong image" to tourists (Curtis and Arreola 1991). Reynosa's zona was constructed in 1948 after the former zona, established in the city's center in 1925, was destroyed in a fire. Some residents of Reynosa believed that those who wanted la zona to be moved away from the city's center burned down the old prostitution zone. The city has since grown around la zona.

About three hundred people worked (and fewer lived) in la zona, including sex workers, strippers, bartenders, food vendors, security guards, pimps, and waiters. Boystown was officially regulated by the local government, which provided health officials and municipal police security guards. Sex workers had to pay out-of-pocket for their mandatory gynecological exams and testing for sexually transmitted infections. Only cis[3] women were allowed to work here.

Boystown was located in what was widely considered an impoverished, dangerous, and drug-saturated *colonia*, or neighborhood, called Aquiles Serdán. Residents considered Boystown, as well as the city of Reynosa, to be territory of the Gulf Cartel. Owners of buildings inside the enclosure were rumored to include both high-ranking narcos and other locals. Sex workers were required to pay a weekly sum to narcos, who used threats, bribes, and acts of violence to demand compliance from Reynosa residents. People in Reynosa from 2008 to 2009 tended to use the terms *la maña, los narcos, los mafiosos, los malos*, and *los mañosos* interchangeably to refer to people associated with drug trafficking organizations. The Gulf Cartel controlled the drug trade in Reynosa. The Gulf Cartel, one of Mexico's oldest drug organizations, began smuggling alcohol and other items into the United States during the Prohibition era (1920–1933). During the time of my research, the Gulf Cartel had an alliance with the Zetas, a paramilitary group originally composed of Mexican military deserters recruited to serve as a private army for the Gulf Cartel. However, in early 2010, the Zetas split from the Gulf Cartel and started battling for territory in Reynosa.[4] The *narcoeconomy* was so embedded in every other aspect of social and economic life that, as Muehlmann argues, it was impossible to distinguish the inside versus the outside of the industry (2013). Most people I met in Reynosa, whether they were teachers, dentists, graphic designers, or sex workers, had family members, friends, bosses, or clients who were narcos. Locals noted that drug organizations had long run their city, often in collusion with local law enforcement and politicians. But fear and violence spiked substantially after federal troops and federal police inundated their city to combat drug cartels.

Like many women there, Lucía cited money as the impetus for her sex work. In contrast, American missionary Stacy White specifically sought to live among and build relationships with poor Mexican sex workers like Lucía. Lucía's and Stacy's relationship was structured by inequalities between the United States and Mexico: while Lucía saw the zone as an escape from poverty, it was precisely living among the poor that made la zona attractive to Stacy. Lucía and Stacy developed meaningful and intense friendships with each other and with other sex workers in Reynosa's prostitution zone, and both claimed to have found Jesus there, in part mediated by their relationships with each other. Lucía's and Stacy's motivations for migration and settlement show how the Mexico-US border differently enables Americans and Mexicans to not only access economic value but also create other moral, social, and spiritual value(s).

Love in the Drug War follows the projects of these two kinds of migrants who came into a particular alliance in the city's prostitution zone. The book is based on twelve months of ethnographic fieldwork and archival research in Reynosa, Tamaulipas, where I conducted fifty-seven open-ended interviews with a variety of border city residents, primarily missionaries and sex workers. I socialized with them, observed their interactions, and took detailed field notes. I also conducted research at Reynosa's municipal archive and interviewed and socialized with men between the ages of sixty-five and ninety who were members of the "Historical Society of Reynosa" and the "Veteran's Club of Reynosa." I recorded their accounts of how Reynosa and its prostitution zone had changed. Additionally, I draw from blogs kept by missionaries and handwritten memoirs that two sex workers wrote in notebooks. The question propelling my research was how the difference created by the border shaped the projects, relationships, and subjectivities of two kinds of migrants and how that difference brought their projects in Boystown into a distinctive alliance. While the term "project" carries some weight of neoliberal corporate baggage, I use it to refer to the migrations of people which they usually undertake with particular goals, or at least with the sense that their actions would lead to a better life for themselves or others. The US-Mexico border is a site upon which migrants project their fantasies about better lives, a place that offers them the means to pursue intimate, economic, and moral projects. This book explores the relations of love and obligation that inspired people to journey to Reynosa, as well as the intimacies they forged there. It also examines the factors that ultimately caused most of these migrants to abandon their projects in Reynosa and return to their places of origin. Sex workers could barely earn a living because the economic crisis, the swine flu, and drug violence kept clients away. Furthermore, sex workers and missionaries were among many of Reynosa's residents who feared bodily harm and death as the Mexican and US "wars on drugs" led to increasing militarization and conflicts with drug organizations.

Love in the Drug War approaches the border as not merely a divider between two geopolitical territories but also a mediator of various relationships. The US-Mexico border itself is primarily imagined and written about as a space of violence and inequality. *Love in the Drug War* shows how people forge intimacies and love here. It is not that love is other to violence, coercion, and inequality. On the contrary, these uglier dynamics are very often part of love relationships. While many of the relationships I write about were structured by deep inequalities, I highlight their interdependencies by viewing both sex workers and missionaries through the same lens: love and obligation. Both mission work and sex work are forms of labor that people tend not to recognize as work: mission work might be construed as purely virtuous and sex work purely vice. Seemingly opposed, I reveal alliances and similarities in these projects.

Thirty-three-year-old Stacy was always cracking clever jokes in a Southern accent that came from living most of her life in South Carolina and Oklahoma. She was the daughter of a former pastor and a bubbly Mary Kay saleswoman. Stacy was a high school cheerleader and had spent her adult life working for short-term mission teams and at coffee shops. About five feet tall, she had brown hair and eyes and a nose ring. She often wore flared jeans, flip-flops, and button-down shirts. In 2004, after making a short trip to Reynosa, as Stacy tells it, Jesus told her to move there "to love the women and men of Boystown." After selling whatever didn't fit in her truck, Stacy left Tulsa for Reynosa, ready to spend the rest of her life there. For the first fifteen months, the security guards would not let her inside la zona, perhaps because she spoke little Spanish at first and looked like neither a sex worker nor a client. Saddened that she did not yet know the names or stories of the people inside, Stacy spent her first fifteen months "prayer walking,"[5] or walking while praying, around la zona's periphery.

One day while prayer walking around Boystown, Stacy met Kilo, a drug dealer in charge of a block in la zona and pimp to twelve women inside. Kilo later died in what was rumored to be a motorcycle accident, but was perhaps a murder. Following Kilo's death, the collective mourning within Boystown enabled Stacy to develop rapport and relationships with many who lived and worked there. Because people in Boystown knew that Stacy and Kilo had become close before his death, they inquired about her conversations with him. The security guards, who previously turned Stacy away, started to welcome her. She spent six years praying for la zona's women, as well as chatting, watching *telenovelas*, and sharing meals with them. She also took short-term teams of missionaries into Boystown to give baked goods and manicures to sex workers as well as to clean rooms, sing songs, and plant gardens for them. These short-term teams also constructed a house two blocks away from la zona that she hoped would become a "modern-day monastery," providing temporary housing and skill training for sex workers who wanted to leave la zona as well as child care for those who continued to work there. Stacy also planned to live there. During my year of fieldwork, Stacy's "Team Boystown,"[6] as she called it, grew from one to four members, and they almost finished building the monastery.

The first day I entered la zona with Stacy, we were not able to find Lucía, Stacy's "Mexican mother," a kinship relation that Lucía had initiated. Every Sunday, as long as Lucía was not drunk, Stacy gave her a ride to visit her seven-year-old granddaughter, Luz. Lucía had told Stacy, "If you want to make sure I'm not drunk, you should probably come to pick me up before noon." On this Boystown morning, we did not find Lucía, and several of her friends told us that she was in a drug rehabilitation center. The day I finally met her, she wore a blue top, a gold-colored necklace, a flowery skirt, and socks beneath tattered dress shoes. Lucía was known for her quick wit, her habit of asking for money, and her gorgeous handwritten poems. Lucía often wrote poems for missionaries and for me that called us *hijas* (daughters) or *hermanas* (sisters, perhaps in Christ), addressed how much she cared about us and wished the best for us, and included biblical references and scriptures. A former sex worker, she was missing several teeth, had lost an eye to domestic violence, and had a weathered face that made her appear much older than her fifty-seven years. Lucía wore a makeshift patch of folded paper towel that she stuck in her glasses over her missing eye. She held a shiny purse given to her by another sex worker. Laughing, she exclaimed, "I may have no money, but I have a purse!" A few months later, I conducted my first formal interview with Lucía at a McDonald's in Reynosa, a spot chosen by her granddaughter. Because she had quit using crack cocaine and drinking *huachi*, an inexpensive malt liquor, Lucía was eager to give me her *testimonio*, or testimony, which is a genre of telling one's life story, often a story of redemption, that culminates in finding God. Such *testimonios* were often given before a religious audience or to evangelize others. Lucía told her tale as she had many times before on the public radio and in church services.

Lucía had lived in la zona for thirty-four years; she was the first of three generations of women in her family to live most of her life there. Although she started working in la zona in the mid 1970s to support her family, she soon started spending all of her money on drugs. Her youngest daughter, Ana, who lived with her, also became addicted to crack cocaine. Lucía's trip to rehab included what she later recounted as a miracle: after she was not able to walk for seven days, God healed her, and he also granted her the strength to avoid crack cocaine and alcohol. At the time this book was being written, she was still not using drugs. Lucía attributed this miracle, in part, to her "daughter" Stacy.

Lucía, Stacy, and other sex workers and missionaries who met in la zona had complex obligations to each other and to the people and deities who had inspired their migrations. These obligations were gendered; they were infused with expectations about what a good woman should be. Lucía and Stacy had intense disagreements and misunderstandings and sometimes upset each other. They also expressed love for one another, and each claimed that the other had brought her closer to God. Lucía received gifts, favors, and monetary help from and through Stacy. Stacy received the story of a miracle—Lucía's story of redemption—that she repeated to her contacts transnationally. Lucía's story helped Stacy, as well as Christians throughout the English-speaking world, to feel closer to God. Sex worker narratives of redemption also were part of the information that individuals and churches considered when deciding to support Stacy's project in Reynosa with prayer, labor, or money. The inequalities of the Mexico-US border structured their relationship.

Reynosa as a Mexican Border City

The self-proclaimed dyke Chicana feminist writer and poet Gloria Anzaldúa has said that the US-Mexico border is an open wound (*una herida abierta*) "where the Third World grates against the First and bleeds" (Anzaldúa 1987, 3). Through a mixture of poetry, prose, autobiography, and theory that code-switches between English and Spanish and draws upon indigenous concepts, Anzaldúa eloquently describes the violence enacted upon Mexicans and indigenous people by the United States. She describes the borderlands as a space of violence and inequality that enables the policing of racial, sexual, and linguistic minorities. But she also views the borderlands as a space of contradictions that forces people to simultaneously hold conflicting worldviews which can lead to new forms of consciousness and connection.

While this ethnography centers love, the violence of the borderlands is its backdrop. An important body of research has ethnographically examined the violence and inequalities of the borderlands, with a focus upon the militarization of the US side of the border, the deaths of migrants crossing the desert (De León 2015; Magaña 2011), the impacts of neoliberalism (Wright 2006), and the war on drugs (Campbell 2009; Muehlmann 2013). Efforts to "control" the border and keep people from crossing—such as Operations Gatekeeper, Hold the Line, and Safeguard, in heavily trafficked areas like

San Diego, El Paso, and Nogales, respectively—have only diverted human traffic to much more dangerous, and sometimes deadly, crossing areas.[7] Jason De León has argued that these policies have used the desert as a weapon to kill migrants in order to deter others from crossing (2015).

The geographical space of the border, with its militaristic, capital-producing institutions on both sides (including maquiladoras, drug organizations, and prostitution zones), is a material manifestation of relationships between local, national, and international discourses and interests. Border industries and unregulated US capital shape the landscape, economies, and social spaces of Mexican border cities like Reynosa as well as the embodied and commodified relations across the border that constitute the focus of this book. US demand for sex, drugs, and inexpensive labor has respectively fueled the prostitution, drug trafficking, and maquiladora industries. This demand has propelled Mexican migration, both *through* border cities to work in the United States and *to* border cities to work in factories. Money, goods, and bodies flow across the border in both directions, but these flows are blocked and channeled in ways that perpetuate inequalities.

Evidence of the US-Mexico relationship was everywhere in the Reynosa landscape. Mexican military vehicles full of armed men greeted border crossers into Reynosa from Hidalgo, Texas, with automatic weapons. Dentist offices catered to both locals and American tourists, as did *casas de cambio* (currency exchanges), where one could buy or sell dollars or pesos. Most bars, restaurants, and stores accepted both currencies. Scattered across the city, one could find the glowing neon signs of Carl's Jr., Subway, McDonald's, and the Texas-based grocery chain HEB. Ten industrial parks housed more than two hundred maquiladoras, or export-processing factories that manufactured products for foreign companies like General Electric and Maytag. Reynosa's streets were full of license plates from Texas and Tamaulipas. It was not uncommon to find oneself at a stoplight alongside a brand-new Cadillac Escalade (often owned by a high-ranking narco), a new, white pickup of the municipal police (without license plates, rumored to be a gift from a drug cartel), or a makeshift garbage truck (sometimes made of recycled pickup truck beds) pulled by horses or donkeys.

In 2008, when I conducted fieldwork, Reynosa was quickly growing; the census counted 576,173 inhabitants (López Díaz 2008), yet unofficial estimates calculated over one million. Two years prior, it was one of Mexico's fastest-growing cities. For roughly a million Mexicans working in the maquiladora industry, Mexican border cities served as a source of employment (Whittaker 2006; Manuel Meza 2008). Reynosa's economy, once dependent upon cattle work and the oil industry, had shifted to the drug, service, and export-processing economies. In Reynosa, maquiladora workers could earn six to eight US dollars per day. This was slightly higher than the Mexican national minimum wage, which was less than US$5 per day ("Publica Diario" 2007). Furthermore, hundreds of thousands of Mexicans tried to cross the border each year with the hope of earning substantially more than they could in Mexico.

The impetus for this migration can be explained in part by inequalities in Mexico. In 2008, 47.4 percent of the Mexican population lived in poverty ("En la pobreza" 2009), 75.9 percent of the indigenous population lived in poverty (Taniguchi 2011), and the top 10 percent earned twenty-six times more than the bottom 10 percent (Villagran 2011). These inequalities have been intensified by neoliberal policies. Neoliberalism has been called a "new, more aggressive stage of capitalism" (Kelly 2008, 3). Mexico was one of seventy poor countries that were pressured into enacting neoliberal policies.[8] Such pressures followed a long history of asymmetries in the Mexico-US relationship after Mexico gained independence from Spain in 1821 (Erfani 1995) and including those stemming from the 1994 North American Free Trade Agreement (NAFTA). The maquiladora industry, established in the 1960s as the Bracero Program (1947–1964) came to a close, grew considerably after the implementation of NAFTA.

Neoliberal policies in Mexico, as in many parts of the world, have widened the wealth gap and reduced social welfare services. NAFTA flooded Mexico with cheap corn, milk, and other items from the United States. The "agrarian reforms" during the administration of Carlos Salinas de Gortari (1988–1994) led the way toward privatizing communal land, devastating farmers of small and medium-size farms (Broughton 2008; McDonald 1995). These policies increased poverty, unemployment, and underemployment, which left migration or working in the narcoeconomy among the few options available to young men in many parts of Mexico (McDonald 2005). More than half of Mexico's labor force worked in the informal economy (Anderson and Gerber 2008, 129), where they generally earned less, had shakier incomes, and lacked access to basic protections and services. Sex workers in Reynosa, before and after working in la zona, tended to work in other jobs in the informal economy. Many migrants to Reynosa, especially sex workers, said that where they came from, there was "a lot of work, but no money," which made the move to Reynosa appealing.[9]

These factors all contributed to Reynosa becoming a gateway city for Mexicans and Central Americans migrating to the United States or just deported from there. It was a receiving city for internal migration. In 2000, roughly a third of Reynosa's population had migrated from other Mexican states, and the highest percentage had migrated from Veracruz (Ayuntamiento Reynosa 2005). Reynosa was also a point of transit where privileged border residents from both sides could cross freely. Those born in Reynosa considered themselves a minority, claiming that migrants from southern Mexican states and Central America had caused the city's crime and cultural deterioration.[10] Anthropologists have documented similar regional and class dynamics in Ciudad Juárez and Tijuana (Vila 2000; Yeh 2018). Reynosa locals often discussed the "hundreds of new neighborhoods" that had recently expanded the city to accommodate maquiladora workers and other internal migrants. Many garbage collectors, who were often from Veracruz, lived in Colonia 21 de Mayo, a neighborhood not far from Boystown where recent migrants squatted in lean-tos. Although people in Reynosa generally knew that the city was rapidly expanding through these neighborhoods, middle-class locals often distanced themselves from migrants and their poverty by mentioning that they had never set foot in these new *colonias*. While locals complained aloud about migrants, they whispered about narcos and rumors of violence.

My analysis adds to a growing body of literature that demonstrates how the militarization of both sides of the border has escalated wars on drugs, terrorism, and organized crime, rendering life more dangerous for both countries' most vulnerable populations (Campbell 2009; Luna 2018; McDonald 2005; Muehlmann 2013; Vite Pérez 2014). Mexican drug violence is a problem that US capital, citizens, and policies have helped to create. The border between Texas and Tamaulipas is marked by the northbound flow of migrants, cocaine, and marijuana and the southbound flow of firearms and US dollars. Furthermore, US state actions have enabled the ascendance of Mexican drug organizations through interventions into Colombian drug-supply routes, the funding of Mexico's drug war through the Mérida Initiative, and the implementation of prohibitionist and neoliberal policies (Andreas 1995, 1996; Campbell 2009; McDonald 2005; Muehlmann 2013).

Former president Felipe de Jesús Calderón Hinojosa (2006–2012), after a contested win in the December 2006 elections, made combating drugs and violence in the name of public safety the primary focus of his administration. Calderón's critics accused him of using the drug war to legitimize his unpopular presidency. During his six years as president, Calderón deployed 50,000 troops throughout Mexico, while the murder rate nearly tripled:[11] an estimated 45,000 to 55,000 people died of drug violence-related deaths and more than 20,000 people went missing (Molzahn, Rios, and Shirk 2013). Although Reynosa had never been peaceful, residents experienced heightened fear and bloodshed after soldiers and federal police flooded Reynosa's streets in December 2007. Tensions between drug organizations and armed men of the state increased in Reynosa, gun battles became more frequent, and people reported feeling increasingly vulnerable to violence.[12] The more generalized sense of crisis was intensified by the 2008 global economic crisis and the 2009 swine flu pandemic. This profoundly changed life in Reynosa for all residents, and fear of bodily harm made it harder for sex workers to earn a living, for missionaries to spend time with sex workers, and for all parties to fulfill their obligations to others.

The economic and semiotic power of the border informs the relationships people forge in the borderlands: what brings the most goods and people to the geographical space of the US-Mexico border is the way it creates the differences out of which people create value. My use of the term "value" is in line with how it has been employed by anthropologists who have sought to theorize how human action is deemed important in ways that include but exceed the economic (Foster 2008; Graeber 2001; Munn 1986).[13] In contrast to the ways in which abstract models represent economic actors, many people do not single-mindedly pursue self-interested, profit-maximizing individual goals (Mauss 1967; Malinowski 1962; Polanyi 1957; Sahlins 1974; Strathern 1988). Instead, they devote their time and attention to relationships, activities, and things that they find meaningful and that make life worth living to them. Anthropologists speak of value as a robust and multifaceted social totality whose inner gradations and differences are representations of what people find meaningful, while in turn inspiring the ideas and activating the actions that reproduce or alter these meanings (Foster 2008; Munn 1986; Graeber 2001). For the sex workers and missionaries I examine, value making is a dynamic, social, and intersubjective practice tied to their conceptions of what it means to be a good person, a good mother, a good woman, or a good Christian. Here, I trace the dynamics through which these people create value. I focus on this process as an expression of their ideas about justice and propriety, such as have been discussed in the rubric of moral economies (Thompson 1971; Scott 1976; Griffith 2009); and as a practice that emerges out of relationships of love and obligation, such as those identified in the circulation of gifts and commodities (Mauss 1967; Gregory 1982; Strathern 1988; Weiner 1992; Chu 2010). In particular, I show how missionaries' and sex workers' moral, spiritual, and economic obligations both issue from and propel their migration projects.

Money is one of a variety of material and immaterial things exchanged and circulated among sex workers and their family members, clients, and missionaries. Both sex workers and missionaries struggled with these forms of exchange—in their relationships with each other as well as with other people and deities. Received wisdom holds that sex and money—or other spheres such as intimate and economic or private and public—either are or ought to be separate.[14] And yet social scientists have made a strong case that intimate and economic realms are intertwined.[15] Ethnographers have challenged a sharp division between "prostitution" and "noneconomic" sexual or intimate relationships by highlighting the many different social forms that commodified intimacies can take (Agustín 2007; Brennan 2004; Cheng 2010; Cole 2004; Hunter 2002; Kulick 1998; Zelizer 1994). Recognizing that almost all intimate relationships have some economic elements, sociologist Viviana Zelizer argues that people not only find forms of payment to match their intimate relations but also carefully delineate boundaries between these different kinds of social relations and their corresponding monetary transactions (Zelizer 2000, 826).

Not only was money exchanged between missionaries, their Christian publics, and sex workers, but so were prayers, stories, rumors, and baked goods. These exchanges reflect human investments of time and attention, and they create value. I track the circulations of bodies and "their various extendable and convertible substances" (Chu 2010) in and out of the prostitution zone as well as in and out of relationships of moral obligation, in order to analyze the moral economies of sex workers and missionaries in Reynosa. These obligations are not always fulfilled in the ways that are expected or hoped, and debates about them are especially revealing when trying to understand these moral economies. Sex work requires the exchange of not only sex but also a great degree of emotional labor,[16] much like other forms of care work (Agustín 2007; Brennan 2004; Chapkis 1997; Ehrenreich and Hochschild 2003). The framework of emotional labor is also useful in thinking about the work done by missionaries, pimps, and drug trafficking organizations.

The difference signified by the border is a large part of what shapes this process of value creation. The US-Mexico border is a site where people use difference to create value—both economic and other kinds. As Josiah Heyman argues, border cities are nodes between different territories through which value steps up or down in the world system (Heyman 2004, 305). In the border region, mobile capital "steps down" for low-cost labor and resources in Mexico, and "steps up" to sell products to consumers in the United States for higher prices. Heyman explains that the differential regulation of mobility allows for an easy circulation of consumers, tourists, and managers who can profit from these value changes. Mexicans, in turn, have a difficult time "stepping up" to get higher prices for their labor. People's abilities to make use of the value-producing capacities of the US-Mexico border are differentially blocked and enabled in Mexican border cities (Heyman 2004) in ways that asymmetrically distribute risks and rewards as well as security and insecurity among bodies and spaces. The difference between the legal statuses of prostitution between the two countries did more than just allow sex workers to earn money in a prostitution zone that historically catered to American clients. It also allowed American missionaries to build relationships with sex workers who gave them "different reflections of Jesus" that missionaries believed increased all parties' intimacy with God and expanded his influence. Migrants and border residents mobilized the meaningful difference created by the border through projects that create economic, moral, social, and spiritual value(s).

This book highlights relationships enabled by the US-Mexico border that largely go unseen. Most of the research on the US-Mexico borderlands has focused on El Paso/Juárez or San Diego/Tijuana. Furthermore, most scholarship about the migration between the United States and Mexico has focused primarily on migration from Mexico *into* the United States, while my study examines short- and long-term migration from the United States to Mexico along with internal migration in Mexico. Although the border is imagined to be a stable line or zone, it is more akin to an ever-shifting process. The appearance of stability is partly due to a number of institutions and actors that are sometimes competing and sometimes working together. The border is a culmination of the way people imagine it, the way people use it, and the material things that constitute it (which also must be imagined). I approach "the state" and "the border" as mutually constitutive and sharing similar traits, as they are ideological projects with material effects that both reflect and constitute the social world. The (social) space of the US-Mexico border is produced by ideologies as well as political and economic structures. In turn it produces social life, shaping subjectivities and relationships. Part of what makes up the border are these different ways in which the migration of people, the movement of goods, and attempts by state and nonstate actors to defend territory are drawn upon and manipulated to create value.

Both borders and love are usually thought about in dyads—relations between two countries or two people. The relations examined in this book are likewise often seen as binary: Americans and Mexicans; missionaries and the populations they seek to rescue; drug organizations and the populations they invoke fear in. Although I am, in part, writing against dichotomies, this book is inhabited by people who engage in dichotomous thinking. Many of the cultural categories used to interpret the world are perceived as dichotomies—or opposites—and as coconstituting—meaning that one cannot exist without the other. Often a hierarchy of value is created between the two—some examples are Male and Female, and Black and White. The characters in this book reproduce these categories at different levels—what Irvine and Gal (2000) call fractal distinctions. Irvine and Gal provide the example of an ideology that saw a European West opposed to an Oriental East. Along with these oppositions came qualities and attached values that were seen to be iconic—including a barbarism inherent in the East and a civility and technological advancement in the West. Fractal distinctions occur when, even within Europe, an East/West dichotomy is reproduced—the southeastern part of Europe was considered to be the least European and most backward part of Europe (Irvine and Gal 2000, 63), and by the early twentieth century the word "Balkan" became a pejorative word meaning "backward" (63). Some dichotomies, such as Good Mother/Bad Prostitute, US/Mexico, and Civilized/Savage, also operate fractally in Reynosa. Fractal distinctions are not carbon copies; they often come with changes of meaning at each level. Furthermore, they are not stable categories permanently laminated upon the identities of subjects. They are invoked in certain contexts, and they can change through time.

This borderlands ethnography pushes toward a queer reading of both borders and love by thinking in multiplicities and considering a wide range of border intimacies through the lenses of love and obligation. Overriding flat ideas of sex workers and missionaries—as "good" or "bad," "heroes" or "victims," "objects" or "agents"—I view relations in groups of three or more to develop my analysis of the intimacies of the borderlands. The border emerges as a character of sorts in the book, as it plays a mediating role in the relationships between humans (and sometimes with God). My analysis of the love triads between sex workers, missionaries, and God has led to applying this triadic approach to understand other border intimacies. Missionaries were invested in monogamy, while sex workers were both stigmatized by monogamous assumptions as well as in some ways seen as facilitating the possibility of marriages to be stable. I use a polyamorous concept of the triad—a relationship between three entities that all have relationships to each other—to interrogate the queerness of such relations. I show that missionaries envisioned queer futures with sex workers and sought to build relationships and cohabitate with sex workers rather than husbands in a triad between sex workers, missionaries, and God. I expand this triangulation to understand other border-mediated intimacies. I give a queer reading of the intimacies of sex work, drug work, and mission work, the whore stigma, and the politics of respectability in la zona. In addition to the triad of sex worker-missionary-God, I also draw attention to the triad between a wife, husband, and sex worker (chapter 1) and how the figure of the sex worker's child mediated the relationships between sex workers and other sex workers (chapters 3 and 4), sex workers and pimps (chapter 3), and sex workers and missionaries (chapters 5 and 6). I also examine the triangulation between elite Reynosa residents, US citizens, and internal migrants (chapter 1). I do not propose to replace a binary with a triad in any permanent way, but will use the triad as an intermediate exercise to reveal greater complexities.

Sex Workers, Missionaries, and God in Reynosa's Prostitution Zone

The five-minute drive to Reynosa's zona from the international border (figure 2) went through a few downtown blocks and then took a curved road, passing by a migrant shelter run by Catholic nuns. On many days, migrants stood outside, sometimes accompanied by donkeys. Approaching la zona, neon lights glowed "Welcome to Lipstick," inviting clients to the biggest and nicest strip club in Boystown (figure 3). After paying twenty pesos to an armed guard, patrons entered Boystown by car, on foot, or in a taxi. Bright yellow, pink, and sea-green paint adorned many of the rooms and buildings, some freshly painted and others showing the passage of time. One part of la zona resembled the ruins of an abandoned city, with the remains of night-clubs delineated by weed-choked walls crumbling above old mattresses where crack cocaine users sometimes slept. A couple of the higher-end strip clubs donned neon signs advertising their establishments, but most bars had signs hand-painted onto their facades.

Inside the walls were strip clubs, brothels, bars, and taco stands, as well as long, narrow structures composed of "accessory rooms"—small, adjacent street-facing rooms rented by sex workers to solicit and service clients (figure 4). Women who worked in accessory rooms made one hundred to three hundred pesos, roughly between US$8 and US$24, for fifteen to thirty minutes of work.[17] On a "bad day," one woman said, she could make at least four hundred to five hundred pesos. It would take a week to earn that much in a maquiladora. Most of the women I came to know in la zona worked in these rooms, and some lived in them. Wearing lingerie, schoolgirl outfits, or miniskirts, sex workers posed in their doorways to attract clients walking or driving by (figure 5). Some donned "stripper heels," others flip-flops. Some, like Sofía, preferred to work in the evening because they could make more money or evade the scorching summer sun. Others, like Rebecca, preferred daytime hours to avoid drunken and troublesome clients. Rent for an accessory room cost three hundred to five hundred pesos per week, and sex workers also had to pay a total of about two hundred pesos per week for health inspection, garbage service, and a protection fee to the drug cartel in power.

While most of the sex workers I spent time with worked in accessory rooms, this was only one of several types of sex work available in la zona. Women who worked in the major strip bars tended to come from urban areas (like Monterrey), had bodies sculpted in part by silicone, and charged much more for their services than those who worked in accessory rooms. Inside and outside of la zona, sex workers sometimes reached agreements with bar owners who allowed them to solicit potential clients in exchange for socializing with bar patrons and encouraging them to buy drinks for themselves and the women. Later, the woman could negotiate with the client and take him to a room, often in the back of the bar, for sexual services.

Most of the sex workers in Boystown were in their early twenties, although I was told that girls as young as thirteen or fourteen worked there. I spent most of my time with women who were between the ages of thirty and fifty-seven. Many were single mothers, and family members in other towns usually cared for their children. Although it was not necessary to have a pimp in Boystown, many women had been brought to Reynosa by pimps. Women with pimps tended to be in their early twenties, came from small towns in or near the state of Puebla, worked in accessory rooms, and lived in apartments outside of Boystown. Both the law and popular culture construct images of pimps as predatory men coercing, exploiting, and brutalizing victimized women. Those who participate in the moral panics about sex trafficking circulate racializing images of pimps and sex traffickers reminiscent of similar discourses during the "white slavery" panic of the nineteenth century (Agustín 2007; Bernstein 2010; Kempadoo et al. 2005). Sex worker activists as well as researchers have challenged these assumptions, showing the great diversity of relations among third parties and sex workers (Hannem and Bruckert 2017; Weitzer et al. 2014; NSWP Global Network of Sex Worker Projects 2016).[18]

Some of the crack-addicted sex workers in la zona lived and worked in accessory rooms, and others worked in bars; some worked independently, and others had pimps. But for all these differences, most of the crack-addicted sex workers' money went toward drugs. As the women with drug addictions grew older, they usually retired from sex work and ran errands for sex workers in order to pay for food, rent, and/or drugs. Women who had neither pimps nor drug addictions usually lived in accessory rooms and worked to send money to their families each week via Western Union. Yasmina Katsulis found in her research among sex workers in Tijuana that while most of them worked for what she called "milk money" (basic provisions for themselves and their children), a smaller number worked for drugs or socioeconomic mobility (Katsulis 2009).

While Boystown was the city's only official prostitution zone, sex work was prevalent in bars, dance clubs, strip clubs, and streets elsewhere in the city, especially in El Centralito, the neighborhood where the bus station and railroad station used to be located. Business there had been declining since the 1950s, but strip clubs and *fichera* clubs remained and sex workers still solicited clients in them. As *ficheras*, women were paid the equivalent of one US dollar to dance to a song with a man. Dance salons where women work as *ficheras* exist throughout Mexico. *Fichera* clubs used to be prevalent inside la zona, but at the time of my research they were only found outside of it. Some *ficheras* only danced for money and for fun, while for others, *fichar* (dancing for money) gave them the opportunity to meet potential clients, whom they would take to a nearby hotel.

Most sex workers who migrated to work in la zona hoped to earn money to improve their lives and those of their families. The history of prostitution zones in Mexican border cities is intimately tied to Mexico-US relations. While no longer a major profit generator in border cities, sex work was historically lucrative, in part, due to American demand. Prostitution zones first emerged on the border as the result of an economic depression in Mexico at the end of the nineteenth century (Curtis and Arreola 1991). Border cities attempted to lift their economies by appealing to the US market. Prostitution zones at this point were small and not very profitable, because Americans could legally purchase sex, as well as alcohol, in the United States. However, the US prohibition of alcohol in 1920 pushed many Americans across the border to find experiences now illegal in their own country—not only drinking alcohol but also gambling, cockfighting, bullfighting, boxing, and prostitution. As a result of increased tourist traffic, Mexican cities experienced rapid growth and prosperity. Prohibition produced profit as US citizens traveled to border cities. Curtis and Arreola explain that "the border towns emerged as convenient yet foreign playgrounds, tantalizingly near but beyond the prevailing morality and rule of law north of the border" (1991). Although tourism died down during the Great Depression (1929–1939), it revived again in the war years and through the 1950s, when border cities catered to young American military men in search of "erotic diversions" (Curtis and Arreola 1991). The sex workers I met in Reynosa, however, mostly served Mexican clients, because fewer and fewer Americans were crossing the border.

Although prostitution was not illegal in Reynosa, sex workers were haunted by the whore stigma. Sociologist Erving Goffman's concept of the stigma analyzes how certain classes of people who are considered to be "not normal" navigate the stains upon their identities (Goffman 1963). Gail Pheterson (1986) was the first to officially coin the term "whore stigma" in an academic context, but the concerns she writes about were long before outlined by sex worker rights activists. The slippage between women who are actual sex workers and those who are stigmatized for presumed sexual excess is captured in the slurs "whore" in English and *puta* in Spanish.[19] Because of this slippage, engaging "whore" as a concept can help reveal intersections between gender, race, and class. Melissa Gira Grant suggests that perhaps "whore" is the original intersectional[20] insult (2014). In Ciudad Juárez, as in many parts of the world, suggesting that a woman *might have been* a sex worker is enough to explain her rape, mutilation, and murder—discursively shifting the blame from perpetrator to victim (Wright 1999).[21] As Melissa W. Wright demonstrates, in Juárez, local discourses surrounding the rape, mutilation, and murder of young, dark-skinned, and poor women blame the victims, and even their families, conjecturing[22] that they may be prostitutes or loose women due to their locations both geographical (the street) and temporal (at night). That most of the victims of the Ciudad Juárez feminicides were not working in the sex industry demonstrates the larger social implications of the fact that, as Anne McClintock notes, the whore stigma disciplines all women (1992, 95). As many intersectional feminists have pointed out, this disciplining does not happen evenly, but is more harshly applied to low-income women who have been racialized as sexually excessive. Although sex workers in Reynosa did not live in a city famous for killing women, they constantly worried that they might be murdered and dumped in public space. The astoundingly high rate of murder of trans women of color in the United States, especially black trans women, is another example of the intersectionality of the whore stigma. While some of these murdered trans women were sex workers, it is also likely that the stereotype of the trans sex worker structures violence and fear toward trans women (see Aizura 2014). As Aren Z. Aizura notes, paraphrasing the insights of other scholars (such as Snorton and Haritaworn 2013): "the most vulnerable gender non-conforming bodies subject to institutional abandonment almost always occupy a position as racialized other to the nation or to whiteness; whether as migrants with precarious access to social and administrative citizenship status; as people of colour trapped in the institutional enclosures of anti-blackness; as inhabitants of the structurally adjusted global south; or as the colonized subjects of multiple imperial and colonial states or wars globally, or multiple racial otherings" (2013, 130).

The whore stigma is not only intersectional but also queer in relation to the normative collision of notions of "good" and "right." My use of queer is influenced by Michael Warner's suggestion that queer theory is defined against the "normal" rather than against "the heterosexual" (Warner 1993, xxvi).[23] I follow Cathy Cohen's thinking about queerness as that which is other to white, middle-class heteronormativity (Cohen 1997). From this point of view, "queer" can describe people who engage in exclusively heterosexual activities yet whose practices are deemed excessive or dangerous. Cohen uses the example of black single mothers on welfare. Sex workers, in many contexts, are among the poor and racially marked populations whose bodies become a site of discipline in the name of the public good. As Patty Kelly, in her ethnography of a zona near Mexico's southern border, argues, the state's registration and regulation of sex workers stigmatizes poor women in the name of hygiene, modernity, or the public good (2008).[24] Several of the sex workers in this study considered themselves lesbians or had other cis women as partners, but it is not because they were in same-sex relationships that I discuss them as queer. Rather, I use queerness as a lens to think about their practices and relations because they are marked with the whore stigma.

Sex workers in Reynosa were well aware of the whore stigma. While earning money motivated their work, framing their labor in a way that constituted them as good mothers and good women was an important part of creating value. Sex workers and the missionaries who sought to love them used the border to fulfill gendered kinship obligations and create value. Women's gendered kinship obligations were one of the major reasons for which sex workers migrated to work in la zona. Like Denise Brennan has noted in the Dominican Republic, I have found that in Mexico, "poverty and the responsibilities of single motherhood are the most decisive factors that inform . . . women's choice to work in . . . [the] sex trade over other labor options" (Brennan 2004, 45). I agree with Kelly that it is a "combination of cultural norms, obligation, need, guilt, and familial love that compels many women to work for their families" (Kelly 2008, 187). Kelly also holds that "their position within a patriarchal gender system . . . expects women to unselfishly serve their families as daughters, mothers, and spouses, without reward" (2008, 187). Castañeda et al. (1996), who, based upon their research in Mexico City, give public health advice about the transmission of HIV for commercial sex workers, go so far as to suggest that health officials emphasize women's roles as mothers to get them to use condoms. Feminist anthropologists have shown how a narrow view of the relations of reciprocity between men has overlooked many ways in which women contribute to politics and social reproduction (Collier and Yanagisako 1987; Munn 1986; Strathern 1988; Weiner 1992).[25] Feminist researchers have also demonstrated the great effort it takes to reproduce kinship ties (Di Leonardo 1987; Weiner 1992).[26] This book shows how sex workers created value through framing their labor as the work of social reproduction. This book also shows how kinship ideologies enabled differentially valued templates for motherhood that informed how sex workers thought about themselves and each other and structured their home and work lives.

Sex workers exercised agency in relation to the whore stigma and grappled with the politics of respectability.[27] They argued for the social value of their work by discussing their roles as counselors to clients and by emphasizing how they created an outlet for the sexual desires of "bad men" who would otherwise rape women (chapter 1). They also framed their sexual labor as fulfilling obligations to their children, pimps, and families (chapter 3). Some sex workers also distanced themselves from the whore stigma by marginalizing other sex workers—critcizing the dependency of women with pimps or the mothering capacities of drug-addicted women (chapter 4).

Motherhood was a key concern to sex workers and intersected in important ways with the whore stigma and the politics of respectability in la zona (chapter 1). Sex workers' status as mothers became relevant to their management by drug organizations (chapter 2) and the department of public health (chapter 3). Chapters 3 and 4 show how sex workers judged themselves and others as mothers, and chapters 5 and 6 show how missionaries were similarly invested in the mothering capacity of sex workers. Children were often an absent presence in the triangulations between sex workers and other sex workers, or missionaries and sex workers. "We, as mothers, are to blame," I was often told by sex workers (chapters 3 and 4), sometimes as self-castigation and sometimes as a way of blaming someone else for being an inadequate mother. With the utterance "we" in the three instances explored in these chapters, sex workers aligned themselves with an imagined community of mothers and demonstrated values important in la zona.

By engaging in long-term ethnographic fieldwork, anthropologists have shown how political and economic transformations sparked by neoliberal policies have shaped intimate relationships, love, sex work, and transactional sex[28] throughout the world (Cole and Thomas 2009; Hirsch and Wardlow 2006; Padilla et al. 2007). Some of these studies involve relationships between local sex workers and foreign, often white, sex tourists (Meiu 2017; Mitchell 2016; Rivers-Moore 2016; Stout 2014). A shortcoming of this study is its limited data about sex workers' relationships with clients. Although I hoped to include clients more fully, I was only able to interview a few. The client interviews were limited because I was in la zona during sex workers' working hours, and I did not want to scare their clients away by proposing interviews with them. However, I did observe that some clients had more long-term relationships with sex workers, paid them for both sex and other forms of companionship, or gave them gifts like perfume, food, televisions, and cars. Some clients supported sex workers financially so that they could leave Boystown or gave them money to pay bills during times when they could not work.

My analysis of missionaries' relations with sex workers was influenced by scholarship about the relations between clients and sex workers, as it helped me to look for nuances in relations that are forged under the backdrop of inequalities. Scholars of sex work have countered hegemonic views of predatory clients by showing exchanges in addition to sex and money: intimacy, love, authenticity, or alignment with a gender, race, or class (Bernstein 2007; Frank 2002; Mitchell 2016; Rivers-Moore 2016). Many of these studies examine parts of the world where larger numbers of sex tourists forge commodified intimacies with sex workers and bring foreign money into places where gender roles, sexual practices, and subjectivities are being reshaped. George Paul Meiu shows how, as former ways of reaching social adulthood became increasingly difficult to attain, young men in Kenya deployed stereotypes of "primitive" African warriors to establish transactional sex relationships (and other intimacies) with European women (Meiu 2017). In Brazil, Gregory Mitchell shows how primarily European and American gay tourists propelled by racialized ideas about Brazilian masculinity and sexuality have formed intimacies with local men who do not identify as gay (Mitchell 2016). In both Mitchell's and Meiu's work, race and gender performances add to the erotic appeal of locals for those who travel to meet them. The missionaries I study target Mexican sex workers because of some combination of ideas about their genders, sexual behaviors, races, and class positions. To call this ethno-erotic might take the comparison too far, but this book seriously considers the erotics of the mission encounter. As Bernstein writes about men in the tech industry who seek out the "girlfriend experience" with sex workers rather than a temporally bound, sex-for-money transaction, the missionaries I studied similarly sought out longer-term relationships with sex workers than those typical in the mission encounter that seeks to convert people.

The mission encounter, as well as the other intimacies forged in la zona, contained both normative and queer elements. Queer theorists and the anthropologists working in this tradition have shown how heterosexual kinship is linked to straight time—a time linked to an imagined progression in which people become men and women who follow normative paths toward adulthood, often including reproduction and the accumulation of wealth or property (Boellstorff 2007; Freeman 2010; Halberstam 2005; Meiu 2015 and 2017). Most of the sex workers and missionaries who participated in this study were clearly invested in normative ways of building a life, and my work reveals the queer intimacies often forged in the service of these normative paths. Meiu uses the term "queer moments" to refer to the way that young men subverted normative expectations of the relationship between temporality and aging: through their monetized relationships with European women, young men were able to become elders more quickly than was the norm (2017, 194). Missionaries, sex workers, and drug workers also produced queer moments. Drug workers and sex workers not only had to hide their "vice"-associated intimacies from family and friends but were said to earn "easy money," a designation that indicated a queerness in the relationship between time and money (chapter 1). Sex workers and missionaries were invested in certain forms of normativity, but sex workers engaged in stigmatized intimacies and missionaries contemplated long-term relationships with Boystown that they suspected other Christians might frown upon (chapter 5).

Even if some aspects of missionaries' relationships with sex workers echo relationships between sex workers and clients, missionaries are key generators of a moral panic surrounding prostitution that often collapses important distinctions between sex trafficking and sex work. Evangelical Christians and anti-prostitution feminists have joined forces in the anti-trafficking movement often in collusion with state attempts to police borders and to deport or imprison people involved in various aspects of the sex industry (Bernstein 2010). My project rejects an a priori assumption that migrant sex workers are victims of sex trafficking and instead examines sex workers' agency as migrants while keeping in mind the structural vulnerabilities they often encounter (Agustín 2007; Brennan 2004; Cheng 2010; Dewey 2011; Kelly 2008; Zheng 2009). The conflation of "sex worker migrant" and "trafficked victim" not only assumes that all sex workers are victims but also takes attention away from the exploitation of other people like agricultural workers and domestic workers (Agustín 2007; Brennan 2014; Cheng 2010; Hoang and Parreñas 2014). Hoang and Parreñas push for a move against discussions of "trafficking" in favor of "forced labor," in order to highlight the structural factors that make migrant workers vulnerable to different kinds of exploitation. They argue that trafficking discourses see the problem as evil people and the solution as jailing them, whereas global inequalities, labor laws, and the criminalization of migration are the factors that lead people to be vulnerable to forced labor (2014).

This question of agency is particularly thorny for analysts of sex workers and those whose projects concern them. It is crucial to find better ways to discuss agency when researching sex work and the rescue industry. Many popular, academic, and legal discourses construct sex workers as a priori victims. However, women who enter the industry without the coercion of a pimp do so after identifying it as the best of a handful of other tedious and potentially dangerous jobs, often because it is better paid. Positing sex workers as always already victims becomes logically unsustainable in the case of legal and popular discourses surrounding migration and sex trafficking in the United States. While Mexican migrants are discursively and legally constructed as "illegal" aliens who break the law by crossing the border, if a woman has migrated to sell sex, she can be discursively and legally constructed as a victim rather than a criminal. In the case of sex workers and others who are assumed to be victims, it is especially important to analytically attend to agency, or else one risks perpetuating this idea of victimhood.[29] However, the concept of agency is burdened with the fantasy of autonomous individuals who enact their independent wills. Both popular culture and academic discourses surrounding these industries implicitly assume that people are or should be sovereign subjects, or self-contained, autonomous individuals in control of their lives. Some scholars have moved beyond the individualized human as the locus of agency or sovereignty by developing nonautonomous and nonsovereign[30] concepts of agency. This question of agency is hard to pin down when writing about missionaries in the rescue industry. Missionaries are generally granted agency as either willful heroes (by their Christian publics and other members of the industry) or colonial agents (by their critics, who are often academics). In contrast, a lens of nonsovereign love and obligation allows me to address questions of agency without presupposing willful, autonomous sovereign subjects.

Thus, this book builds anthropologists' challenges to assumptions that sex workers are victims of clients and pimps. It does so by similarly complicating sex workers' relationships with members of the rescue industry, showing how these relationships are as complex as sex workers' relationships to clients and pimps. Furthermore, the relations of sex workers with their family members are often just as coercive as their relationships with other people. Forms of love and intimacy exist alongside forms of coercion in many of these relationships. I agree with critiques of the rescue industry that show how projects that seek to "help" sex workers, generally with good intentions, not only fail to ultimately provide material assistance to them but also often make their lives more difficult by limiting their mobility (Agustín 2007; Cheng 2010). My reading of missionaries is critical of their attempts to turn sex workers into former sex workers but also critical of my own biases. I employed the anthropological method of cultural relativism—trying to understand a culture on its own terms—instead of imposing my own value judgments upon it. In my analysis, I refrain from any assessment of what the missionaries are doing as "good" or "bad," or even "harmful" or "helpful," and focus instead upon the exchanges, transformations, and conflicts that result from this encounter as well as the ways that both parties create value through their relationships.

The missionaries' project is structured by a longer history of neocolonial mission encounters in the Texas/Mexico borderlands. The borderlands were first colonized by the Spanish in the fifteenth century and later violently taken over by the United States in the nineteenth century. While Catholic missionaries intervened upon the languages, cultures, and dress of the indigenous populations of the fifteenth century, the US occupation was accompanied by Protestant missionaries, who have been working in the US-Mexico borderlands since the 1820s (Machado 2006). Historically, Protestant missionaries in this region have sought to not only convert Catholics to Protestantism but also "Americanize" the Mexican and Mexican American population, which was seen to be racially and morally inferior (Machado 2003, 2006; Mora 2011).[31]

Border cities like Reynosa are ideal for short-term projects because of their proximity to the United States and the relative ease with which untrained groups can carry out construction projects in Mexico due to fewer legal regulations. Stacy joked that every youth group in the American Midwest has visited Reynosa. Some of these youth groups worked in the short-term teams that provided the money and labor to build Stacy's house near la zona—the house where she planned to both live and build a "modern-day monastery" to serve the people of Boystown (figure 6). Stacy criticized short-term missions (chapter 6) but also called herself a product of them; before moving to Reynosa, she served on facilitated short-term mission teams visiting West Africa, Thailand, and Central and South America.

An estimated two million Americans participate in short-term missions each year (Priest and Howell 2013). Churches send mission teams to border cities like Reynosa, generally for a week at a time, to give their congregants the experience of assisting the poor in a place where poverty is perhaps more exotic than at home. Although I did not conduct a systematic study of short-term mission teams in Reynosa, I spent time with teams associated with three different mission projects. I observed that witnessing the living conditions of poor Mexicans *both* generated sympathy and reinforced American Exceptionalism that associated the United States with freedom, prosperity, and God. These short-term mission trips served as an opportunity for American parents to teach their children to be thankful to God for material wealth. The short-term teams that built houses for "homeless" people, for example, explained to me that they felt fortunate to have what they have in the United States once they saw people in Colonia 10 de Mayo living in lean-tos and using outhouses. Some of these short-term teams, however, assumed that all of Reynosa was like this shantytown, or even drew conclusions about all of Mexico based upon their limited experiences.

Teams from Presbyterian, Apostolic, Catholic, Methodist, Nondenominational, Episcopalian, and Southern Baptist congregations all over the United States provided the labor and money to build Stacy's house during short-term mission trips. Her mission was independently conceived, and she did not officially represent a congregation or denomination. Stacy was financially supported by members of her charismatic, evangelical, nondenominational church in Tulsa. More than any particular denomination, Team Boystown is closely aligned with the New Monasticism movement, which is typically seen to be a subset of the Emerging Church movement (Schneider 2018). While members of Team Boystown never explicitly identified themselves with either of these movements, people they were influenced by did,[32] and Stacy's project was exemplified in a book about the subject.[33] The New Monasticism movement and the Emerging Church movement are primarily composed of young, white, educated, middle-class people who grew up in and eventually rejected suburban evangelical megachurches (Moll 2005; Schneider 2018; Bielo 2011). Opposed to prosperity gospel promises of riches to faithful Christians, participants in the New Monasticism movement have often sought to live among the poor, citing Jesus's mandate to "Go and sell everything you have and give to the poor . . . then come and follow me" (Mark 10:21, cited in Heuertz 2008, and a similar passage in Matthew 19:21). New Monastics seek to build intentional communities in what they call modern versions of the ancient tradition of monasteries, and to transform the world through prayer and social justice. They also believe that becoming deeply engaged with, friends of, and neighbors to racial and economic others is key to both individual and structural transformation of inequalities (Schneider 2018).

Both Team Boystown as well as the organization it became affiliated with, 24-7 Prayer,[34] were part of an imagined community of "followers of Jesus" which prioritized the commandments to love God and love one's neighbor. 24-7 Prayer is a global, interdenominational prayer movement concerned with social justice. When Stacy first met the director and learned about the project, she explained, she and those involved in 24-7 agreed that they shared some basic philosophies. Stacy's involvement with 24-7, which started as a friendship and evolved into an affiliation,[35] gave her a sense of a global community while she was waiting for long-term team members.

Before Stacy had a team, people all over the world who were involved with 24-7 prayed for sex workers and prayed that God would send team members to join Stacy in Reynosa. In my observations, Team Boystown missionaries only occasionally discussed the Holy Spirit and were more likely to discuss God and Jesus, to whom they prayed directly. Through the support of 24-7 and other individuals and missions, Stacy slowly gained contacts and different forms of support from 24-7 as well as other individuals and missions.

Stacy became close friends with other white American missionaries who worked at a school for deaf children in Reynosa. The school teaches deaf children Mexican Sign Language and how to read and write in Spanish while also teaching them about Christianity.[36] They helped her build her modern-day monastery, often describing themselves as a "community" or a "family." One of the members of this team, Abigail, entered la zona with Stacy before she had a team, and once set up a week-long medical clinic for sex workers outside of Boystown. Abigail had excellent Spanish language skills and was good at problem solving and helping people to navigate bureaucracies or access resources they needed. She had grown up in the Apostolic Christian church and had graduated from college. She was very thin, with olive skin, delicate features, and large green eyes that she would make bigger at the end of a sentence for effect. She often wore form-fitting jeans and polo-style shirts. Abigail was not an official member of Stacy's team when I got to Reynosa, but they were heavily involved in each other's lives and projects.

A blonde British woman named Emma joined Stacy's team for eight months after learning about Stacy's project at a 24-7 convention in London. She was no longer part of Stacy's team once I arrived. Ashley and Eleanor were the Team Boystown members, along with Stacy, that overlapped with me in Reynosa. Ashley, a recent college graduate from Tulsa, made a two-year commitment to join Stacy's team. She had short blonde hair and large blue eyes and she often wore long, flowing dresses with sandals. Eleanor, a white South African, had also graduated from college and made a two-year commitment to joining Stacy's team. She was thin and had brown hair and bluish-green eyes. Eleanor played the violin, Ashley sang well, and one of our mutual missionary friends played the guitar, so the three of them often played music together at social gatherings.

I describe people's appearance with details like hair color and the clothing they wore to help my readers keep track of all of the characters in this book, but also for several other reasons. Phenotypical traits and clothing signaled that they were foreign missionaries. Very few women could be found in Boystown who did not sell sex other than missionaries, a few retired sex workers who performed odd jobs, and a few women who worked selling food or other items.

In most contexts in the United States, whiteness is associated with privilege, racially unmarked, and taken as the "norm." Missionaries' whiteness in the prostitution zone was associated with privilege but also racially marked (for other examples of whiteness as racially marked, see Bashkow 2006 and Hartigan 2005). Based upon my observations, I suspect that the missionaries' whiteness helped them, at least initially, in establishing relationships with sex workers. In this neocolonial context, certain phenotypical traits like blue eyes, blonde hair, and light skin were highly valued. Sex workers and other people in Reynosa often commented about how beautiful Ashley's blue eyes were. Several American women who were especially racially marked by their whiteness suspected that people in the prostitution zone might have been so open and friendly to them because of their whiteness. My observations of their interactions led me to suspect the same thing. A missionary also mentioned to me, when discussing how often people requested prayers from her, that she wondered if people in Reynosa thought that God heard her prayers better because of her whiteness and Americanness.

The differences between these missionaries and sex workers was very likely a factor in what made the relationships valuable on both sides. In the quote that opened this book, Stacy noted it was not because of Boystown or Mexico that the sex workers there made her feel closer to Jesus, but because she was spending time with the same kind of "poor and forgotten" people that he had. It seems likely that their status as sex workers would have allowed for this as well, and perhaps their Mexicanness, although it would require even further speculation to try to tease apart whether this Mexicanness was primarily seen as a cultural, ethnic, racial, or citizenship-based. Similarly, for sex workers, it is difficult to detangle the missionaries' foreignness, whiteness, economic privilege, and perceived closeness to God.

The religious differences between sex workers and missionaries was also a factor for both parties. Most sex workers I interviewed identified as Catholic and thus did not pray directly to God but used saints as intermediaries, and they often used missionaries in this way, too. Many of the sex workers also prayed to la Santa Muerte, or the Saint of Death, an unofficial saint rejected by the Catholic Church whose followers include people of lower classes, people associated with drug cartels, sex workers, and LGBTQ people in Mexico and the United States. About 70 percent of the people I met in Boystown had tattoos, necklaces, or candles in their rooms for la Santa Muerte. I saw shrines to la Santa Muerte inside Boystown, elsewhere in Aquiles, and on some of the highways between Reynosa and other nearby towns. These shrines were thought to be erected by people associated with drug cartels. Some sex workers attended Protestant church services by local churches, one of which held weekly services in la zona. Lucía and several other former sex workers lived at a Protestant migrant shelter run by Hermano Domingo, a Oaxacan man who had been deported while working in Texas. He set up a Protestant migrant shelter on land next to the Rio Grande River and not far from Boystown that had formerly been a garbage dump. Domingo allowed migrants to stay for a few nights, but they had to agree to attend church services and work for the shelter to stay longer.

Team Boystown was not trying to convert sex workers to Protestantism, but they did hope and expect that their relationships would change sex workers. For example, Stacy's team hoped that sex workers would develop personal relationships with God and pray to him directly. Many sex workers saw no problem with praying to Catholic saints and la Santa Muerte as well as entertaining the possibility of living with missionaries in the "modern-day monastery, which to them indicated that they would become *hermanas*, or missionaries."[37]

As part of the rescue industry (Agustín 2007; Cheng 2010) that hoped to reform sex workers via God's love and turn them into former sex workers, Team Boystown's project was marked by colonial gestures. Team Boystown was one of many faith-based rescue industries that include not only a "rescuing" people from sex work but also training them for alternative forms of employment. Team Boystown was part of a larger structure of neocolonial missionaries trying to change the sexual behavior of a formerly colonized population. This missionary project both reproduced and actively worked to avoid the stigmatization of sex workers. Several missionaries noted that once they knew the details of sex workers' lives and financial situations, they could imagine themselves making the choice to do sex work under similar circumstances. However, they clearly wanted sex workers to leave sex work and live with their children. In pursuit of this goal, missionaries provided material and emotional support, which sometimes included coercive pressure.

The missionaries who are the subject of this book were aware of many of the forms of violence that had been enacted in the name of Christianity. They were wary of feeling good about themselves as white missionary Christians for having "helped the poor" and of being granted celebrity status in their home churches. Team Boystown missionaries were critical of these dynamics, which nevertheless haunted their project.

Although this book is sprinkled with missionaries' statements discussing sex workers "selling themselves" or the dehumanizing nature of prostitution, they did not engage in moralizing discourses about prostitution as sin. While they believed that God wanted people to commit themselves to either monogamous marriage or celibacy, when I asked missionaries about sin, especially related to sexuality, they consistently emphasized God's grace rather than damnation. They explained that God had grace for people, even if they did things he didn't want them to do, and missionaries sought to exercise this grace toward others instead of judging their actions. Team Boystown did not judge sexual sin as worse than other kinds of sin and emphasized that everyone is a sinner. Team Boystown missionaries and some of their friends criticized how "the church" judges sexual sin as worse than or different from other sin. Many of the sex workers did believe in God, but local churches, for the most part, did not reach out to them. This might have made Stacy's assurance that God loved them especially meaningful. Sex workers told me that they felt judged by other Christians but not by Team Boystown members. Eva told a story about a Mexican Protestant missionary who had told her that she was fat because the devil was inside of her. She used this story to express how different Stacy and her team were.

The relations I examine are marked by inequalities but also include great tenderness. Hirsch and Wardlow's comments about companionate marriage and love in the couple-form ring true for my analysis as well: "We argue that to study gendered relationships it is necessary to attend both to the socially, politically, and economically structured inequalities within which couples negotiate *and* to the possibilities for tenderness, pleasure, and cooperation that exist in spite of these inequalities" (2006, 3). The kinds of love examined in this book include intimacies and obligations. Love includes physical and moral care. Love in this book is also heavily tied to stigma. In some cases, people stigmatize those they love, and in other cases, protecting a loved one from stigma is an important part of caring for them.

The way that I theorize love comes from an emic use of the Spanish verb *obligar*—to obligate—which sex workers used primarily when describing their relations with pimps. Sex workers in Reynosa used *obligar* to refer to situations ranging from the threat of force to subtler coercion or social mores. Sex workers usually did not use *obligar* to describe familial relationships, except when pimps used sex workers' children to oblige them to earn money. Indeed, such obligations were sometimes coercively created by pimps or family members, sometimes internally motivated, and often informed by gendered expectations of a good wife, daughter, sister, or mother. Obligation was often tied to love for a pimp, a child, or other family members. I expand this theorization to analyze a wider range of relations between sex workers and their children, between sex workers and missionaries, and between missionaries, Christian publics, God, and drug organizations. With my expanded etic conceptualization of *obligar*, I analyze relations that neither sex workers nor missionaries would have used this term to describe. These obligations were sometimes imagined as forged by self-sacrificing love and generosity, sometimes through threats of force, and usually entailed elements both burdensome and desirable. By using the concept of *obligar* to theorize love, I show how love and coercion are linked. It is through these relationships of love and obligation, and for their sake, that people create value.

My analysis pushes toward a view of love and obligation that is distinctly nonsovereign, an alternative to the idea that human beings are sovereign— that they are in control of their own destinies as self-contained, autonomous units enacting their wills. Both states and individuals are commonly thought to be sovereign. A handful of political theorists argue for a nonsovereign conception of personhood and agency that emphasizes how humans are fundamentally dependent upon one another and thus not in control. While political theorists usually approach nonsovereignty from an engagement with Western liberal theory, anthropologists enter into this conversation through ethnographic fieldwork with people who have diverse conceptions of personhood.

Anthropologist Jessica Cattelino has usefully developed an analysis of sovereignty that does not presume autonomy. In her ethnography of Casino-era Seminoles in Florida, Cattelino not only demonstrates how Seminoles enact sovereignty "in part through relations of *interdependence*, for example through economic exchange and political and legal negotiations with other sovereigns" (Cattelino 2008, 17), but also uses this model to highlight the interdependent condition of sovereignty for the United States and other nation-states (162). Cattelino argues for a "relational account of sovereignty as forged through relations of interdependency, obligation, and reciprocity among sovereigns and peoples" (17).

I start with an assumption that life is unpredictable and that people are not completely autonomous or in control of their destinies. Obligations to other humans and sometimes deities entangle humans in relationships of interdependency that are enabling and disabling, burdensome and desirable, coercive and supportive, sometimes simultaneously. The nonsovereign aspects of both love and obligation are key to value creation. This study's participants valued some forms of interdependency as well as states of being in or out of control more than others. Using insight from ethnographic research, my methodology emphasizes the interdependencies and obligations inherent in social life and investigates the politics of nonsovereignty in Reynosa. By analyzing the relations between a Christian God, state actors, drug organizations, differentially empowered migrants to a Mexican border city, and the people for whom they labor, this study highlights the ways in which they create value(s) through their relations. People create value through hierarchies of nonsovereignty and debate about the extent to which people should be independent or in control. For example, in la zona, many sex workers saw other sex workers who worked for their own profit, for their pimps, or for drugs as inferior to those who worked for their families. Thus, a sex worker who was completely independent and in control of her money was looked on negatively, as was a sex worker whose money and actions were perceived as controlled by her pimp or drug addiction. The sweet spot of nonsovereignty for the politics of respectability in Reynosa's zona was a sex worker whose money went to her family dependents. Missionaries also thought that one should follow God's will, but they sometimes criticized missionaries who put everything in God's hands and did not, for example, secure a way of earning a living.

Love in the Drug War can be read as an ethnography of nonsovereign love and obligation. I approach differentially empowered migrants through the lenses of love, obligation, and interdependency, and thus address the question of agency without assuming sovereign, autonomous, willful, individualized subjects. The kinds of value(s) at the heart of my analysis stem from everyday relations in the borderlands, which are usually not seen or tracked: the relations between sex workers and their children, missionaries, and drug trafficking organizations. I show how these people create value through their obligations and for their sake, often in ways that are mediated by the US-Mexico border. Sex workers and missionaries described their migration projects as motivated by relations of love and obligation. Sex workers and missionaries alike valued certain forms of nonsovereign love and agency over others. I chart the ways in which conflicts about these relationships can be read as arguments about the politics of nonsovereignty and interdependency.

My Relationship to the Subjects of the Book

This project springs from prior research about the Ciudad Juárez femicides that began in the 1990s in which the bodies of murdered women repeatedly turned up in public spaces. Convinced of the urgency of critically examining how working-class women's sexuality is policed in Mexican border cities, I decided to study sex work in a city not far from Reynosa. I took an exploratory trip to this city with a man I would become romantically involved with who had grown up near the prostitution zone and who had many contacts there. When I broke up with him, he told me that if I pursued my project in that city, he would follow me there and ruin my reputation so that I would be unable to conduct research. He warned, "You wouldn't be the first woman to disappear at the border," a threat particularly terrifying for its resonance with the Ciudad Juárez femicides I was studying at the time.

To fend off his threat, I turned to the neighboring border city of Reynosa. I gained contacts in Reynosa through my parents' small evangelical church on the south side of San Antonio, Texas, which has a mostly Mexican American working-class and lower-middle-class congregation. The new contacts, a pastor and his wife, headed my parents' "sister church" in Reynosa. During my preliminary research trip, they arranged for me to stay at a Christian orphanage for several nights. This was a difficult trip. Although everyone was polite, they seemed to assume I was also a Christian, and I felt uncertain as to whether I would still be welcome if I were to correct them. During the trip, the director of the orphanage told me of his intention to prevent same-sex sexual behavior among the children by having them sleep in separate beds. I felt concerned that my hosts might discover that I was not a Christian and my partner was a woman.

Although these concerns led me to make different arrangements for my next exploratory trip, one of the young Americans volunteering at the orphanage serendipitously put me in contact with the missionary Stacy White. Stacy and her team visited la zona regularly; with them, I was able to safely enter la zona and make contacts there. In time, I came to know the missionaries well, and their project became a crucial component of my research.

It is important for me to note how my own position impacted my fieldwork and analysis. I grew up in an evangelical church in San Antonio not so different from the ones missionaries also grew up in. My Mexican American mother was raised Catholic, and my white father converted my mother's whole family to Protestantism. I eventually rejected my parents' religion, so my parents were delighted to find out that I would be spending a year doing fieldwork with missionaries in Reynosa.

As I studied the intimacies of the mission encounter in Reynosa, one of my key methods involved forging intimacies with both sex workers and missionaries. I was sometimes mistaken for a missionary or sex worker, depending upon where I was, how I was dressed, and who I was with. I spent time with sex workers and missionaries both separately and together. Missionaries were both a focus of my research and my way of gaining entry into la zona. In order to do my research, I needed the missionaries to accept me. I worried that they would not if they knew I was not a heterosexual monogamous Christian, so my first six to nine months of fieldwork involved a great deal of secrecy and a few lies. I was an outsider in both worlds who developed intimacies in both worlds and could "pass" depending upon my situation and context. Sex workers, missionaries, and I built intimacies by sharing details about our lives and by joking. With the sex workers, the version of myself that I shared was close to the one I share with some of my closest friends in the United States—only choppier and less coherent as my Spanish is not as good as my English. I was out to sex workers before I was to missionaries.

My time in Reynosa was one of palpable fear due to the city's militarization. It was not unusual for gun battles to break out between soldiers and people associated with drug organizations. Furthermore, the cartel in power infused local subjectivity with anxiety. Out of concern for my own safety and that of the participants of this study, and due to the general climate of fear, I employed methods suited to this complex environment, such as snowball sampling to make contacts. While I did not initially intend to research drug trafficking organizations, they shaped social life to such an extent that their inclusion in my research became necessary. As Howard Campbell notes, conducting ethnographic research in a drug war zone, which is a climate of paranoia and mistrust, causes unique methodological difficulties (2009). After only a few days in Reynosa, I hoarded printouts of my field notes, fearing they might make their way from the garbage into the hands of narcos, who could kidnap and torture me or the participants of my study. The first time I talked to a public official in Reynosa about my research, she said, "You're writing about the prostitution zone in Reynosa? I'm surprised you're still alive! It's run by some powerful people." At the time, I was also hearing rumors that public officials and policemen worked for drug organizations, and that the one local official who spoke against drug organizations had been publicly executed. These rumors shaped not only the people I write about but also my own sense of vulnerability, my perception of the field site, and the methods I employed, speaking to the problem of ethnographic research in tense and violent political situations.

To find a host family, I searched online social networks such as Couchsurfing and Hospitality Club designed to put travelers and hosts in touch without the exchange of money. There I found Verónica and Antonio, two bilingual Mexicans in their early twenties who would become some of my closest and most trusted friends in Reynosa. Initially, I stayed with each of their families for several days, but I ended up staying with Verónica's for the first nine months. Before I moved in, they were five people (a twelve-year-old, a fifteen-year-old, a twenty-year-old, a mother in her forties, and a cousin who was visiting to work in a maquiladora) and three dogs living in a very small two-bedroom house. I paid rent but was given the role of sister and daughter by the family. The father occasionally visited and tried to convince me to cook and iron for him. Within the first two months, the visiting cousin and Verónica moved out, and once my fifteen-year-old sister discovered she was pregnant, her fourteen-year-old boyfriend lived with us, too, and I shared a room with them. I eventually moved out, both because I sensed that my sister needed more space to prepare for the baby and so I could interact with the missionaries more. The timing worked well as one of Stacy's missionary team members, Ashley, was moving to Reynosa and needed a roommate.

After living with my Reynosa family for nine months, I lived with the missionaries for three, participating in the daily activities of my housemates. Throughout this year I visited Boystown several times a week, sometimes with missionaries and sometimes alone, to talk with sex workers and observe interactions among them as well as with the missionaries. Stacy's team of missionaries provided me safe entry into Boystown, as entering with them led the guards to assume that I was a missionary too. Once I met sex workers and others I might interview, I explained that I was an anthropologist. Through Stacy's contacts, I conducted interviews as well as life, work, and migration history narratives with missionaries and sex workers. I came to know many other missionaries, as we lived across the hall from two male missionaries whom we spent time with when we were not in Boystown. While living with Ashley, I participated in almost all of her daily activities, visiting Boystown, occasionally attending "house church," and socializing with other missionaries. In addition to more routine social events, I also traveled to Oklahoma for Stacy's wedding and went on several vacations with missionaries. These activities allowed me to make observations and forge new contacts. I engaged in sex workers' quotidian activities just as I did with the missionaries, although usually limited to their daytime leisure and working hours. I chatted with groups of sex workers and missionaries, prepared and shared daily meals with them, celebrated birthdays, threw bachelorette parties, and attended funerals. On one occasion, two missionaries and I accompanied a sex worker to her hometown when she decided to stop working in la zona. These activities gave me access to the interactions between missionaries and the sex workers they moved to Reynosa to love.

Participating in the daily activities of my host family and the missionaries, including crossing the border between Reynosa and McAllen, Texas, allowed me to understand the ways in which some of Reynosa's more mobility-privileged residents took advantage of the difference created by the border. Missionaries crossed the border about once per week to run errands, buy groceries, and, a few times a year, spend time with their families in Tulsa and Houston. I crossed the border with my Reynosa family usually once a week to buy groceries that were cheaper on the US side, to make payments on my host mother's US department store credit cards, and to buy used clothing in markets on the US side that I would then sometimes accompany her to sell at markets on the Mexican side. Mexican border residents with visas could easily cross to shop, and while it was not officially allowed, some Reynosa residents even worked in McAllen once they crossed over. One of my friend's mothers, for example, crossed once a week to work as a housekeeper. None of the sex workers I met in la zona were able to cross the border with such ease.

Living with Verónica's family taught me about important aspects of social life in Reynosa. My host sister's pregnancy revealed how savvy *reynosenses* were about the costs, benefits, and strategies involved in deciding on which side of the border to give birth and what kinds of citizenship documents to secure for one's child. The deep social embeddedness of drug organizations became apparent to me in living with Verónica's family, as I learned from my host sisters how many of the people with whom we regularly interacted were somehow involved with drug organizations. I found myself going to swimming pools and nightclubs with the children of jailed drug traffickers and retired hitmen. I spent time with men in their late teens and early twenties who did low-level cartel work like crossing drugs over the border or guarding hostages. Although people from Reynosa incessantly talked about narcos, both in terms of celebrity-like gossip and on a deeper level of fear and safety, they conducted these conversations in whispers.

Furthermore, crossing the border on behalf of some of my contacts in Reynosa who could not legally do so allowed me to understand some of the inequalities in the mobilities blocked or enabled by the border security apparatus, as well as the anxieties they created. On one particular trip from Reynosa to San Antonio, I crossed the border with my host mother's money to pay her department store credit card bill, as well as a with a prosthetic leg to be returned to a one-legged migrant from Honduras who had managed to extralegally cross the border on crutches. On my return, I reentered Mexico with a visa for one of my sex worker contacts that I hid between the pages of a book. I was asked to pick up this visa from my friend's former employer, who ran clandestine brothels in Texas, and to pretend that my friend was a housekeeper for my aunt in Reynosa, because she did not want her former employers to know that she was a sex worker. Along with my friend's visa, I hid party favors—lacy thongs, a game called "Pin the macho on the man," and some edible underwear—for a bachelorette party that a missionary, two sex workers, and I were organizing for Stacy. The missionaries ultimately opted not to use the more scandalous items because they were uncomfortable with them. Because I often crossed with items that were, if not illicit, certainly grounds for further questioning by border officials, I was often nervous when crossing into the United States. Stacy's tips for border-crossing included lots of lip gloss and a big smile. My own experience usually involved the authorities questioning me about the Frida Kahlo tattoo on my shoulder. I made it visible each time I crossed, because while I was not sure why they were so interested, it was a welcome distraction from the varied and difficult-to-explain wares with which I was crossing. Mindful of their potential power to block our mobility or make our day difficult, whether I was with my middle-class host Mexican family or missionary contacts, we answered questions carefully. Both the US Customs and Border Protection and the US Immigration and Customs Enforcement were permitted to search and seize laptops (and hold them indefinitely) as well as to copy data. But while both the surveillance of the US security apparatus and the cartel in power were sources of stress for me and made my project in Reynosa harder, my US passport empowered me with a sense of relative safety and ease of mobility. These surveillance apparatuses much more negatively affected the lives of the sex workers and other Mexicans and Central Americans whose projects are examined in this book.

Book Overview

This book is divided into three parts. Part I sets the stage for the political and moral economies of sex work and drug work in Reynosa generally and la zona in particular. Chapter 1, "Dinero Fácil: The Gendered Moral Economies of Drug Work and Sex Work," demonstrates how the moral and occupational careers of border residents were shaped by industries that cater to US demand for "vice" activities. This chapter discusses the "necessary evil" status of both drug trafficking and prostitution industries, their status as "easy money," the queer intimacies fostered by them, and how premature death was an expected outcome for both.

Chapter 2, "Rumors of Violence and Feelings of Vulnerability," argues that rumors of violence intensified both the power of drug organizations and the vulnerability of locals. When Reynosa residents shared rumors of violence, I claim, they spread not only terror but also intimacy. Sex workers were among the most vulnerable to cartel actions, as they worked in the territory of the Gulf Cartel, who mobilized them to protest the military presence of the city.

Part II focuses upon the moral economy of sex work in la zona and the intimate obligations of sex workers. I triangulate these relations by showing how sex workers' children were invoked in sex workers' relations with each other. Chapter 3, "Stigmatized Whores, Obligated Mothers, and Respectable Prostitutes," examines how sex workers responded to the whore stigma and created value(s) in relation to their clients, children, and colleagues. Through an analysis of emic and etic uses of the concept of *obligar*, I compare two instances in which sex workers and those for whom they labor used geographical distance to leverage or fulfill obligations in order to show the similarities between obligations to pimps and obligations to parents, children, and other family members.

Chapter 4 examines sex workers who were seen as *not* to be working for their obligations. "'Sometimes We, as Mothers, Are to Blame': Drug-Addicted Sex Workers and the Politics of Blame" centers on the suicide of the sixteen-year-old daughter of a former sex worker. This chapter argues that drug-using sex workers embodied negative value and negative hope—they were cited as evidence of la zona's potential to make the lives of one's family members worse instead of better. They were thought to engage in one *vicio* (prostitution) in order to feed another (drug addiction), using their sexual labor to fulfill bodily desires rather than reproduce families. Non-drug-using sex workers criticized crack cocaine users for being bad mothers. They established themselves, by contrast, as respectable sex workers and good mothers.

Part III turns to the intimate, economic, moral, and spiritual projects of missionaries, which were dependent upon their relations with sex workers. Chapter 5, "The Love Triad between Sex Workers, Missionaries, and God," examines the beliefs, goals, and actions that constitute Team Boystown's project. Team Boystown hoped that sex workers would become former sex workers and cohabitate with their children. I argue that Team Boystown created value by engaging in a form of gendered and gendering intimate labor through the forging and nurturing of triadic relationships. In these love triads, each element mediated the relationship between the other two, creating value by expanding intimate relations with God and by turning humans into agents of his will. Missionaries shared the stories of love triads in a way that expanded God's influence among a wider (mostly Christian and English-speaking) audience.

While chapter 5 focuses on missionary expectations and actions, chapter 6, "Love and Conflict in Sex Worker/Missionary Relationships," looks at the results of these actions. This chapter argues that missionary/sex worker relationships were complex and marked by interdependencies as well as a mutual concern with instrumentality, or using one another. Some missionaries and sex workers had close relationships that both parties considered to be love, friendship, or kinship. Missionaries wanted sex workers to leave la zona to fulfill God's wishes for their lives, and sex workers sometimes perceived actions toward these ends as helpful. Some sex workers pointed to the moment of a missionary telling them that God loved them as the turning point in their lives that led them to leave la zona and live with their children. However, missionary actions were sometimes coercive, and sex workers sometimes resisted missionaries' attempts to change their actions. This chapter focuses on observations of sex workers and missionaries' relationships as well as conflicts about pressuring sex workers to leave Boystown, fights among sex workers about who would get to live in Stacy's house, and rumors that missionaries wanted to buy the sex workers' babies.

The Conclusion synthesizes arguments from various chapters to offer insights about love and obligation, the whore stigma, and the figures of the narco and the racially marked migrant in the borderlands. I show how drug violence after militarization led to the decline of la zona and discuss how the events in Reynosa from 2008 to 2009 foreshadowed much of the violence that overtook great parts of Mexico in the coming years, making life harder for the most vulnerable.

PART I

DRUG WORK AND
SEX WORK IN REYNOSA

CHAPTER 1

Dinero Fácil: The Gendered Moral Economies of Drug Work and Sex Work

While balancing her sick and crying eighteen-month-old son on her hip and stirring pasta sauce on the stove, Frida, a sex worker, expressed her fear that her son might one day choose to earn "easy money" by selling drugs, as she noted that many young men do in Reynosa. Originally from a small town outside of Mexico City, she told me that people in Reynosa "don't like to work" and instead make a living selling drugs, used clothing, or used cars from the United States. Frida suggests that people who earn a living from buying and selling across the US-Mexico border are lazy. I heard others linking "easy money" to "laziness" or "not liking to work" in discussing both maquiladora work and sex work. Frida's fear that her son would get involved in drug work was one of the primary reasons she wanted to leave Reynosa; other factors were that her relationship with the father of her child was dissolving, she was having trouble making ends meet due to a lack of clients, and she feared her son would eventually learn what she did for a living and be bullied at school. Many sex workers shared her concerns. They all constantly calculated the potential risks and rewards of their stigmatized and sometimes dangerous labor for the people they loved and were obligated to.

This chapter examines the moral economy—shared sociocultural values surrounding economic behavior—of morally ambiguous and relatively lucrative enterprises tied to the creation of economic value on the border. I use David Griffith's definition of a moral economy[1]—what is considered to be proper or just economic behavior in a local setting (Griffith 2009, 484)— to show how drug trafficking and prostitution were viewed by their practitioners and by others. Both drug trafficking[2] and prostitution are pleasure industries that reflect the commodified intimacies of the US-Mexico relationship. They have prospered in Mexico in part because the United States has prohibited activities deemed vices. The economic potential of the step-like value transformations facilitated by the border enable border residents to have particular kinds of occupational careers, like factory worker, drug worker, or sex worker. Sex workers as well as other people in Reynosa often discussed prostitution as a "necessary evil" and a form of "easy money." This chapter asks what these common sayings about prostitution and other kinds of labor reflect about the moral economy of these industries in Mexican border cities.

I first examine the way that meanings surrounding identity and sexuality in Reynosa (especially for the upper classes) operate in relation to the internal others of migrants from southern states and the external others of Americans. I show how the whore stigma in Reynosa fused class, racial, sexual, and regional anxieties and judgments. I then turn to how the sociocultural values surrounding these ways of earning money influenced the moral careers of drug and sex workers in gendered ways. I use Erving Goffman's notion of a moral career to trace the expected stages of people's conceptions of themselves in relation to social structures such as stigmas or institutions (Goffman 1961 and 1963). Moral careers link events that happen to an individual with societal expectations about what will likely happen to certain categories of people.[3] Through moral careers, people working in these industries were expected to pass through particular paths or stages. The moral and occupational careers of drug workers and sex workers can resemble each other, but their differential social valuation expresses deeply embedded gender hierarchies. The moral careers associated with these industries not only shaped the lives of drug workers and sex workers but also informed their risk of death and the tenor of their posthumous reputations.

People never talked about what might be the opposite of easy money, but a joke told to me by one of the Veteran's Club members went something like this: A young boy who grew up on a farm was given important advice by his father: "Be sure that you marry a woman who has rough hands. If a woman has rough hands, it means she's a hard worker and will help you work on the farm." One day, the young man met a woman who was absolutely gorgeous, and he shook her hands and found that they were really rough, so he decided to marry her. Once they were married, he found that she was really lazy and just laid around all day. The wife didn't help around the house. She didn't work on the farm, either. Finally, the man asked his wife how it was that she had such rough hands.

The punchline had something to do with the woman being a stripper whose hands were made rough by sliding down a stripper pole. Although I did not find the joke funny, it helped me to understand that "easy money" might be contrasted with agricultural labor, although in Reynosa it was also used in contrast to skilled labor that required education and training. Migrants to Reynosa told me that where they came from, there was a lot of work but little money; they were "not afraid of work," they assured me, but could not support their families on those wages. People in Reynosa expressed moral ambivalence about work and workers in these industries by designating prostitution, drug trafficking, and maquiladora work as "easy money." They understood these forms of labor as "easy money" in part because workers could earn more money, much more quickly, than they would be able to with other unskilled (or in some cases, even skilled) labor. "Easy money" was sometimes a distinction reflecting the queering of the relationship between time and the accumulation of money and was sometimes also a way to judge the labor of sex workers and racialized others as not real work. A queer reading of these kinds of work and these lives illuminates their separation from normative (publicly) monogamous heterosexual marriage and nuclear family structures, as well as how people fostered alternative intimacies that they cloaked with secrecy. This chapter also shows sex workers' agency in relation to the whore stigma: they recovered their respectability by emphasizing the social benefits of their labor.

The Whore Stigma on the Mexican Border

The walls of Reynosa's historical museum are filled with photographs of border town shops advertising the sale of "Mexican Curios," souvenirs embodying stereotypes of Mexicanness marketed to American tourists. On a trip to the neighboring border town of Nuevo Progreso, Tamaulipas, among the curios I saw were clay figurines of big-bellied, sombrero-wearing men asleep under cacti and sculptures in the style of Aztec artifacts depicting couples in a variety of sexual positions. These objects are the trinket-trophies that depict the foreigner's imaginary of a place and sell the image of lazy, sexually charged Mexicans to Americans. While Mexican and US intellectuals have talked about curios as a "necessary evil" that "border folks *have had to accept* in order to earn a meager existence" (Alvarez 2003, 38, emphasis my own), the development of the border curio industry like the one depicted in Reynosa's historical museum was criticized by nationalist elites who thought it demeaning to create such images of Mexico, even if only to cater to the foreign market (Alvarez 2003, 37).

Sex work in many border towns has assumed a similar status to Mexican curios as "necessary evil" that catered, at least historically, to the foreign market. In downtown Reynosa tourist areas in 2008–2009, one could purchase stripper keychains and piñatas. In south and central Texas, groups of fraternity members have historically traveled to prostitution zones in Mexican border cities to see a curiosity marketed as Mexican: the Donkey Show, a live spectacle in which a Mexican sex worker performs oral sex upon and has genital contact with a male donkey.[4] In his Internet account of the Donkey Show on storistic.blogspot.com, a student from the University of Texas at Austin tells his story with simultaneous disgust and enthrallment of the "donkey-whore" having sex with a donkey. He writes, "You will not believe what they do with donkeys in Mexico," referring to the Donkey Show as "one of the most depraving acts of humankind." Similarly, a cartoon image from *Vice* magazine's 2008 Mexico Issue, one of four "World's Finest Mexico Jokes" in the issue, depicts the spectacle of bestiality between a Mexican prostitute and a donkey written all over the streets of a Mexican city (Ryan 2008). In the cartoon, a street covered with signs and posters advertising the Donkey Show, some lined in lights, others shaped like donkeys, is given the caption, "Broadway in Mexico." In this instance, we are told that the show worth seeing in Mexico is that of a woman having sex with a donkey, and an industry marketed to Americans in border cities becomes representative of Mexico. This is a familiar trope about the relationship between Mexico and the United States: although Mexico is geographically close and politically and economically tied to the United States, it is also socially, morally, and racially distanced from it. These images, which reproduce a racialized other through the iconic linkage to animal sexuality, are informed by coconstituting racializing and sexualizing ideologies. As other scholars have established, such a linkage of racially marked people with deviant sexuality relies upon a Civilized/Savage and Human/Animal distinction that has historical precedents in slavery, colonialism, and scientific racism (Davis 2001 [1983]; Povinelli 1997; Somerville 1994; Stoler 1997), which continue to be invoked in a range of contexts today (Hill Collins 2004; hooks 1992; di Leonardo 1997; Lutz and Collins 1998).[5] It is important to note that although the association of racially marked populations with deviant and excessive sexuality has been used to justify a wide range of violent, exploitative, and oppressive practices, some sex workers and non-sex workers have found forms of agency and even pleasure through the deployment and contestation of these stereotypes (Cruz 2016; Shimizu 2007; Miller-Young 2015).

The political stakes of the relationship between the sex worker's body and humanity can be seen in another cartoon from the same spread in *Vice*. This cartoon depicts a mother and father smiling and watching a little boy jumping with excitement while a blindfolded girl hits a donkey-shaped piñata. Blood and a severed hand, foot, finger, eyeball, heart, bones, and intestines spill out of the piñata as the mother exclaims, "I filled the piñata with murdered hookers!" This cartoon grimly satirizes the famous Ciudad Juárez femicides that began in the 1990s, in which the bodies of women who were murdered (often after being raped and tortured) were found in public spaces. The cartoon puts their remains into a piñata, one of the few pieces of Mexican material culture familiar to US residents and another bit of shorthand for the whole country. Like local discourses in Ciudad Juárez, the cartoon relies upon the assumption that the women killed were sex workers and makes the murder of sex workers seem normal.

In many different cultural contexts, the figure of the prostitute is a negative exemplar of corruption, vice, and moral degeneration, the prototypical example of realms that are thought to be mutually corrupting and therefore should be kept separate—sex (and the private or intimate) and money (and the public or economic). It is important to note that, at least in the case of cis and trans women sex workers who serve cis male clients, corruption and degradation are projected onto the body and subjectivity of sex workers, not onto those of their clients. Anne McClintock ties the scandal of prostitutes to the question of gender and property, arguing that prostitutes, by charging for sexual services, "transgress the fundamental structure of the male traffic in women" as well as challenge the idea that "women do not own property in their own persons" (1992, 76–78). In some historical and cultural contexts, as McClintock points out, the law has deemed both wives and prostitutes unable to be raped, because wives were considered to be the property of their husbands (although their rape by another man is "a crime against a man's property in a woman") (1992, 76–78).

Kinship systems help constitute gendered subjects, and this is certainly the case in Mexico, where the Virgin/Whore dichotomy, influenced by Catholicism and a particular reading of a colonial history, provides a powerful template for women's gender and kinship roles (Rubin 1975). In Mexico, the Virgin/Whore dichotomy is embodied by the symbolic mothers of the nation, la Virgen de Guadalupe, Mexico's patron saint, and la Malinche, Cortez's indigenous translator and mistress, who is a symbol of betrayal (Paz 1961). Mexicans sometimes refer to themselves as "*hijos de la Chingada*," or "sons of the raped woman," referring to the rape of indigenous women during colonization, which Octavio Paz has linked to the figure of la Malinche. Mexican women try to align themselves with the sexually chaste "good" virgin mother while trying to distance themselves from the "bad" whore (Bakewell 2010). Men want to imagine their own mothers as virginal and, when trying to insult other men, compare their mothers to *la chingada* (Bakewell 2010).

Anthropologist Claudio Lomnitz suggests that the association of the

Mexican border cities with vice activities for US patrons could be seen from some Mexican perspectives as a threat to Mexican nationalism. Applying a Goffmanian[6] distinction to poor or peripheral countries' management of their national self-image, Lomnitz frames the part of the city that is presented to tourists, including the nice restaurants and hotels, as the "front stage," and the part of a city that the government would rather hide, including poverty and illicit activities, as the "backstage." He argues that because the prosperity of Mexican border towns has historically come about from prostitution, sweat shops, bars, and abortion clinics that catered to US clients, Mexican border cities become the "backstages" to US border cities and thereby have been seen as threatening to Mexican nationalism. He writes, "The fact that Mexican cities constitute the backstage of US cities threatens nationalism's foundational credo: modernity is for the nation's own benefit and not for foreign outsiders" (Lomnitz 2001, 138).

Border residents are often posited by residents of other parts of Mexico as "not really Mexican" due to the cultural taint of proximity with their northern neighbors. In September 2007, I gave a guest lecture in Mexico City to a group of fourth-year university students at an elite art school. In preparation for the class, they read an excerpt from Gloria Anzaldúa's *Borderlands/La Frontera*. One young woman, highly disturbed by the reading, commented that Anzaldúa's mixture of English and Spanish did not reflect the way that "Mexicans" speak, and, quite simply, was ugly. She and several others debated the reasons that they found the *mexicanidad*, or Mexicanness, of the border resident to be suspicious; they mentioned that people on the border use English words, pay for goods with dollars, and are far removed from "Mexico." A month later, commenting upon a paper I presented at a workshop in Chicago, a professor of anthropology from the outskirts of Mexico City asked me, "How are you going to study *mexicanidad* on the border? It doesn't exist there." Interestingly, Reynosa residents had similar complaints of Mexican Americans, whom they called *pochos*. I heard many complaints that pochos spoke both Spanish and English poorly, mixed the two languages, and felt superior to *reynosenses* because they lived in the United States and earned dollars.[7]

Both nationalism and regional rivalry become implicated in respectability. If Mexican cities are "backstages" to US border cities, *zonas de tolerancia* are "backstages" to the other tourist areas of border cities and places where "respectable" people go. And prostitution is, perhaps, a backstage to heteromonogamous marriage. La zona enables a public image of respectability to other parts of the city of Reynosa, as Reynosa in turn allows McAllen, Texas, to look cleaner and safer.

I conducted interviews with men between the ages of sixty and ninety who were members of the "Veteran's Club of Reynosa" and the "Historical Society of Reynosa" about the history of the prostitution zone. In their stories, the relationship with the United States was always highlighted. When people in Reynosa discussed Americans (*americanos*), whom they sometimes called gringos, they were usually referring to the unmarked category of white Americans, and they usually specified if they were including African Americans or Mexican Americans in their statements. One man who authored books about the history of Reynosa told me that during World War II, when American men were at war, their wives and girlfriends would travel to Reynosa for liaisons with Mexican men, and that he and his friends would go "fishing for gringas." Once the war was over, he said, American men wanted the same privileges (to sleep with Mexican women), which is why the prostitution zone was built. This origin story of prostitution in Reynosa interestingly suggests that Mexican men had sexual access to American women before American men had access to Mexican women. This story is also consistent with the common belief in Mexico that American women are easy to have sex with. A man from Matamoros, Tamaulipas, used to tell me jokingly, "If you want to have sex with a Mexican woman, you have to either pay her or marry her. But American women love to have sex for free. That's why I try to bring as many gringas to Mexico as possible." In both of these stories, American women are seen as easier than Mexican women because sex with them is free of either monetary obligations or obligations associated with the marriage contract.[8] One sex worker in Boystown, Marisela, after I interviewed her, asked me if she could ask me a question that she had wanted to know the answer to for years but had been too embarrassed to ask anyone. She told me she had heard that in the United States, girls have their hymens removed by doctors when they are young so that they are not discriminated against for being virgins. The perceived sexual availability of American women could also be seen as a sign of either sexual immorality or sexual freedom.

This idea of sex for "free," as distinguished from a clear monetary transaction through prostitution or an obligation through the marriage contract, had recently become an important part of sexual practices in Reynosa. My contacts between the ages of eighteen and thirty-five told me that it was in style to have "frees," a phrase spoken in English, meaning a one-night stand free of any kind of commitment or obligation. Young people would go out with their friends and meet friends of friends with whom to have "frees," either in a hotel or a car. They found "frees" at nightclubs, bars, and a weekly event called "El Roll" where young men and women would get dressed up to drive very slowly in circles around a several-block radius, drinking in their cars and interacting with people. One sex worker, Sofía, mentioned the possibility of having a free with another woman. When she described to me her interactions with an attractive butch woman she had recently flirted with, I asked her if she might date her. "No, I don't think so," she responded, "perhaps we'll have a free, but nothing else."

Another kind of arrangement was described to me that was not quite "free," but also not exactly characterized as prostitution, and thus might be more adequately called a form of transactional sex. I was told that young men in Reynosa had no need to visit the prostitution zone because women whom they called *putillas* or "little whores" that they met at clubs would have sex with them for free, but expect to be taken out for dinners and drinks and given spending money. But these kinds of transactional sex encounters were much more likely to be seen as a cause of concern when they were done by nonlocal women.

Ideas about sexual behavior were constructed in relation to not only Americans but also the "internal others" (Schein 1994) of migrants from southern Mexican states.[9] Mexico is known for its regional rivalries.[10] Both in Juárez and in Reynosa, local discourses linked internal migrants who work low-wage jobs (often in factories) to whores. Wright provides examples of American managers linking workers with sex workers,[11] and I have observed similar discourses from Reynosa locals about internal migrants from southern states. While I conducted formal interviews or asking informal questions about prostitution in Reynosa, middle- and upper-class "native *reynosense*" consistently mentioned promiscuity as a problem in the feminized industry of maquiladora workers, in which mostly nonlocal, working-class women worked. A pejorative word for racially marked low-wage laborers in Reynosa, including sex workers, was *veracruzano*. The term would normally be used to refer to people from the Mexican state of Veracruz, and indeed many of the internal migrants in Reynosa were from there and had migrated north to work in the maquiladora industry, the service industry, the sex industry, and other low-wage jobs. But the term "veracruzano" shifted to include anyone who migrated from elsewhere, had dark skin, and appeared poor.

Veracruzanos were widely thought to be unattractive due to their dark skin, straight hair, short stature, and "tacky clothes." I heard several people refer to veracruzanos as *veracruzchangos* (*chango* is a slang term for a monkey), and a woman who lived in Reynosa for twenty years told me that women from Veracruz are "like monkeys" as they "don't shave their armpits." Reynosa locals claimed that veracruzanos polluted their culture by migrating to Reynosa. It was commonly stated that one could spot a veracruzano on the street. "They all look alike," Karen, a dentist, told me, "as if they were made from a mold." Thus, as racialized poor migrants, veracruzanos were phenotypically and sartorially, rather than geographically, pinned down. One day Karen and her other dentist friend, Roberto, discussed vera-cruzanos with me while we waited for tacos at an outdoor stand:

> Karen: "[In our dental practice in Reynosa] we get three types of clients: *americanos*, *mexicanos*, and *veracruzanos*. The veracruzanos are another species! [laughs]"
> *Roberto uncomfortably clears his throat and looks at Karen while slightly nodding his head toward the person preparing our tacos who is directly in front of us and two feet away from our faces.*
> Roberto: "Heil Hitler! Karen is a racist."

This instance of Roberto calling Karen a racist surprised me for two reasons. When the three of us were in private twenty minutes before and Karen told me that she and Roberto were among the few attractive, light-skinned and blue- or green-eyed people in a city of "dark little veracruzanos," Roberto laughed in agreement. At the taco stand, I imagined that his calling Karen a racist was prompted by his realization that the woman serving our tacos might be considered a veracruzana. This interchange further surprised me because my anecdotal knowledge was that Mexicans usually claim that racism does not exist in Mexico. It seems that veracruzano essentially became a euphemism for *indio*, or indigenous person, which, as Lomnitz and other scholars have noted, is a category that has conveniently changed to fit contemporary contexts. Lomnitz explains that during the colonial period in Mexico, Indian was a "racial" and legal category of persons, but during the nineteenth century, the term Indian "fus[ed] racial and class factors: for the urban middle and upper classes, any poor peasant was an 'Indian'; that is, the category 'Indian' came to mean those who were not complete citizens" (Lomnitz 2001, 41, 52). It also seems likely that the category of veracruzano as it was used in Reynosa was haunted by the racialization of the state of Veracruz, an early slave port with the highest population of people of Afro-Mexican descent, which has historically been associated with blackness (for more on blackness in Mexico, see Bennett 2009; Cruz Carretero 1989; Martínez Maranto 1994; Restall 2009; Sue 2010, 2013). Official and popular narratives of *mestizaje* in Mexico have erased both anti-indigenous racism as well as blackness from Mexican history. In this case, a fractal distinction served to erase the class-based and racialized elements and to posit the critique as mere regional rivalry.

In line with racialized othering, the supposed sexual behavior of veracruzanas was also of concern to those who shunned them. While I was conducting formal interviews or asking informal questions about sex work, middle- and upper-class people who were born in Reynosa consistently mentioned

promiscuity as a problem among maquiladora workers and other veracruzanas. Rigoberto, a *cronista* and member of the Historical Society of Reynosa
whose former responsibilities as a public official entailed controlling sexually transmitted diseases in la zona, told me,

> Women come to Reynosa from Veracruz or Chiapas to work in maquilado-
> ras. Some have AIDS, and they give diseases to men. We don't have any kind
> of sanitary regulation for them because they're not prostitutes. They're not
> public women. Sometimes they have sex just for fun; sometimes they do it
> for money, because their salaries aren't enough. A man doesn't know who
> he's going with.

Rigoberto also indicated that maquiladora workers were bad for the local economy, telling me that his friends who owned businesses that profited from prostitution were suffering financially because maquiladora workers go out with men who pay for "dinner, drinks, dancing, everything. And
later, in a hotel or in a car, they have sexual relations without being precisely a prostitute." Rigoberto suggested that the sexuality of veracruzanas
was more dangerous outside of la zona than inside of it because they could
not be controlled by the state. Sex workers' status as public women in la zona
allowed them to be visible and disciplined.

Like drug work and sex work, maquiladora work was often referred to
as "easy money." Several people mentioned to me that veracruzanos tend to
work in maquiladoras "because they're lazy." Several of my local and middle-class contacts argued that maquiladora workers did not care about ad-
vancing their lives or studying to get better jobs. Even Sofía, a sex worker,
used the example of a maquiladora worker as someone who earns easy
money for easy work as part of her argument against communism. A maquiladora worker, Lauren, reproduced the slippage between "easy money"
and "easy work" in relation to her own occupation: she told me she loved
factory work because it was easy; she did not have to have prior experience
and could learn to do a new job quickly. However, in the same conversation, she told me about her health problems resulting from repetitive factory
work as well as the difficulties of having to work long hours during the night
shift. In this case, despite the apparent difficulties of her work, she still defined it as easy due to the lack of specialized skills and education necessary
to do the work.

People who considered themselves to be "from Reynosa" frequently dis-
paraged veracruzanos among themselves, complaining that Reynosa used
to be a small town where everyone knew everyone, thus romanticizing the
days before veracruzanos arrived and lamenting that locals were becom-

ing extinct "like dinosaurs." In both casual and formal settings, locals emphasized *just how local* they were, asking questions like, "How many of you are 100 percent from Reynosa?" and telling stories about their families' long histories in the area. A distinction was made between those who were "from Reynosa" and those who were not, and negative qualities were associated with those who were not from Reynosa.

By placing such semiotic weight on veracruzanos, Reynosa residents not only distanced themselves from the racialized and class-based category of indigenous peasant but also blamed outsiders for the city's problems. They painted their city as a metropole in contrast to the peripheral Veracruz. Locals from Reynosa often repeated this joke: "veracruzanos always complain that Reynosa is ugly and say that Veracruz is beautiful. Do you know why it's beautiful? Because no veracruzanos are there." Although seemingly perturbed when veracruzanos criticized their city, many locals were not likely to disagree that Reynosa was ugly, corrupt, and dangerous. Young people sometimes took pride in how dangerous their city was, wearing T-shirts that said, "I survived growing up in Reynosa" with an illustration of a person being forced into a car, or "Welcome to Reynosa, Tatatamaulipas," onomatopoetically infusing the name of the state (Tamaulipas) with the sound that a machine gun makes, "tat tat tat." However, people who had the means (and, in the case of cross-border travel, visas) to travel were more likely to "get identity" from other cities like Monterrey, Nuevo Leon, or McAllen, Texas, Reynosa's "sister city" across the border. Carlos told me, "Gringos often think that all of Mexico is poor. They don't know we have large buildings. They've never been to Monterrey." Several months later, sipping an Appletini (apple martini) over dinner, Lizet emphatically stressed to her friends, "I don't even know where to go out in Reynosa. I always go out in McAllen." Doing one's shopping in Texas was a symbol of status—young people would write "McAleando" on their Facebook status updates to tell their friends that they were shopping and eating out in McAllen, and Antonio told me that when he was young, the rich kids brought their lunches to school in bags advertising that they had shopped at Abercrombie and Fitch or Gap like American consumers. While the upper classes expressed their cosmopolitanism through their links to other cities, they also established their identity through distancing themselves from internal others like veracruzanos.

Reynosa locals fractally reproduced US ideologies that construct Mexicans as a threat to the social and national fabric. A Reynosa native told me, "Now that the veracruzanos are here, I understand how you [Americans] must feel being invaded by Mexicans."[12] At all levels, speakers tried to distance themselves from veracruzanos.

Even people from Veracruz complained about the "bad" veracruzanos. Veracruzano subjectivity was shaped by racializing ideologies assuming their lack of culture and laziness and was fractally reproduced by some veracruzanos who wished to distinguish themselves from the bad ones. When I was invited to a carne asada with a family from Veracruz one night in their front yard, various members of the family made the point to differentiate themselves from other veracruzanos, telling me stories about veracruzanos' laziness, apathy, lack of manners, poor hygiene, and lack of interest in their children's educations. With wide eyes and frowns of disgust, the mother of the family explained to me that when she would drop her seven-year-old daughter off at school, the other parents she encountered (who were largely from Veracruz) wore pajamas and slippers and arrived wild-haired and un-bathed. She added, "They should wake up earlier so that they can bathe and put on a skirt or something. It's a school, not the market. But I wouldn't even go to the market dressed like that!" She added, "I know that when these people lived in Veracruz they had more pride and cared more about having manners and looking respectable. I don't know why they lost all culture when they came here." In this case, not only were the negative qualities associated with veracruzanos fractally reproduced among veracruzanos in a way that aligned the speakers with signs of middle-class respectability, but also the geographical space of the US-Mexico border was seen as causing people to lose their culture. This fractal, like many described by Irvine and Gal (2000), is not an exact replication of the original distinction. It includes within it an implicit critique of the (social) space of Reynosa, its inhabitants, and its supposed lack of culture as a border city.

Even sex workers, most of whom would be considered veracruzanas, complained about them, and it was women with pimps who were most likely to be discussed in this category (chapter 3). The oldest intersectional insult was most pronounced in Reynosa through the whore stigma facing poor, dark-skinned, low-wage migrant laborers. My ethnographic examples indicate that ideas about identity, sexuality, culture, and work in Reynosa are intimately defined in relation to both the external others of Americans and the internal others of veracruzanos.

"The Difficult Life of an Easy Woman": An Introduction to the Moral Economy of Prostitution in Boystown

People in Reynosa widely considered prostitution to be "easy money," but this often slipped into an assumption that it was "easy work" performed by "easy women." Sex workers responded to this stigma by emphasizing the difficulties of their jobs and the ways in which their labor was socially beneficial. The idea of prostitution as a "necessary evil" was both an important aspect of the moral economy of sex workers and a hegemonic idea with a much larger history that serves to uphold gendered expectations of appropriate sexual behavior.

People both inside and outside la zona widely rehearsed and sometimes contested the notion that prostitution was "easy money." Occasionally, sex workers themselves would refer to their work as easy. Marisela told me that working in prostitution in Reynosa was much easier than working as a stripper back home in Puebla, where she was also expected to complete chores at home including cooking, cleaning, and child care. However, most sex workers denied that their work was easy. A former sex worker in her fifties from Cuba, nicknamed la Cubana, wrote in her handwritten memoir, *Abismo* (Abyss, Chasm, or Hell), which she entrusted to me, "The oldest profession in the world is not the way many people imagine it to be—it is not easy." Cubana, who was in her late forties, had big eyes, freckles, and short, curly hair. She had what looked like homemade fading black tattoos on her back and arms, one of them depicting la Santa Muerte. She wore a long, flowered nylon dress with flip-flops and had a large belly; sometimes she would trick new girls into thinking she was pregnant. Her memoir listed some of the difficulties of sex work, including men who are rude and smell bad. She wrote that when clients open their mouths they smell like lions, and when they take off their shoes they smell of a hundred years of collected waste. Cubana added, "There are men who pay you miserably little for pleasure and later they demand more." Most of the complaints I heard from sex workers in relation to clients were about men either trying to pay them less for services or to negotiate extra services without paying more. Sex workers were offended by these negotiations. Several other sex workers shared Cubana's complaints of bad-smelling men. Rebecca complained that while sex workers were expected to be recently bathed and nice-smelling, clients did not hold themselves to the same standards. In the winter, because many sex workers did not have hot water in their rooms, achieving this cleanliness was laborious. They had to use an electric device to heat water in a bucket to have hot water for a sponge bath.

Lola, who started working in prostitution when she was thirteen and usually worked in clandestine brothels in the United States, told me that her family believed her work to be easy. Lola was eighteen when I met her, and she only lived in Reynosa for a few months. She claimed that her family stigmatized her for the work she did yet was happy to spend the money she sent home. In my interview with her, Lola told me about some of the difficulties of sex work that her family did not recognize, including violence, often switching into a second-person accusation:

> Everyone in my family wants a part of the inheritance. They don't have a right to my money, not even one peso of my money. I am the one who built the house; you do not know what I risked over there [the United States]. You don't know about the times when you have to deal with a crazy person, like the day when I was tortured in a room. You do not see it. You think that it's easy and such. [. . .] For this reason, I tell my brothers if they want the luxury goods that I have, they should work. They always tell me "you're vulgar," "you are this and that," and I say to them, "Do you know what? Thanks to this vulgar person you're eating. Where do you think that all of the money that you spend comes from? And now you're going to the beach with my money; it should give you some shame."

In Lola's tirade to her brothers, which she may or may not have delivered directly, she countered the idea that sex work is easy work. She argued that her corporeal and intimate labor, which she transformed into the money that her family used to buy food, vacations, houses, and cars, included risks and vulnerabilities her family did not recognize. Furthermore, she defined her family members as lazy, nonworking hypocrites who lived off of her money yet criticized her for the way in which she earned it. In so doing, Lola defined herself as morally superior for the difficult and risky work she performed in order to provide for her family.

Lucía also denied that prostitution is easy. In the memoir that she handwrote for me, which she subtitled, "The Difficult Life of an Easy Woman" (*la vida difícil de una mujer fácil*), she wrote:

> I wanted to really tell part of the story of my life, if this can even be called a life. Apart from the sadness that this life entails, the woman who works in prostitution suffers the worst humiliations; she has to become submissive to satisfy the basest instincts of men who solicit her services. Therefore the life and the work of the prostitute is truly the most difficult life that can exist. Once I heard something that I will never forget. Someone commented to me, "The life of prostitutes is the easiest and most comfortable life." But later someone told me something contradictory, "We all truly are ignorant of the life that these women lead, and I argue that an easy woman has a difficult life." Since I left this damned zona with the help of God, I started to truly meditate on this phrase, and I came to the conclusion that truly soci-

ety takes pleasure in treating with an air of contempt women who, for one reason or another, dedicate themselves to this profession.

Lucía argued against the idea that the lives or work of "easy women" was easy, and she pointed to the negative sociocultural valuation of sex workers as one of their problems.

Another sex worker, Sofía, voiced a similar opinion. Sofía was in her mid-thirties and from Tampico, a coastal city south of Reynosa. She had facial features that reminded me of an Olmec head statue—a round face, a wide nose, and almond-shaped eyes—and one of her eyes was slightly lazy. She was usually wearing thick glasses and sweatpants rather than contact lenses and lingerie when I saw her, because I usually visited la zona in the day, and she worked at night. Sofía was one of the handful of sex workers who preferred sexual and romantic relationships with women. Similarly to Lucía, she stated, "We are the marginal and forgotten of society. People forget that we have a family, that we have a story, that we are human beings." Sofía's and Lucía's comments about the dehumanization of and contempt for sex workers are reminiscent of Simone de Beauvoir's argument that the main differences between the married woman and the prostitute are 1) the length of the contract and 2) the fact that the married woman is respected as a full human being and the prostitute is "denied the rights of a person" (de Beauvoir 1953, 556). De Beauvoir sidesteps the many different possible configurations of each institution as well as the fact that it is possible to be both married and a sex worker. It is important to remember the specific cultural and historical contexts that differently shape intimate and economic relations between people of different genders. But de Beauvoir importantly gestures toward the whore stigma that places different social valuation on wives and prostitutes.

De Beauvoir also reminds us that in contexts where men are more empowered to earn money, women depend upon relationships with men (either a husband or clients) in order to survive economically. Eva also invoked this idea of sex work as an alternative to marriage. Originally from El Salvador, she fled while pregnant during the 1980s to Mexico to escape El Salvador's civil war after several family members and the father of her child were killed. When I met her in 2008, she was in her mid-fifties and had been working in Boystown for two years to support her four children and five grandchildren, who lived outside of Mexico City. When Stacy introduced me to Eva for the first time, I immediately noted her glowing golden-brown skin and bright brown eyes framed by lashes made thick with black mascara. She wore black two-piece lingerie with a see-through, fishnet tube-top dress, flip-flops, and an ankle bracelet. Her hair was bleached honey-blonde and pulled back into a ponytail, and her lips were lined in fuchsia and filled in with light pink lipstick.

Eva said that she believed sex workers to be more responsible than women outside of la zona because sex workers are strong and work to support their families, while many women outside of la zona stay with husbands that beat and disrespect them. Perhaps Eva conflated these two actions—working to support a family and leaving a disrespectful and abusive husband—because this was her experience. Before she became a Mexican citizen, her abusive husband threatened to have her deported when she tried to leave him. In Eva's case, prostitution made surviving economically without her husband possible, although she found her work in Boystown to be dangerous and difficult, especially because of the violence and insecurity caused by the drug war. For some women, having temporary intimate and economic relationships with many men gives them more independence than they experience with one man under the marriage contract or less formal relationships.

De Beauvoir reminds us that the whore stigma is one of the greatest problems sex workers face. The dichotomy between respectable mothers and disreputable prostitutes creates stress for sex workers, because working in prostitution, an industry associated with vice, robs them of the claim to being virginal, virtuous, and thus "good" mothers as well as full human beings. One of the many ways that sex workers responded to the whore stigma was through engaging the idea of prostitution as a "necessary evil" to describe their important function of keeping crazy men and rapists off the street. While pointing out the social benefits of economic behavior is one feature of a moral economy (Griffith 2009), the idea of prostitution as a necessary evil is also reflected in legal and popular discourses surrounding prostitution. Sofía claimed, "We are a necessary evil. Many of the men who come to us are bad men who have complexes, fantasies, and psychological problems. Some are married, some want to have sex with men, some want to be hit, some are crazy. If we didn't exist, they would walk the streets." Sex workers saw themselves as making the streets safer for other women by becoming the primary recipients of deviant male sexuality; if men could not find sexual release with sex workers, they would rape other women.[13]

I also heard *men* throughout Reynosa make this argument, almost word for word. Not only sex workers but also men outside of la zona told me that men would be more likely to rape women if they didn't have the outlet of prostitutes for their sexual energy.[14] This thinking aligns with Mexican law: in Mexico, although prostitution is stated in some legal documents such as Mexico City's penal code to be offensive to church and society, the law tolerates prostitution as a "necessary evil" on the grounds that men possess a voracious sexual appetite that could not otherwise be contained. Historian Katherine Bliss notes that the idea of prostitution as a "necessary evil" came together with ideas about containing disease in various versions of the Reglamento para el ejercicio de la prostitución in Mexico City modified by Mexican officials between 1879 and 1926 (the original version was imposed by the French in 1865 during their rule of Mexico):

> The registration, inspection, and surveillance of sexually active prostitutes was based on the modern science of hygiene, but the Reglamento's spirit of tolerating male sexual promiscuity and containing disease among a group of "deviant" women resonated with older Catholic beliefs that prostitution, although a sin, was also a "necessary evil" that could prevent greater problems like rape or seduction from threatening the moral order. (Bliss 2001, 3)

The idea of prostitution as a "necessary evil" was invoked by Saint Augustine, who argued that tolerating prostitution was preferable to what might come about if brothels and harlots were to be eliminated from society (Guy 1991, 13). Saint Thomas Aquinas held this view in the thirteenth century, believing that prostitution prevented the graver sins of adultery and homosexuality (Guy 1991, 13). The Catholic Church largely tolerated prostitution in the Middle Ages (Rossiaud 1988).

Sex workers and other women in Reynosa similarly normalized male sexual promiscuity. Sofía said that men are "unfaithful by nature," which I also heard on several occasions by non-sex workers. Women would advise one another not to leave unfaithful boyfriends. A dentist in her mid-thirties, after breaking up with her boyfriend, was told by her mother that she had to learn that men were unfaithful and accept it, or she would never get married. She took her mother's advice, and although she knew that her next boyfriend probably had sex with other women, she was happy to at least have the special status of official girlfriend. Her approach evokes the oft-repeated saying that a man may "*tener muchas capillas pero una sola catedral*," using the hierarchy of Catholic chapels and cathedrals to describe the hierarchical ranking of a man's lovers as secondary to his wife. It was fairly common for men to have more than one family, sometimes in different cities and occasionally one on either side of the US-Mexico border, but the legitimate wife was the cathedral. I knew people on both sides of the border who did not learn about the extended family members of the *capillas* or *catedrales* of their fathers or grandfathers until their funerals.

Although the triangle between a sex worker, a client, and his wife strayed from the ideal of monogamy, it was, to a certain extent, legally and socially tolerated (for an analysis of the triangulation between strippers' clients, their wives, and strippers, see Frank 2002). One of Sofía's frequent clients, a married man she also considered to be a friend, would often give her money and gifts, and continued to do so and talk with her on the phone once she left Reynosa. While she was still in Reynosa, this man offered on several occasions to rent an apartment for her and support her as a mistress. Sofía told me that while she considered his offer, she would never accept it. I knew that most of her relationships outside of work were with women and assumed this to be the reason that she would "never" become this man's mistress. I asked, "Oh, is it because you only would want a woman as a partner?" She answered, "No. It's because he has a wife, and it's wrong. It's different from when I'm working in la zona, because if I'm his mistress, I'm a threat to his marriage. And I don't want to ruin anyone's marriage." Having a sexual relationship and friendship with a man that was part of her job was morally acceptable. She was merely fulfilling her duty as part of the "necessary evil" task of providing a sexual outlet for men. Prostitution was seen as a complement to, rather than necessarily at odds with, heteromonogamy in the triad of sex worker, husband, and wife. However, if outside of la zona Sofía were to allow herself to become a mistress, this would be morally dubious and "wrong." Both kinds of relationship involve forms of transactional sex as well as friendship and intimacy, but the categorization of one type of relationship as a job helped to free Sofía of culpability in relation to a marriage.

The idea that men's sexual behavior is beyond their control not only leads to the justification and legal toleration of prostitution as "necessary evil" but also has wider gendered implications. First, if men cannot control their sexual behavior, they are less likely to be culpable for sexual violence. The other side of the coin of the gendered double standard is the surveillance of women's sexuality. Men, in this view, can be seen as having a certain kind of nature, while women are defined by their reproductive roles and distinct sexual behaviors, which must be controlled. The system that registers sex workers and forces them to be "public women" stigmatizes a group of women while, in theory, keeping other women safe and pure. As Bliss (2001) notes, the existence of public women upholds the moral order by preventing men from seducing or raping other women. Thus, providing "public women" for voracious men also keeps nonprostitute women virginal or monogamous.

Sex workers also highlighted the care aspect of their work—including forms of emotional labor. Sofía said that some men didn't want to have sex, but rather would visit to tell stories or talk about things that bothered them, adding, "We are psychologists and givers of advice." Eva pointed out that some men cried with them, and that sex workers knew secrets that not even the clients' wives knew. In this case, sex workers compared their emotional labor to nonstigmatized professions in order to demonstrate its social value.

Cubana was less concerned about respectability than many of the other sex workers and spoke with the greatest pride about being a sex worker. Cubana said, "For twenty-five years, I was the best whore (*puta*). Twenty-five years. The best here. For this reason, everyone knows me." She claimed to earn more than other women, who she said would only be paid one hundred pesos because all they did was take off their underwear and open their legs. She earned more because she was sexy in bed—she talked dirty to clients, gave them oral sex, and had sex with them in a variety of positions.

Cubana's pride in working as a *puta* was an anomaly, perhaps because talking openly about sex is less taboo in Cuba than it is in Mexico. When having serious discussions about their professions, sex workers in Reynosa almost never uttered the word "prostitute" or "sex worker" and usually opted for the vaguer *nosotras* ("us") or would say *trabajar en eso*, or "this line of work." In interviews and serious conversations, instead of referring to la zona, women tended to use the deictic *aquí*, or "here" to refer to what happened in la zona and *afuera*, "outside," to refer to what happened outside of la zona.

In la zona, many sex workers felt a moral obligation to maintain what they called a *doble vida* or double life, bearing the stigma of prostitution while protecting their families from the stigma as well as the knowledge that they engage in sex work (chapter 2). Sex workers often worked far from their families as well as kept secrets from them to maintain a double life. La zona fostered queer intimacies because the space itself and many of the relations that proliferated in it were taboo and had to be shrouded in secrets. Some of the queer intimacies fostered by sex work were with clients, other sex workers, and drug workers. Sex workers engaged in nonreproductive sex with men for money. Relationships with clients were complex, varied, and sometimes lasted years, and while instances of coercion and disagreements were not uncommon, sex workers and clients sometimes developed relationships that included emotional intimacy and affection. Clients would buy gifts for sex workers or buy them groceries when they were low on money. Sex workers' relationships with each other were similarly complex: while I observed a great deal of mistrust and fighting among them, they often referred to each other as family.

Parallels and Intersections between the Moral and Occupational Careers of Drug Workers and Sex Workers

In the 2010 Mexican film *El Infierno*, directed by Luis Estrada, Benny is deported from the United States after living there for twenty years and returns to his small town in rural Mexico only to find it completely overtaken by the drug trade. He becomes involved with the girlfriend of his recently deceased brother, a sex worker with a teenage son. Due to a predicament of his girlfriend's son that requires a large sum of money, Benny begins to work for a drug organization. After Benny complains to his sex worker girlfriend about how difficult it is for him to have to kill people, she says, "One can get used to anything, except not eating." Her comment about work in the drug industry is perhaps also a commentary about prostitution—an understated comparison of two "easy money" industries that outsiders often believed to be easy but insiders argued was difficult.

I had heard this phrase "One can get used to anything, except not eating" word for word from Sofía, when she explained to me her difficulties as a beginning sex worker in Boystown. Sofía knew that flirting and drinking with men would be part of her job when she arrived in la zona, but she also claimed to be unaware that she would have to have sex with them. Although she found having sex with clients to be "horrible" at first, she got used to it. Her story of innocence and coercion may also be a way of establishing herself as a respectable woman. Other sex workers told similar stories. Both a sex worker in Reynosa and a sex worker in a popular movie uttered the same statement about getting used to difficult work being preferable to going hungry. Women working in maquiladoras could have just as easily said it too. This statement points to ostensibly "easy money" involving corporal and moral difficulties not always recognized by outsiders.

This chapter opened with Frida's concern that her son would grow up to be a narco if she were to stay in Reynosa. Several other poor women (a maquiladora worker, two sex workers, and a woman who sold snacks in la zona) expressed to me their fears of having their sons grow up in Reynosa because of the temptation to become involved in the drug trade. Antonio, a graphic designer in his early twenties who grew up in Reynosa, told me, "In Reynosa, little boys don't dream of growing up to be Superman or Batman. They want to be narcos when they grow up."

People in Reynosa considered both drug use and prostitution to be vices, and middle-class people indexed their respectability by indicating that they did not use drugs ("not even marijuana"), but sex workers were more heavily stigmatized than drug workers. Killing people (which cartel members sometimes had to do) was considered to be morally wrong. Yet drug workers benefited from the valuation of their work as sexy, cool, and a way to acquire money and power, while sex workers grappled with the whore stigma.

This is consistent with Campbell's point that in Mexican border cities, "drug trafficking is considered an inevitable, rather than shocking, fact of the border economy" (Campbell 2009, 31). The knowledge of the importance of drug money to the local economy might be one reason that work in this industry was less stigmatized. A dentist with her own practice told me she made her money "honestly," but her business suffered when the drug business was making less money, because the local economy was so dependent upon drug money. Drug cartels are often deeply socially embedded in communities as well, and people are often likely to turn to them for help (Diaz-Cayeros et al. 2011). *Reynosenses* did not usually criticize drug work on moral grounds unless it was negatively impacting their lives or projects through violence, intimidation, or taxation.

Reynosa residents feared narcos but also treated them like celebrities. Reynosa residents in their forties and fifties told me that everyone had always known which families made their money through smuggling and trafficking, but that they had only recently started to be seen as celebrities. This social value given to narcos was reinforced by larger elements of *narcocultura*, including the cult of la Santa Muerte and the popularity of *narcocorridos*, ballads that heroize drug traffickers to the beat of danceable music. The celebrity status of drug organizations was sometimes intertwined with techniques of intimidation. When several narcos wanted to have drinks with a friend at a bar, Jessica said, they would simply enter a bar, and their armed guards would not let anyone leave or enter or use their cellular phones. The narcos would buy a bottle of alcohol for every table and flirt with women, who knew that they must respond positively to these advances even if they were not interested.

I experienced a similar dynamic once, while enjoying cupcakes at a birthday celebration with a group of missionaries and sex workers in the prostitution zone. A man who was rumored to be a high-level member of the cartel, and who undoubtedly had some power in la zona, tried to get my phone number, set up a date with me, and get me into his shiny new SUV. I tried to avoid a date or a car ride in a way that would not anger him, as I assumed that he had the power to both hurt me and make my research more difficult. I smiled and flirted back just enough to validate his masculinity, yet I emphasized that I was engaged. Pretending to be heterosexual, monogamous, and respectable, I told him that it was important to me to be a good girlfriend, and that good girlfriends do not give their phone numbers to men or hang out in their cars or houses.

Several other women told me that they employed similar maneuvers to get out of tricky situations with narcos, but it is also true that many women in Reynosa sought out these men to gain access to luxury goods and money. Young people in Reynosa reported that plenty of women would try to date narcos so that they could be bought nice things and nice clothes. Although these instances of transactional sex are not defined as prostitution precisely, people in Reynosa discussed them as being a form of prostitution. Indeed, I found that while both local and migrant mothers feared that their sons would grow up to work for drug organizations, they feared that their daughters would date or marry narcos. Jessica's schoolmate, Esther, traded sexual favors with older men, including narcos, for money and name-brand clothes while in high school. Jessica and Antonio told me that Esther was a self-proclaimed sex addict and was stigmatized by many of her classmates. Jessica said that although Esther came from a humble family, her marriage to a narco bought her a new, expensive SUV, straight teeth (because he bought her braces), fake fingernails, and a nice body (he paid for breast implants). One of my close *reynosense* friends who migrated to Europe while I was in the field confided in me that she hoped her youngest sister, Yaneth, would move to Europe to live with her: "What kind of a fucking life awaits Yaneth in Reynosa? To marry someone connected to narcos like [my other little sister]?" Thus, women who wished to capitalize on some of the value produced by the drug industry usually had to do so through intimate relationships of various types (often transactional sex) with narcos. Poor young men aspired to be like narcos because they were seen as powerful and rich, and poor young women often aspired to date or marry them to access luxury goods or as a technique of upward mobility.

That little girls did not aspire to be prostitutes but little boys aspired to work for drug cartels brings home their gendered social valuation. While a prostitute was a prototypical image of the worst kind of woman one could be, the successful, high-ranking narco is arguably a prototypical image of successful masculinity in Reynosa as well as increasingly throughout Mexico, especially for young men from poor families. Muehlmann (2013) discusses the high-ranking narco as representing successful masculinity, sex appeal, wealth, and power. Although few of the men in her study achieved great wealth, this image was an important force attracting men into the drug trade. The moral careers of drug workers also meant that leaving the drug industry left them with declining prestige, money, sex appeal, and self-confidence. Muehlmann found that while men in her study were quick to identify as narcos and would even exaggerate their involvement, the relatively few women who were involved would downplay their involvement and explain it in terms of family obligation and sacrifice for their families, especially their children, much like sex workers in Reynosa did (2013, 53–55). However, a few successful female drug traffickers have been able to harness respect in a male-dominated field (Campbell 2008). These examples suggest that both drug work and sex work might violate conceptions of what it is to be a good woman.

Both drug workers and sex workers are likely to have greater purchasing power than many people working in other aspects of the economy. They also face unique occupational risks, including death and drug addiction. But it is ultimately the gendered meanings attached to these jobs that make them so differently valued. While little girls did not dream of being prostitutes, there was concern on the part of missionaries as well as other sex workers that children in the neighborhood might end up in this profession—the moral careers of children in the neighborhood were, in a sense, predetermined at birth.

A rhyming local adage predicted, "*De Aquiles Serdán, nunca saldrán*," or "Those from Aquiles Serdán [the neighborhood la zona was located in] will never leave." This phrase was often heard in Reynosa, and it suggests that those born in la zona would have limited mobility—presumably because poverty, drugs, and prostitution would limit their occupational careers.[15] A point of speculation among other sex workers was the whereabouts of the children of sex workers who were addicted to crack cocaine. They were imagined to have been adopted or purchased by American families, killed in order to sell organs to Americans, or kidnapped by drug organizations to make child pornography marketed to Americans. In these rumors, migrants, sex workers, and their children either complete families or in some way serve Americans: they are killed to sustain life for American bodies or they are raped to provide sexual satisfaction for American pedophiles. These rumors indicate that the subjectivity of sex workers in Reynosa entailed an anxiety about the vulnerabilities of their bodies and those of their children in relation to both drug cartels and to US capital, which, of course, are deeply intertwined.

The occupational and moral careers of those in the drug trade and the sex industry included overlapping connections and similar struggles with work and family. Diego's experiences in drug work provide a good example of how the values of family, money, and work were weighed in the moral economy surrounding the drug industry. I met Diego because I had already interviewed his sister, Jessica, who was a friend of mine, and his mother. Diego's mother and sister urged me to interview him because he had worked for *la maña*, struggled with a drug addiction, and lived inside of the prostitution zone for a few months. Diego was over six feet tall and had a muscular build and black tattoos on his arms. He started using drugs while working in low-level jobs for the cartel in which he had twenty-four-hour shifts. He explained to me that working in the drug industry so commonly resulted in addictions for the cartel's workers that the cartel in Reynosa had its own rehabilitation center.[16] Diego had also been to rehabilitation centers in Reynosa and Monterrey. His mother slipped drugs into his soda one night and dragged him into the trunk of his car, and he woke up in a rehabilitation center in downtown Monterrey.

During my first interview with Diego, he told me the little he remembered about life in la zona, explaining that he was not sure if he lived there for weeks or for years because of his heavy drug use. He lived in a bar with a much older sex worker, Gabby, who had mostly retired but still sold sex to special clients. Gabby owned the bar and collected money from other sex workers who worked there. Diego said he was in a relationship with Gabby, and he was also a pimp to the other women who worked in the bar, whom he ordered to iron his clothes and cook for him as well as to have sex with clients. He also told me that he felt ashamed that he had sex with both women and men for money when he was living in la zona.

Diego and I became good friends. One day, as we were lounging on my couch, he told me that he wanted to tell me the truth about something. He confessed that when he had come back to Reynosa from Monterrey a few weeks before, the impetus for his return was a job with the cartel making US$1,500 a week. Diego had never before made that kind of money, but he explained that he had a good record because he had worked trafficking drugs across the border as a teenager and guarding hostages later on. However, the person who was going to give him the job was angry that Diego had shaved his head and told him that he could not have the job until his hair grew back. Diego explained that the cartel only employed people who were well-dressed and clean-cut for these kinds of positions so that they would not look suspicious. When I asked him what the job would entail, Diego replied, slowly, with a frown, "I don't know. Probably kidnapping people, hitting them. Maybe killing them. I don't know. I've never done that before. I've seen it happen, but I've never done it." We were both quiet for a few moments. I told Diego that it was difficult for me to imagine him beating up people and killing them because I thought of him as loving and tender. He agreed that he was kind and gentle with me and with his family, but he reminded me that I had never seen him angry and explained that he had another, darker side. Diego explained that although he didn't want to kill people for a living, the dire state of the economy made this job tempting. But the worst part about working for narcos, Diego said, was that it would require completely cutting off contact with his family and friends, to keep them safe. "Would you hang out with me if I worked for them?" he asked. "Probably not," I replied, "because I would be afraid." I told him that other people might not have many options, but that he did: he could work with family members in Texas, and his aunt in Reynosa had offered to pay for him to go back to school. I said, "Diego, it's better to be middle class and have family than to be rich and have no family, or perhaps to be dead." I rubbed my hand over his buzzed head, thinking about what might happen once his hair grew back.

After this conversation, I worried about Diego. Whenever I did not hear from him for several days, I was convinced that either he had gone back to using drugs or had taken the job working for a drug organization and had cut off contact to protect me. His plan to cut off ties with family members while working for the cartel is similar to sex workers' double lives, which will be more fully examined in the next chapter. In both industries, although one might acquire money more quickly than in other lines of work, such duality is a precondition for this work to be morally acceptable. The double life is necessary for sex workers because of the stigma that a sex worker is morally expected to shield her family from. In the case of those working for a drug cartel, it is the safety of their family members rather than their reputations that are at stake. Diego also referenced a duality of selves very much like the double lives described by sex workers when he told me that I don't know his other side, the side of him that made it possible to beat and kill people as part of his professional duties.

Both drug work and sex work created separation from normative forms of intimacy and cohabitation and fostered other forms of intimacy that could be thought of as queer. They are seen as "other" to habitation in a normative heterosexual (publicly) monogamous nuclear or extended domestic unit, the heteronormative and reproductive family that the state promotes. Furthermore, both drug work and sex work are considered to be morally ambiguous. Cartel membership involved the keeping of public secrets and homosocial bonds (which are beyond the scope of this study). I heard of and occasionally witnessed intimacies between sex workers and drug workers: I learned about two instances of older sex workers being given free rent by those who owned blocks of rooms inside of Boystown. I also saw Eva and El Grillo—the man who worked for the cartel who was in charge of collecting rent and performing other managerial tasks for the block of rooms that Eva lived and worked in—develop a friendship over time. El Grillo gave Eva certain responsibilities such as selling condoms and showing new sex workers the ropes, but I also witnessed a joking banter between them. El Grillo and Eva seemed familiar with each other's personal lives, and he was familiar with her good cooking. They joked that many people suspected they were involved romantically, but characterized their relationship as that of brother and sister.

The moral careers of drug workers and sex workers included premature death by homicide as a likely possibility. Sex workers worried that they would be killed and buried in unmarked graves. Men working in drug trafficking and those who knew them could also imagine their deaths. During my reunion in Mexico City in December 2010 with Eva and Sofía, Eva gave Sofía's seventeen-year-old son, Sergio, a similar rationale to the one that I had given to Diego for why he should not work for a drug organization. Sergio accompanied us on the trip, along with his fourteen-year-old pregnant girlfriend, Susana. We were all chatting in the room I rented for us at a bed-and-breakfast. While I had known that Sofía's son had once been a drug user, I was unaware that her ongoing stress and preoccupation about his well-being was in part due to the fact that he had been working for a drug cartel in Tampico. During our three-day reunion, Sergio told stories about being trained by the cartel in the jungle, being deprived of food and water, and having to drink from murky green ponds. He also told a story about a shootout where he was one of the only survivors; he witnessed his friend get shot in the hand. Eva and Sergio talked about the red color that bullets leave in space as they pass by, as well as what they feel like entering the body—at first more like heat than pain. They compared techniques of intimidation used by the cartels in Mexico to the practices Eva witnessed in El Salvador during the Civil War. Sofía told us that while her son was with *los mañosos*, she prayed a scripture every day that Ashley, an American missionary, had given her. Once Sergio came back home, Sofía said, several friends who also had missing sons asked her to pass along the scripture, because it appeared to have worked. Eva then began to reprimand Sergio, "You need to behave yourself (*compórtate bien*). Don't go back with those people." Sergio replied that he had left the cartel in September, which was the reason that he was working in Mexico City and could not return to Tampico. He told us that he had no intention of going back to them. Eva said,

> You need to be good, because now you're going to have a child. If you work for them, you will likely die, and Susana is pretty, she will find another father for the child, but it won't be the same. A man will tell a woman, "I love your child and will raise it as my own," but they never do, and it becomes even worse once they have another child together. You don't want that to happen to your child, do you? Don't let the money tempt you. It's not worth it. You will die young. It's better to have a long life and less money. We all start at the bottom. Look at my daughters. When they moved here [to Mexico City] they could only afford a tiny apartment. They had nothing and slept on the floor. Now they have six beds, a television, and many things. It's still humble but they're happy. You should find a way for Susana to live with

you and you can start from scratch like this. Tell her parents that we all start with nothing.

Eva threatened Sergio with the idea of his own death, and she tried to convince him that being alive and able to be in contact with his family was more important than making a lot of money. Emphasizing the importance of life over wealth, and the moral obligation to try to stay alive in order to fulfill one's obligations to one's children, Eva's comments demonstrate the values shared by many other poor women in Reynosa. Her comments recognized that familial obligations come with financial obligations, as she mentioned the pressure that Sergio might feel to provide for his family. However, she warned him that economic gain was not as important as ensuring that he would be alive to raise his child. Eva's statements similarly weigh the intimate costs and economic benefits of working for the cartel. She urged him not to be seduced by easy money, emphasizing the familial obligations that his death would make him unable to fulfill. This was one of the very few occasions in which I heard people in Reynosa addressing the obligations of fathers. The obligations of mothers, in contrast, were perennial.

Sex workers worried about the fates of their bodies after death. Wright argues that discourses surrounding both the femicides in Juárez and drug-related violence (of which men are usually the casualties) constitute both kinds of murders as "normal" in gendered ways (Wright 2011). Politicians placed the blame for murders upon the victims to exonerate themselves. Politicians made the murders of women seem like the women's fault by implicating that they were sex workers, while suggesting that drug traffickers were rational businessmen only killing other criminals. Because the moral career of both sex workers and drug traffickers normalize their murders, their occurrence is ordinary—not a cause for investigation. Once a precedent has been set that finding bodies with certain kinds of markings suggests the imagined profession of the victim that negates their victim status, almost anybody might be killed with impunity as long as the sufficient signs are written upon the corpse (Luna 2005).

Conclusion

The gendered and commodified intimacies involved in the US-Mexico relationship shape not only opportunities for work but also meanings surrounding gender, sexuality, and labor. The identity of Reynosa's elites was formed in relation to various significant others, including Americans and internal others from southern Mexico. Proximity to a relatively wealthy country that officially prohibits particular vices plays a role in creating the "backstage" of Mexican border cities (Lomnitz 2001). Ideas about normative and nonnormative sexual behavior were mapped upon the landscape of Reynosa through the creation of the prostitution zone. Boystown is an even further fractalization within the city of Reynosa—a space to contain "vice" so that the rest of the city can paint itself as virtuous. The US-Mexico border shapes the occupational careers of Mexican border residents by creating gendered opportunities for relatively quick profit. The prohibition of drugs, prostitution, and at one time alcohol in the United States has pushed US demand-based pleasure industries to the Mexican side of the border.

Although drug work and sex work were both considered "necessary evils" in certain ways and were both relatively lucrative compared to other professions, it was easier for men to create social value through their labor. Border residents worried that their sons would work for cartels (as indeed many have) and that their daughters would marry or date cartel members. Calling drug work and sex work "easy money" reflected the moral ambiguity of these industries and their queerness. A slippage between easy money and easy work became a way of criticizing workers as lazy. People inside these industries rejected these criticisms and pointed out the difficulties of their work.

Little boys wanted to grow up to be narcos, but little girls did not aspire to be sex workers, because while drug work was seen as a symbol of successful masculinity, sex workers were marked with the whore stigma. The culmination of racial, class-based, regional, and gender hierarchies became most apparent in the way that internal migrants from Veracruz, as well as other poor, dark-skinned migrants who were also called veracruzanos, were blamed for social ills in Reynosa. The whore stigma was widely deployed against veracruzanas, not only at those who were sex workers. In some cases, those who were not officially sex workers were seen as more dangerous. Sex workers created value by emphasizing the "necessary" part of "necessary evil" and by arguing that their stigmatized work was socially important.

Drug and sex workers' work fostered both normative familial separations (geographical and informational) as well as queer intimacies (outside of the normative family structure and shrouded in secrets). The lives, subjectivities, deaths, and posthumous reputations of drug workers and sex workers, as well as those assumed to engage in this kind of work, were shaped by the ways in which death was considered to be a normal occupational hazard for people who worked in these industries.

CHAPTER 2

Rumors of Violence and Feelings of Vulnerability

We have considered the nuances of *dinero fácil*—how money earned through drug trafficking and sex work is and is not easy—and here we dive deeper to see how these economic exchanges are caught up in violence, power, and intimacy. During Reynosa's drug war, people nurtured intimate connections with the people they cared about by sharing rumors about violence. This story was first told to me in whispers at a fiftieth birthday party in McAllen, Texas, by a man who, like many of us at the party, lived across the border in Reynosa, Tamaulipas.

> A woman in a car sat waiting at a traffic light for several minutes after it had turned green because a brand-new Lincoln Navigator with tinted windows and US plates was idling in front of her. She didn't honk her horn. Finally, a man got out of the car and approached her, laughing. "My friend and I had a bet," he said. "I told him that if you honked, I was going to kill you, and if you didn't honk, I was going to give you five hundred pesos." Opening his jacket to expose his gun, he handed money to her and said, "You win."

My host mother later forwarded me an email of the first-person account of the same story, which ended in a warning to the loved ones of the narrator to exercise caution and to avoid honking their car horns. This story was told to me as an act of care to help me safely navigate the city by car. But these rumors also summoned fear at the moment of telling that would resurface as I drove around the city.

The primary forms of power held by drug organizations that I discuss here are tied to coercion grounded in violence—the power to kill or let live—as well as in the economic ability to purchase loyalty and impunity. This kind of power is best described by the expression *plata o plomo*, silver or lead, which is the choice narcos offered between accepting currency (in exchange for cooperation) or a bullet (death). *Plata o plomo* is a key method through which drug organizations have woven themselves into Mexico's political fabric. Howard Campbell (2009, 16) shows how *plata o plomo* has proved integral to relationships of "corruption and collusion" between drug traffickers and Mexican police, as well as judicial and military forces.[1] Although this story told to me at a birthday party rehearses *plata o plomo*, its protagonist was not granted the opportunity to choose between silver and lead; she was a pawn in a deadly game she did not know she was playing. In this rumor *plata o plomo* appears, at first glance, to be a mere game for narcos' amusement rather than a political/economic strategy. Yet the fear generated by the rumors that snowball from such (possible) acts reinforce their political and economic power. The takeaway of this rumor, like many circulating in Reynosa at the time, was that one should be vigilant and treat narcos with respect and deference.

Rumors like this have shaped affective atmospheres of terror, especially as Reynosa has become further militarized by the Mexican state in what was an attempt to combat narco-trafficking and its attendant torture, killings, and threats.[2] As Reynosa residents spread rumors of violence, borders between narco-controlled territory and state-controlled territory shifted in and through their bodies. I argue that in such atmospheres of terror, rumors of violence have a particular kind of contagious performativity that conditions affective responses and inculcates both fear and intimacy. Rumors are performative speech acts in the sense theorized by J. L. Austin (1962): they are utterances that do not merely describe but also *accomplish* something in the social world.[3] Performative rumors of violence shape the way power feels. These rumors had corporeal and social effects, creating intense sensations in bodies that led not only to collective fear but also to shared intimacy. These stories produce shared bodily intensities such as a rapid heart rate, a slowness of breath, and a hyperawareness. In the first part of this chapter, I draw on theories of performativity, conspiracy, and affect to show how sharing rumors about violence spread both fear and vulnerability. The second part of my discussion examines how Reynosa residents generally, and sex workers specifically, changed their spatial practices in response to both affective atmospheres of terror and the content of rumors. These effects first occurred among Reynosa's less-empowered populations, like sex workers, and eventually among populations that historically felt relatively safe in border cities, such as American (sex) tourists and missionaries. I conclude with how this particular manifestation of fear and precarity led to the decline of the prostitution zone for sex workers, missionaries, and clients.

Because narco power and state power overlap at various levels, they are often indistinguishable to the populations that reside in their territories. Fear forms an important part of the power wielded by drug organizations, which have diversified economic strategies to include protection rackets, extortion, and kidnapping. The spread of terror makes their other enterprises profitable (see Campbell and Hansen 2014), and drug organizations clearly take part in actions meant to spread fear. But this chapter focuses on how practices of the resident population likewise contribute to atmospheres of terror.

Contagious Rumors and Bodily Intensities

When Sergio and his pregnant fourteen-year-old girlfriend joined my reunion with Eva and Sofía in Mexico City in 2011, we all exchanged news and gossip, reminiscing about funny things we had experienced together but also repeating rumors of the gun battles and murders that took place in Reynosa.

One morning, as we were all eating a breakfast of orange juice, coffee, and spicy egg dishes, the narco-stories of the day began. Although we were pretty sure that we were a safe distance from Reynosa's narcos, Eva spoke in hushed tones as she told us a story about two "little old women" shopping at a market in downtown Reynosa. While one woman loudly recounted a rumor about narcos, the other remained quiet and looked nervous. The loud woman was later found dead, with a severed finger in her mouth. A note was attached to the corpse: "Keep quiet if you don't have anything to say." Our eyes widened, we breathed deeply, and we looked at one another in silence.

All of us felt Eva's story that morning about the old woman with a finger in her mouth on an affective level. Affects are intense sensations in the body resulting from external stimuli, and they are noncognitive, nonconscious, and nonrational (Gould 2009, 19–20). Rumors shape emotions, actions, thoughts, and subjectivities, but they are first experienced at the level of affect.[4] While emotions are largely individual, affect is intersubjective and bodily transmitted, and, as Sara Ahmed (2010, 39) notes, "contagious" (see also Herrmann 2015; Richard and Rudnyckyj 2009). "Ordinary affects," as Kathleen Stewart (2007, 2–3), has written, "are public feelings. . . . Their significance lies in the intensities they build and in what thoughts and feelings they make possible." My bodily response during Eva's story was a fight-or-flight adrenaline surge and a rapid heartbeat. In an attentive state of increased psychological and physiological tension, I breathed slowly and leaned in to hear Eva's whisper. But while shared, even public, surely these affective intensities were experienced in different ways by different people. As Lauren Berlant (2008, 4) notes, the emotional states linked to affective structures are not predetermined. Ben Anderson (2009, 78) defines the affective atmosphere as "the shared ground from which subjective states and their attendant feelings and emotions emerge."

Stories of narcos' exploits were followed by long moments of silence and intense eye contact; sometimes there were tears. That day, Eva broke the heavy silence by affirming for us all: "That is why I need to leave Reynosa." When I asked her if she could think of any kind of solution to what was happening in Mexico, Eva said that all we could do was pray, and she assured me that God must have kept her alive for a reason. Although living in territory contested between drug organizations and state actors put Eva at risk, she ultimately had faith, or at least hope, that God's sovereignty would prevail. In the meantime, she spread rumors.

While designating a narrative as a rumor or a conspiracy theory calls into question its truth-value, this is not my intention.[5] My analysis of rumors, rather, is in line with that of scholars of conspiracy theory who do not attempt to assess the veracity of narratives but rather examine them to make sense of particular political conditions in which available information is incomplete or inconsistent (Butt 2005; Fenster 1999; Keeley 1999; Stewart 1999). Stories like the one told by Eva proved vital for transmitting information to one's friends and family, in part because people associated with drug organizations effectively controlled the press. While I knew as early as 2008 that the press was not free in Reynosa (and *reynosenses* knew this long before I did), this information circulated only in rumors until surfacing in the US and Mexican press in 2010. That year, Mexico was the second-deadliest country in the world for journalists (Heslop 2011), and during a two-week period, eight journalists in Reynosa were kidnapped; two were released with a warning, one died after being tortured, and four are still missing (Pérez Arellano 2013; Stevenson 2010). Many gun battles in Reynosa went unreported by the local media,[6] so people depended on rumors for information.

Moreover, the violence and inequality in the neoliberal and heavily militarized Reynosa of 2008 and 2009 created fertile ground for rumors. Rumors and conspiracy theories can operate as critiques of larger power structures by people with little access to power (Comaroff and Comaroff 2001; Hoskins 2002; Kirsch 2002; Masquelier 2000; White 1997). Rumors are one means through which people react to collective experiences of inequality, exploitation, and political violence, and the circulation of rumors intensifies during times of extreme exploitation and suffering (Butt 2005; Kirsch 2002;

Masquelier 2000; White 1997). Mexicans have relied more heavily on gossip than on official information sources because the national public sphere has rendered itself untrustworthy by excluding many voices due to power asymmetries (Lomnitz 1995, 36). Rihan Yeh (2012) further demonstrates asymmetries in the Mexican public sphere through her analysis of Tijuana's two publics: a hearsay public constituted of the lower classes, and a bourgeois public that rested on a "we" of citizenship that distanced itself from poverty and criminality. The absence of a free press in Reynosa led to a particularly dynamic hearsay public in Reynosa, but Reynosa also contained a bourgeois public composed of elites who considered themselves to be locals. In private, these *reynosenses* whispered complaints that narcos were taking over their city, and in public they loudly attributed the city's problems to migrants from southern Mexico and Central America. For the purposes of my discussion, I have focused on what Yeh (2012, 716) would call the "hearsay public" register.

During the drug war, rumors of violence had performative effects—their contagion circulated affectively and increased perceptions of risk and vulnerability. Performative rumors played an important role in constituting power relations they might, at first glance, appear only to describe. I am thus interested in what kind of work rumors in Reynosa *do*. Performatives cannot be evaluated in terms of truth. Their success requires felicitous conditions that allow them to do the things in the social world that they name. I do not know if an elderly woman was found with a severed finger in her mouth. The local press in Reynosa did not publish such things. The absence of a free press and the fact that people periodically received evidence of violent acts created the conditions of possibility for such rumors to be especially poignant. Howard Campbell (2014, 64) shows how narco-propaganda has propagated terror in Mexico through public acts of violence, media censorship, and written statements, videos, and music. Reynosa residents were active consumers of narco-propaganda, including my host family, which crowded around a computer to watch YouTube videos of Reynosa's gun battles. Some were filmed by news reporters, while others were taken on cell phones and put to the soundtrack of *narcocorridos*.

One of my host sister's friends, Josiah, who was a low-level worker for the Gulf Cartel, claimed that the song "Fiesta en la sierra," by the musical group Tucanes de Tijuana, was an accurate reflection of the ties between narcos and politicians. The song is set at a lavish ranch party in the mountains where Mexican politicians and high-level narcos socialize together. Invoking the "we" of the Gulf Cartel and referring to the mayor of Reynosa, Josiah said, "We put him into power." Politicians were elected as well as killed to the beat of *narcocorridos*. When Juan Antonio Guajardo Anzaldúa, Rio Bravo's former mayor running for reelection, was gunned down with five other people in broad daylight in November 2007 (Sánchez et al. 2007), the Tucanes de Tijuana allegedly played at a party at Reynosa's Holiday Inn put on by a drug organization to celebrate his death. While the death of Guajardo was devastating for some of my missionary contacts who were friends of his and his family, it was also difficult for other locals I spoke to, who saw this as evidence that local politicians who tried to fight narco corruption would be executed.

The circulation of rumors and threats, and the occasional display of dead, mutilated bodies, sometimes with messages attached, generated a public both passive and terrified. Iterability is partially responsible for the power of narco-stories (Derrida 1982). In stories like the one narrated by Eva, narco power emerges with few constraints, as almost absolute and God-like. Stories of narcos threatening, killing, and mutilating people as well as controlling various aspects of political life snowballed through rumors, in effect magnifying the power of drug organizations. Whether or not narco-stories accurately reflected the social world, each rumor's circulation constituted a further iteration of this power. The subject in most of these rumors, the agentive actor in each sentence, was a supposed narco; the verb was torture or murder; the direct object was a person that the speaker and listener were afraid they might become. Consequently, each telling and retelling of a narco-story spread both imagined and felt narco power and created subjects regulated through fear. In Reynosa, the circulation of rumors of violence led to embodied affects such as fear and anxiety that changed the way people experienced their own vulnerability. Rumors form an important part of discursive power; their presence changes how people talk and think about the world and imagine their place in it. As we will see below, vulnerability was gendered, raced, and classed, but the circulation of narco-stories contributed to atmospheres of terror that created increasingly vulnerable-feeling subjects all around. The repetition of violent narco-stories not only expressed cartel power but also amplified it. According to Danilyn Rutherford (2012, 101), every violent act may be considered performative insofar as it "says" what it "does." I argue that in environments of terror, even *rumors* of violence are performative in this way. Hearing narratives about incidents of assault, kidnapping, torture, and murder does not hurt people in the same way that experiencing or witnessing violence does. Yet while rumors may not create the physical violence they name, they have performative effects, producing a sensation akin to what subjugation feels like. Narco-stories produce the anticipation of pain just as they produced the terror of the apparently unchecked power of narcos.

All rumors, like all speech acts, have performative capacities. Rumors of violence differ in that they recapitulate previous violent acts and contagiously shape how power feels for the people circulating and listening to these stories. As in Derrida's conception of iterability, some rumors have been circulated so many times and in so many contexts that they have become spatially, temporally, and substantively separated from original acts of brutality. Some narco-stories surely named events that never occurred, but *reynosenses* witnessed violent acts often enough to sustain belief in rumors. Yet despite, or perhaps because of, the distance between the violent act and its performative citing, rumors continue to draw on the power of violent acts. As with Michael Taussig's (1986) concept of epistemic murk, what happens in the imagination adds force to the power of fear in an environment of terror. These gaps between the evidence of violent acts and perceived violence not only intensify fear but can also, perhaps oddly, allow rumors to provide a feeling of comfort, because they help make sense of an uncertain world.

Sharing rumors about torture, murder, and kidnapping produced affective states that allowed for the bond of collective trauma in Reynosa. Stranded in a mutual sense of powerlessness and isolation, migrants withheld information from faraway family members to avoid worrying them. They also nurtured local intimacies through the circulation of narco-stories. Missionaries, sex workers, and I observed that when we traveled to other cities to visit family members, it was difficult to explain how fear haunted us in Reynosa. Indeed, many of us lied to loved ones so as not to worry them.

Rumors of violence in an atmosphere of terror are contagious in part because they help sustain social bonds. Sex workers would often preface a story about narcos with, "I may end up floating in the river for telling you this, but . . ." The "but" was followed by the revelation of a rumor. They divulged stories and speculations compulsively, torn between reluctance and recklessness. They often spoke in whispers, a gesture reflecting both the regulation of fear and the intimacy of trust. These moments of sharing created intimacy in an uncertain world. The take-home message of the narco-story about a gossiping old woman who was found dead with her finger in her mouth was that one should not speak of narcos in public, yet people like Eva spread these stories regardless of risk. They served as a parable-like warning to those with loose lips.

When I asked my closest contacts to repeat these stories for my recorder, they did so hesitantly, tensely, and with fewer details. I suspected, but never asked to confirm, that we feared the same fate: that a high-ranking narco would find my recording and torture and murder the participants of my study or me. I could never tell if this was a reasonable fear or paranoia.

Given the potential risks of exchanging rumors, retelling stories not only created but also reflected trust and intimacy.

Reynosa residents cared for one another through text messages, phone calls, Twitter, and Facebook. On social media, I observed Reynosa contacts warn each other of where they heard gunshots or explosions. Spreading rumors despite the risk constitutes an act of care because disseminating knowledge can, in theory, save those who acquire it from harm. These rumors often have a warning subtext: *Don't honk your car horn. Don't leave the house at night.* Circulating narco-stories was not only a means of caring for one's loved ones; it also worked, on an affective level, to spread terror.

Embodied Spaces of Narco/State Territory

Affective atmospheres of terror had embodied, spatialized, and social effects that changed how people moved through Reynosa generally, and through la zona specifically. Setha Low's (2016) concept of embodied space attends to the human body as a spatial field that both constitutes and shapes space. Low's work not only bridges smaller-scale analyses of bodies and macro-analyses of the social and political world, but also supplements accounts of the material production and phenomenological construction of space with bodies and their affects, mobilities, and feelings. This concept helps explain how terror contagiously spread through bodies in specific kinds of places and altered peoples' trajectories. This terror had material and social effects on border cities as businesses closed and migrants returned to their places of origin. Fear pervaded the embodied habits of whispering rumors, scanning the landscape for new SUVs, and driving carefully. Narco-stories generated temporal and spatial topographies of fear in Reynosa that eventually became generalized to any time and place. As shootings, which had historically occurred at night, started to happen during the day, many *reynosenses* became reluctant to leave their houses at all during particularly violent periods. Affective atmospheres of terror were spatialized, as were the places of intimacy where people disclosed rumors about violence. Particular locations became infused with terror when people heard gunshots or revealed narco-stories. Sex workers would not tell me rumors of cartel activity in coffee shops or restaurants, fearing they might be bugged or that we might be overheard by a high-ranking narco. They waited until we were in my car or their rooms to tell me the rumors that scared them the most.

Even in periods of heightened fear, though, places such as my car, sex workers' rooms, and missionaries' houses remained filled with stories other than narco-stories and affects other than terror. Sex workers gossiped about each other, missionaries spoke about their families, and we planned a missionary's bachelorette party. In Reynosa, I observed and participated more frequently than in any other time in laughter so intense it caused crying, bellyaches, and difficulty breathing. These bodily intensities were the flip side to our terror.

Reynosa residents altered their spatial practices in relation to the content of rumors. Rumors of further violence kept the streets empty for days after a three-hour public gun battle between soldiers and members of drug organizations in which they shot up a school while children hid under their desks to dodge the bullets (*Crónica de Hoy* 2009). My host mother worked at a preschool that was closed due to bomb threats. She and my host sisters stayed in the house for days, complaining about their boredom on social media. But fear of the street extended beyond the fear of dying in a gun battle or a bomb.

Narcos' imagined omnipresence had a disciplining effect. Drivers in Reynosa were especially aware of their behavior around new, luxury-brand SUVs with tinted windows. Attentiveness to visual and spatial cues prompted anxiety, as anyone could be a narco. The circulation of narco-stories spread awareness of corporeal vulnerability and instilled habits of self-surveillance and restraint thought to mitigate danger. Many people avoided honking at stopped cars and exchanged tips for negotiating interactions with armed men who might pull them over while in traffic, which also fueled terror. None of the sex workers I knew had cars, but even on foot, they found it ever more stressful to navigate the city and so became reluctant to leave Boystown, where they felt safer. While money and violence provided the material grounds for narco power, the contagion of rumors spread terror in ways that caused people to alter their spatial practices.

People in northern Mexico during this era associated Reynosa with drug activity and bloodshed. Young men from Reynosa told me that when they traveled to Monterrey (which would, several years later, become as violent as Reynosa), they found that people there assumed that most *reynosenses* had narco ties. Those of us who lived in Reynosa also shared the perception that it was more dangerous than other cities we traveled to. When I left town with sex workers or missionaries, we often felt a sense of relief, like we could breathe. While affective atmospheres become mapped onto space, it is through the space of bodies that they travel and live. Some of this terror lingers in bodies even as they travel to different locations, since affect shapes subjectivity and habitus.

As tensions between state actors and members of drug organizations escalated, sex workers felt increasingly vulnerable to narcos in la zona. Once, when I was standing in front of Eva's room during a moment of downtime, she whispered to me:

We [the sex workers] are in danger here [in the prostitution zone]. Everyone is in danger, but we are especially in danger here. *La maña* [a term at the time used interchangeably with narcos] comes every week to take money from us, and if we do not pay it, they take note, and they will beat us or kill us if we do not pay. I could end up dead, floating in the canal, and my children wouldn't even know what happened to me, because they don't know what I do for a living. They would just know I disappeared one day.

Eva's sense of risk was tied to her location in la zona, her obligation to provide for her beloved children and grandchildren, and her desire to protect them from news of her death and the truth about her work. Migrant sex workers' vulnerability was structured by their stigmatized professions and their visibility in la zona, as well as by the way in which the preexisting apparatus for their control by the state was co-opted by a drug organization. Soon after troops were sent to Reynosa, sex workers noted increasing pressure from narcos, who told them they would have to start paying each week for "protection," but sex workers told me it was *la maña* they were afraid of. In addition to the rent for their rooms, sex workers had to pay an additional two hundred pesos per week, a combined fee for their health inspection, garbage service, and a "payment" to *la maña*. Sex workers were not the only ones who had to pay this weekly sum. Still, the fact that they paid their tax to the cartel along with their health inspections—these two sums probably eventually going to different parties—shows how state power and narco power overlapped in the surveillance of sex workers.

Drug organizations leveraged sex workers' gendered obligations to the state and to their families in order to exert control over them. Sex workers were registered with the health department, and drug organizations tried to mimic some of these state functions. *La maña* asked sex workers to submit a photograph of themselves along with an address to issue them an ID card. Because sex workers were hesitant to talk about matters involving *la maña* in a downtown Reynosa coffee shop they feared might be bugged, Eva waited until we were in my car before revealing that she thought *la maña* wanted their addresses in order to extort or threaten their families. Eva and several other sex workers told me that they were delaying providing these addresses or giving fake addresses, a form of resistance they used to protect their families. "They say they want to protect us," said Eva, "but who are they going to protect us from? They are the ones we are afraid of."

Sex workers occupied a gender, race, and class position that shaped their vulnerability in ways that allowed them to imagine their own murders. I was sometimes mistaken for a sex worker, while at other times I was taken for a missionary. I felt safer when I was surrounded by white, English-speaking missionaries than if I was with other Mexican friends, including sex workers. My perception of my vulnerability shifted depending on my company, because I was aware of the relative impunity for murderers of poor brown women in border cities. Fewer rumors circulated of violence toward American citizens, which was more likely to generate international news. Perhaps affective atmospheres differ based on the color, citizenship, gender, and class of the bodies that constitute them, as such factors shape these bodies' relationship to power and disposability. Over breakfast one morning in Mexico City, Eva told Sofía and me about the closure of Baile, a dance club we had all visited in Reynosa. Internal migrants from Veracruz who worked low-wage jobs frequented Baile, where men paid women the equivalent of a dollar to dance with them. Sofía and her friends occasionally danced at this salon to earn money and solicit clients. Eva told us Baile closed because a room full of freezers was found stuffed with corpses missing vital organs. "They say most of the victims were veracruzanas," she said, "and la maña sells their organs to Americans and rich people in Mexico." More than just a gruesome piece of gossip, Eva's story expressed anxiety about the vulnerability of poor, racialized bodies marked with the whore stigma in relation to narco power and predatory US capital.

In 2008, I started to hear rumors that Central American migrants on their way to, or just deported from, the United States were being found in mass graves, following their kidnapping and torture, as well as the extortion of their families. I began to see newspaper coverage of these events in 2010.[7] Eventually, Mexicans started to fear that they would disappear like Central Americans. On the so-called Highway of Death in 2010 and 2011, Mexican citizens were among those forced to exit buses; some were raped, and most were never seen again (Ramsey 2011; Torres 2011). Mexicans, too, began to fear that taking a bus might lead to their murders and disposals in mass graves. As the contagion of terror spread, the differences that once separated more from less vulnerable bodies faded. When residents of Reynosa talked about narcos, the image that came to mind was usually the all-powerful cartel boss. Although most of the young people working for the cartel had low-ranking positions and little power, it was not always clear to outsiders where a cartel member resided in the hierarchy of the paramilitary organization, and those involved could index the authority of the cartel to make themselves seem more powerful and knowledgeable.

Rumors shaped the way that bodies moved around space in Reynosa. Shortly after federal troops were sent into Reynosa in December 2007, every business selling alcohol, including in la zona, was given orders to close at 10 p.m. and remain closed until 10 a.m. Newspapers speculated that these were military orders. However, a city-level public official in Reynosa in charge of media relations stated that neither the city government nor the state or federal authorities had imposed the curfew (Osborn 2008). Reynosa residents believed *la maña* put the curfew into place. In one common explanation, narcos attempted to limit the local economy in order to mobilize local resistance to the military occupation. During this period, many people in Reynosa took extra care to remain inside at night because of rumors that those on the street after 10 p.m. would be shot.

A march against narco violence in August 2008 in Mexico City included hundreds of thousands of people using their resisting bodies to reclaim space, and this was only one of many marches throughout the country. Yet no such march against narcos occurred in Reynosa. Locals noted that Reynosa residents would never organize an anti-narco protest due to either apathy or fear. Even so, *reynosenses* did protest the military presence in Reynosa in early 2008 and early 2009. One march included a thousand people, most of whom were involved in the night-time tourist industries such as bars, restaurants, and clubs and worked as waiters, sex workers, taxi drivers, and *mariachis* (*Proceso* 2008). The protesters accused the military of human-rights abuses and demanded they leave Reynosa. Yet many locals told me that the protests were not organized by concerned citizens, but rather by narcos.[8] A woman living in a squatter area in Reynosa who had protested told me that *la maña* offered her and her neighbors bags of food and money to pile into buses and protest.[9]

Narcos and soldiers enacted their territory battles in the space of la zona via the bodies of sex workers. A week before one of the marches, men who appeared to be soldiers blocked the exit and entrance of la zona with what seemed to be military vehicles. Toting guns, they assaulted sex workers and clients. In retrospect, sex workers speculated that *la maña* had committed these acts of intimidation and violence dressed as soldiers to encourage sex workers to join the protest against the military. Several days later, a man wearing a ski mask who identified himself as part of *la maña* told sex workers that they must join the protest or else lose the right to work and be punished with spankings on bare buttocks with a large wooden paddle. These spankings, *tablazos*, formed part of an alternative penal system for offenses that would not warrant torture or murder. Sofía told me that narcos visited jails to give *tablazos* to everyone accused of either rape or beating women or children "before they [were] sentenced by the law." When Eva was sick and unable to march, someone from *la maña* threatened to give *tablazos* to her good friend Sofía, who had been made responsible for making sure that all her colleagues marched. Eva and Sofía lived on the same block in Boystown, often ate meals together, and would watch each other's rooms when the other left town to visit family. By assigning responsibility to one woman, narcos used established intimacies to force cooperation. Once Sofía left la zona to return to Tampico, Eva was given responsibilities originally assigned to Sofía, and she risked punishment if other sex workers did not comply with orders.

The spatially delimited zona, with its intact regulatory apparatus, made it easier for *la maña* and the health department to manage sex workers. The spatial features of la zona, particularly the way it was surrounded by solid cement walls with only one principal exit and one entrance that could be blocked to trap people inside—were particularly important for creating a space that allowed for control. Sex workers' bodies proved particularly vulnerable in confrontations between narcos and soldiers. "They put us on the front lines," Sofía explained. "If someone was going to die in that situation, it would have been us." That sex workers were threatened with physical force and economic sanctions instead of bribed with money indicates that *la maña* possessed a power over sex workers that they did not have over some other Reynosa residents.

According to local narratives, narcos both masqueraded as state actors— dressing as military officials—and acted as civil society—organizing protests and using both gifts and violence to coerce people to participate. Whatever the truth of these reports, the attribution of these roles to narcos implies their power to generate fear and compliance. In militarized Reynosa, rumors gave credit to narcos for almost all acts of violence and politics. That Reynosa residents believed protests to be fueled by narco threats and bribes indicates how they imagined power to work in their city.

Following the militarization of state interventions at the border, the intensification of cartel power resulted in the breakdown of institutional and political differentiation in the minds of the public. In response, the public engaged in a range of communicative and interpretive practices such as telling each other stories of brutality and tweeting about locations of gun battles, practices that sustained interpersonal social obligations under circumstances of extreme anxiety and risk. Ironically, the same narco-stories that manifested cartel power in the public sphere also provided border residents a private space in which to foster intimate ties and practice care.

Intensified Vulnerabilities and Blocked Intimacies in la Zona

The intimacies sex workers, clients, and missionaries formed in la zona were blocked by drug violence as many people became afraid to visit la zona or eventually left Reynosa. The factors that made Reynosa a popular destination for foreign sex tourists and missionaries were overshadowed by those visitors' fear of drug organization activities. Depictions of narco violence in the US media, another kind of terror-spreading rumor, proliferated from 2008 to 2010.[10] American citizens I interviewed reported feeling less secure in Mexican border cities. Tourism had already seen a decline, and media coverage of the violence in Mexico had a significant impact on Reynosa. Tourism revenues dropped by half in 2010, following already sizable reductions in 2008 and 2009. Tourism itself dropped 40 percent in Tamaulipas between 2009 and 2010, and thirty-eight restaurants in Reynosa closed that year (*Milenio* 2010). Meanwhile, residents' responses to fear were structured by inequalities of mobility. The privilege of leaving Reynosa for safer places was accessible to Americans (including missionaries and anthropologists) and Mexicans with visas or savings. Most sex workers, like other low-earning workers in the informal economy, left Reynosa only to return to hometowns similarly inundated by fear and bloodshed.

For sex workers, the decision to leave la zona was the result of a complex calculation of factors related to their intimate obligations. So few clients visited that they barely earned enough to pay their rent, much less send money to their families or save for the future. Rebecca, a sex worker from Puebla who was saving her money to attend nursing school and buy a car, rhetorically asked me: "If I'm only earning enough to pay my expenses, what's the point?" Some sex workers credited their relationships with missionaries and God as factors influencing them to leave Boystown and Reynosa, and missionaries spread these stories to their Christian publics. The decisions of others to leave were sparked not only by drug violence and reduced earnings but also by personal factors. Frida had entered prostitution because she was coerced by and fell in love with a pimp. After terminating that relationship, she continued to work to support her children. Frida eventually left la zona because she feared that her son, who was still a baby, would grow up to work for narcos or to be teased by other children for having a sex worker as a mother. Furthermore, she had a sense that her relationship with her son's father was dissolving. Sofía, who had considered leaving for years, finally took action when her teenage son, Sergio, went missing after escaping from a drug rehabilitation center in their hometown of Tampico. He had left the drug organization and gone into hiding near Mexico City for a year. When he returned to Tampico to meet his infant daughter, he was kidnapped from Sofía's house. Like many young men in Mexico, Sergio is assumed by his family to be dead, although his body has not been found. Thus, although fear of dying at the hands of narcos and a generalized anxiety were factors compelling sex workers to leave Reynosa, their intimate relationships were also profoundly affected by the increasing power of drug organizations.

Foreigners faced difficulties forging intimacies with Mexican sex workers as militarization increased tension in Reynosa. Sex workers were wary of strangers after being abused and intimidated by armed men in the events surrounding the protests. Stacy stopped taking short-term teams into Boystown and instead had them construct the monastery two blocks away. Several missionary groups canceled even construction trips after seeing US media depictions of Mexican violence. Team Boystown stopped entering la zona during periods of increasing tensions as the Zetas and the Gulf Cartel split and fought for territory. Some of Stacy's team members told me that although they had once had "favor with the Gulf Cartel," they did not assume that the rival cartel would extend the same welcome to them. It is notable that in Reynosa, even missionaries needed informal alliances with drug cartel representatives to carry out their work, indicating a certain alignment between God's territory and narco territory.

Missionaries' decisions to leave required weighing Reynosa's risks and rewards in relation to their intimate obligations to God, sex workers, children, Christian publics, and spouses. Stacy was also forced to schedule an early cesarean to avoid a gun battle that was rumored to block the road to the hospital. After Stacy's daughter was born, gunfire and explosions kept the family up at night. In May 2010, Stacy and her husband abandoned their mission. While drug violence clearly factored into their decision, Stacy indicated that God told them to leave Reynosa.

Police corruption further deterred American visitors. Clients reported increasing robberies and extortions by local police in Reynosa, particularly in Boystown. Chuck, a white American and a frequent client, became hesitant to cross the border because security guards conducted *revisiones*, or inspections, through which they would rob, extort, or blackmail clients. Several clients, as well as many Reynosa locals, believed that Boystown security guards, like the local police more generally, worked for or with narcos. All uniformed representatives of the state—the police, the military—could potentially represent narco power by disguise or collusion. Power in Reynosa became reduced to the random and absolute exercise of violence through a single, undifferentiated agent of corruption. Affective atmospheres of terror extended from their temporally and spatially delimited arenas (at night, in certain neighborhoods, directed at particularly vulnerable populations) to encompass more kinds of people, places, and times of day. Anxiety and suspicion, forged in part through rumor, stymied the border's productivity. Many clients ceased to visit the prostitution zone due to fear of bodily harm, and many sex workers and missionaries chose to leave Reynosa.

Conclusion

Events that took place in Reynosa between 2008 and 2009 foreshadowed what would happen throughout Mexico in the following years: affective atmospheres of terror spread to more and more of the country's residents, and drug trafficking organizations penetrated social, political, and economic life in new, profoundly destructive ways. My analysis of the performativity of violent rumors draws attention to how a climate of terror spread through bodies. Populations terrorized by the threat of bodily harm are affected in ways collective and corporeal that shape space and change the social world.

Through the contagion of affect and the performative power of rumors about violence, narcos became posited as all-powerful. Vulnerable subjects sustained that power by circulating rumors. Eventually, most political acts—whether protests, local ordinances, or military action—were said by Reynosa residents to be the work of drug organizations. I have suggested that rumors of violence in an affective atmosphere of terror differ from other kinds of rumors because they cite prior acts of violence and thus reamplify the power effects of that violence. Terror is contagious because circulating narco-stories create intense bodily sensations that also mark a form of intimacy. The bodies of Reynosa's residents were key sites at which territorial battles between soldiers and narcos were felt. These turf wars had immediate effects on the bodies of sex workers (among others)—bodies used in confrontations between narcos and soldiers.

Rumors of violence spread in such a way that even those who would have been protected by some combination of class, racial, and citizenship privileges eventually felt defenseless. Through the contagion of rumor and affect, a climate of terror enveloped more and more of the population. Affective shifts were in dialectical tension with real acts of torture, brutality, and murder. Perhaps narcos first tested techniques of domination on the most vulnerable populations, like Central Americans without legal status in Mexico, before applying them to the rest of the populace. The decline of Boystown offers a case study of how drug trafficking organizations' ascendance to power and the local population's vulnerability intensified during a period of increased militarization in the US and Mexican war on drugs.

PART II

THE INTIMATE AND ECONOMIC OBLIGATIONS OF SEX WORKERS

FIG. 1. The entrance to la zona

FIG. 2. The McAllen-Hidalgo-Reynosa International Bridge

FIG. 3. The road to la zona

FIG. 4. Sex workers' rooms in la zona

FIG. 5. A sex worker standing in front of her door

FIG. 6. A short-term mission team building the "modern-day monastery"

FIG. 7. Sign stating, "Women's medical checkups are an obligation, not a whim. I worry about your children. Signed, the Department of Health"

FIG. 8. Painting in María's bar-turned-living-space

CHAPTER 3

Stigmatized Whores, Obligated Mothers, and Respectable Prostitutes

A message painted onto the now defunct Las Vegas Nightclub in Reynosa's Boystown (figure 7), situated below an older painting of a naked woman inside of a wine glass, warns, "Women's medical checkups are an obligation, not a whim. I worry about your children. Signed, the Department of Health."[1] Confused by this sign, I asked several sex workers what children had to do with medical exams. They told me that if a woman were to miss her medical checkup, she would be more likely to contract a sexually transmitted infection and miss work. During the time in which a woman would take medication to treat her STI, she would not be allowed to work, and therefore she would not be able to provide for her children. Two obligations became one in this handmade warning: to materially provide for one's children, and to be tested for STIs in order to work in Boystown. This hand-painted sign built upon knowledge that many sex workers worked to support their children, whether or not through the coercion of pimps. Thus, the Department of Health used women's maternal obligations—the relations of love and obligation tied to their intimacies with their children—to aid in their biopolitical surveillance and management. This is one of many examples I observed in which people who claimed to help sex workers used motherhood to aid in their management. In this instance, the use of the Spanish world *obligación* merges a legal and bureaucratic obligation with a gendered moral obligation.

On several occasions I interviewed David, a white American client who lived in Reynosa and frequented la zona almost every day. David had been married for several years to an exotic dancer from Acapulco whom he first met as a client. David believed that his ex-wife's parents knew what she did for a living as she sent home such large quantities of money. He explained to me that he did not see a difference between women who worked for their families or their pimps: "Either their husbands are pimping them out, or their families are pimping them out. I don't understand why they don't just work for themselves." David's wish that sex workers work to maximize their individual profits failed to recognize the complex networks of love and obligation that made up the social worlds of sex workers in Boystown.

Most of these sex workers migrated to Reynosa from rural parts of Mexico to work in la zona in order to try to earn money, but their intimate obligations usually inspired their migrations. Unlike David, I would not go so far as to completely collapse sex workers' relationships with families and pimps, because pimps often had sophisticated techniques of coercion to convince women to work in prostitution, while family members, as far as I know, did not usually know at first about their entry into prostitution (with the exception, perhaps, of women who were born into families of pimps or sold to pimps by their families). However, David's comments do provide an alternate reading to the commonsense assumptions that families are good and pimps are bad.

This chapter investigates the similarities between sex workers' obligations to their pimps and their families. Sex workers in Reynosa used the Spanish verb *obligar* to refer to a range of situations, some of which pertained to the threat of force, but also many that involved more subtle coercion or social mores: the pressure that pimps brought to bear on prostitutes, or sexual situations that blurred the line between consensual and nonconsensual. They usually did not use *obligar* to describe relationships with their families, except in circumstances in which pimps used the children they conceived with sex workers to obligate them to earn money. Nonetheless, sex workers' obligations to family members were sometimes as violent and coercive, or as marked by love, as their obligations to pimps. Although most of the instances I examine involve coercion, I hope that the concept of obligation will highlight the social aspects of these relationships. A sense of obligation was often held internally, as sex workers were concerned with their obligations to be good mothers, daughters, wives, and sisters. Some of these obligations to others were forged through love, others through violence, and some through sex, as pimps from the Mexican state of Tlaxcala were said to be masters at oral sex. My preliminary findings point to an area for future research that disturbs some popular conceptions about the relationships between pimps and sex workers: we will see that according to discourses in la zona, pimps make women fall in love with them in part through cunnilingus.

Many of the findings of this chapter are not new and can be seen in a good deal of the sex worker literature. For example, others have examined how the stigma against prostitution leads some sex workers to lead double lives or to reproduce ideas about "good" versus" bad" sex workers, sometimes by arguing that the "bad" sex workers engage in "bad" sex acts or spend their money on bad things (Castañeda et al. 1996; Castillo 1999; De Meis 2002; Kelly 2008). My study differs from the previous literature through my argument that sex workers' double lives are a form of agency, my analysis of obligations to pimps and family members as a form of nonsovereignty, and my triangulation of relationships which shows how children mediated relations between sex workers.

Obligations of Motherhood

Even before I met her, Sofía had been planning to leave la zona, both because there was little work there and because she did not feel safe. Concerns surrounding her role as a mother, however, solidified her decision to return home to Tampico. On a sunny day in late April 2009, I drove to Boystown to pick up Sofía to go out to lunch. She jumped into my car wearing blue jeans, white sneakers, and a burnt orange shirt with rhinestones on it spelling out, in English: "Rich Girl \$," reminding me of how Boystown was once, to Sofía and many other women, a place overflowing with American dollars and opportunities for quick profit. During our drive to the restaurant, Sofía revealed that her son, Sergio, had been using drugs for three months; unbeknownst to her family, he had been roaming the streets until finally he admitted himself to a rehabilitation center, where he was scheduled to remain in residence for three more months. Sofía was relieved that her son was now in good hands, and proud that he was brave enough to recognize his problem and attempt to fix it. She told me about her plans to return to Tampico, her city of origin, to set up a home and find employment before Sergio got out of rehab. She reminded me that before she worked in prostitution, she was employed as a cashier in a restaurant. Sofía said that the drug cartel presence in la zona had her so stressed out that she was considering searching for another job in Reynosa until she could move to Tampico, where she would surely earn less money.

But Sofía ended up leaving la zona much earlier than she thought. The next day, she and I were planning Eva's birthday party with Ashley and Eleanor, who had joined Stacy's team of missionaries while I was in Reynosa, when Sofía received bad news. Sergio had checked himself out of the rehabilitation center, and her family had no idea where he was. Sofía was so concerned that she decided to leave Reynosa just a few days later. At Eva's birthday dinner at the Sirloin Stockade, Sofía stared into space, checked her phone for new voicemails and text messages, and expressed concern about her son's whereabouts. Assuming that Eva knew about the situation with her son because we had been talking about it all evening, one of us mentioned the rehabilitation center. Sofía looked startled and then, once Eva had gotten up to serve herself more food, said under her breath, "I don't want Eva to know that my son was using drugs."

Ashley, Eleanor, and I agreed to accompany Sofía to Tampico to help her transport her belongings, to meet her family, and to help her find her son. We all felt the weight of this trip. For the missionaries, a sex worker leaving la zona meant that their prayers were being answered and God was doing his work in Boystown. For Sofía, the return home was more ambivalent—she was happy to begin a new chapter with her son but also nervous about making less money. All of us were determined to keep Sofía's secrets. She told us her given name the day before we took a bus to Tampico and explained that her family members believed she worked at a second-hand clothing store. We practiced calling her by her given name in preparation for the trip and expressed our concerns that we might slip and use the wrong name or mention information that would reveal her profession. We were introduced to Sofía's family as missionaries. We agreed on a story to hide the queer intimacies between us forged in la zona because Sofía did not want her family to know 1) that she worked as a sex worker, 2) that the missionaries worked with sex workers, and 3) that I was an anthropologist studying sex workers and missionaries. We were fed by Sofía's family, treated to several free nights in a hotel room, and asked, in return, to talk to and pray for people, including several teenage sons who were in trouble. We were also asked to pray against the swine flu (at the time, in 2008, the epidemic was in full bloom: on our bus trip to Tampico from Reynosa we were given medical masks).

Sergio returned before we arrived in Tampico, but Sofía still went ahead with her move. As we stood together on a beach in Tampico and watched the ocean waves hit our ankles, she explained that she saw her decision to move back home as taking responsibility for her child. Sergio would now live with Sofía's mother until they could save enough money to get their own place. Sofía said she believed her son was crying out for help, demonstrating that he needed his mother with him. "Now I am here," she told me, as we both watched the waves hit our knees. She paused for a second, and then said solemnly, "Sometimes we, as mothers, are to blame."[2] As a mother, she admitted that although she gave her son everything, "what was lacking was my time."[3] "Now I will give him that," she said, "which is why I am here, in Tampico."

These vignettes about Sofía's departure from Boystown exemplify three dynamics present in the lives of many sex workers in Reynosa who worked to support their families: 1) the separation they felt an obligation to keep between their family and work, which often involved lying or keeping information from both family members and one's colleagues in Boystown; 2) concern with maternal responsibility in relation to the time and money one could devote to children; and 3) sex workers' judgment of each other's maternal performances. These concerns gelled together at the dinner table when Sofía told us that she did not want Eva to know her son was using drugs. The missionaries and I sensed that this had something to do with a judgment Sofía thought Eva might make about her capacities as a mother. We were surprised that Eva did not know the full story, because we were convinced that she and Sofía were very close friends; but as will be explored below, keeping secrets from one's colleagues in Boystown, even those one considers to be friends, is a common element of the *doble vida*. Their management of double lives shaped the financial and intimate relationships between sex workers without drug addictions and their children, their relationships with both colleagues and family members, as well as the subjectivity of the sex workers themselves.

Respectable Mother/Prostitute Dichotomy

One way in which sex workers exercised agency in relation to the Virgin/Whore (or Respectable Mother/Disreputable Prostitute) dichotomy and the stigmatization of sex work was by making maternal obligation a necessary part of their roles as sex workers. These categories, like most dichotomies, are considered to be mutually exclusive. However, one way that sex workers created value was by positing their work as part of their maternal responsibilities and thus assuming the identity of Respectable Prostitute. I should note that this is my term—they never called themselves "respectable prostitutes." But it seemed to fit the ways in which women emphasized certain familial obligations as well as criticized each other's performances as mothers. This distinction worked fractally (Irvine and Gal 2000), as sex workers reproduced the Respectable Mother/Disreputable Prostitute division within the category of "Prostitute" in order to define themselves as respectable. What they did not see is how this reproduced the whore stigma that they were all subject to.

The status of both prostitution and drug use as vices (as well as sins) was important to Boystown's moral economy. Obligations (primarily to children and other family members) and reciprocity (with colleagues and friends, including missionaries) were important moral values in Boystown. If a woman was working to fulfill her obligations, the stigma/vice associated with prostitution lost some of its negative moral weight. Prostitution could be somewhat redeemed by linking it to familial obligation, motherhood, and specific expected circulations and separations that mediate and contain stigma.

Some sex workers exercised agency in relation to the whore stigma by making motherhood a moral precondition for prostitution. Sofía blamed the Mexican government for failing to provide assistance to single mothers who had few choices but to work as prostitutes. Eva chimed in that in the United States, the government provided support to single mothers, and even additional support if a mother had a sick child. She said, "My daughter is deaf and mute, and I will have to work the rest of my life to support her. Here, in Mexico, they don't help." Sofía qualified her previous statement, adding that some support for single mothers did exist, but only people with connections were able to access it, thus alluding to the well-known corruption that operates at various levels of government.

Sex workers consistently claimed to work for their families. Most sex workers expressed desperately wanting to leave Reynosa because it was violent, unsafe, and ugly. To make matters worse, as of late, they were unable to make a living there. Nevertheless, many sex workers stayed in la zona because of a sense of responsibility to send money home to pay the living costs of their children or other family members. These financial obligations were often a source of stress. One day as I was sitting in Eva's room with three Team Boystown members (Stacy, Ashley, and Ken), Eva told us that she was angry because she had found out that day that her oldest daughter, Beatriz, was pregnant for the third time. Calling her daughter stupid and irresponsible, Eva reminded us that she was already supporting two of Beatriz's other children. Eva held back tears when she told us that Beatriz wanted to keep the baby. She explained that her daughter was deaf and mute and could not work, and thus Eva would have to work her whole life to support Beatriz and her offspring. For Eva, a new grandchild was a new mouth to feed, when she could barely provide for herself and the children and grandchildren she already had. Because Beatriz was deaf and Eva could not directly have a phone conversation with her, she spent a good part of the day trying to convince her other daughters that Beatriz should have an abortion. Eva told us that she wished she could go home to go resolve the situation, but she did not have money for the return trip. She also supposed that she might go to jail if she were to force her daughter to have an abortion.

I was not surprised that Stacy asked Eva if adoption, rather than abortion, might be a possibility, nor was I surprised that Eva did not consider this. But I was surprised that Stacy did not pursue the matter further, knowing she considered herself to be "pro-life," although she qualified that she did not approve of the judgmental and sometimes violent practices of many anti-abortion Christians. I imagined other missionaries who might tell Eva that abortion was murder or that God might punish her. Instead, I watched Stacy listen empathetically to Eva, as all of us in the room got teary-eyed.

Eva proceeded to tell us the story of Beatriz's birth. Beatriz was the eldest of Eva's four daughters, and Eva was pregnant with Beatriz when she left El Salvador to escape the violence of the civil war in the 1980s. Eva was shot in the leg while pregnant in El Salvador and attributed Beatriz's deafness to this injury. She gave birth to Beatriz alone in the barn of a ranch in Mexico where she lived and worked after leaving El Salvador. She passed out during childbirth for loss of blood, and might have died if someone had not heard her baby crying. Eva and Beatriz were poor; they slept on the floor of the barn, and Eva cut diapers for Beatriz out of old pants. Eva explained that even though Beatriz could be really stupid sometimes, she loved her a lot because they suffered so much together. Thus, while most of Eva's discussion was cast in terms of maternal obligation, she also spoke of love to explain her economic obligations to her daughter. This is also a good example of how love and obligation bring about nonsovereignty: Eva's obligations to her daughter could multiply in ways that she could not control.

The most striking example of motherhood as a necessary precondition for respectability was one I learned about after leaving the field. Rebecca, who was originally from the Mexican state of Puebla, was in her mid-thirties when I met her in front of her room in Boystown. Rebecca was tall and had dark brown skin, broad shoulders, a strong nose, large teeth, and full lips that she painted red when she was working. When I first met her, she wore lingerie that looked like a white two-piece bathing suit with heels, a neat side braid, and small gold earrings. She had a way of posing on a chair in the threshold of her door that allowed her body and long legs to be visible to passersby so that she could attract clients while watching television or reading. An avid reader, Rebecca sometimes tried to engage me about anthropological topics I knew little about myself. Months after we both left Reynosa, I met up with Rebecca in Mexico City, where she was living with her mother. As Rebecca and I walked in search of tacos, she told me about her life after leaving la zona. When I asked about her daughter, she took my hand and said, "Sarita, I have to tell you something. It was a lie. I don't have children." She told me that she lied about having a daughter when she was in la zona because she was afraid of the judgment of the other women who would say, "Well then why are you here, if you don't have children to support?"

Rebecca started in sex work because she needed money for an operation. She continued to work in la zona because she grew accustomed to the money, which allowed her to accumulate savings as well as buy clothing and other items she would not otherwise have been able to afford. Sex work was also good for her self-esteem, because her mother always told her she was ugly, and she had never felt attractive to men before. Rebecca claimed that most women lie about their reasons for working, saying it was self-sacrifice and for their children. Although she presented herself as more honest about her reasons for working, pretending to have a daughter while in la zona was, to her, necessary so that she would be seen as respectable in the eyes of other sex workers, and perhaps also in the eyes of missionaries and anthropologists. Because sex workers' association with vice and sin could only be ameliorated by being recast as fulfilling obligations, preferably to children but also to pimps or other family members, a sex worker free of obligations was morally suspect.

Sex workers exercised agency in relation to the Respectable Mother/Disreputable Prostitute dichotomy by making motherhood necessary to the category of "prostitute" in order to give it relative respectability. Fulfilling one's obligations—to one's children as well as one's colleagues—was an important part of the moral economy of sex work in la zona. Some sex workers pointed to their own respectability in ways that could be read as enacting agency in relation to the whore stigma. However, these same actions marginalized sex workers who were not mothers, like Rebecca, who had to pretend to have children in order to be seen as respectable.

Double Bind of Motherhood

To be a good mother in Mexico, like in many other places, it was necessary to sustain one's children, which involved both a financial obligation and other forms of care. Rhacel Parreñas, who studied the transnational relationships between Filipina migrants and their children, succinctly outlined three types of care normally expected of parents, while noting that the expectations for these types of care vary widely in different societies and cultures:

> (1) moral care, meaning the provision of discipline and socialization to ensure that dependents are raised to be "good" moral citizens of society; (2) emotional care, meaning the provision of emotional security through the expression of concern and feelings of warmth and affection; and (3) material care, meaning the provision of the physical needs of dependents, including food, clothing, and education or skills-training to guarantee that they become producers for the family. (Parreñas 2001, 117)

Migrant sex workers shared many of the same problems as migrant mothers who work in other industries, but because their profession was associated with vice, people thought them to be deficient at providing moral care. What makes sex work different from other forms of migrant labor is that, in some cases, it is the whore stigma itself that propels migration. Although it was legally, financially, and logistically possible, or even preferable, for a sex worker to cohabitate with her child, she would sometimes choose to migrate. She did so because of the stigma attached to prostitution and the ways in which cohabitation was imagined to forfeit moral care. If women were found out to be working in prostitution by people back "home," they could be called vulgar and disreputable. Due to the Respectable Mother/Disreputable Prostitute dichotomy, they would run the risk being deemed bad mothers and bad women. Because the Virgin/Whore dichotomy includes a virginal mother, prostitute mothers were particularly seen to be bad mothers, and it was up to them to prove otherwise.

The stigma associated with prostitution created a double bind for sex workers in la zona, because they often saw themselves and judged each other as unable to provide both material and moral care to their children. Although many sex workers worked to support their families, providing one type of care (material) for them by means of sex work would risk preventing or rendering suspect another type (moral care). Emotional care was also an important part of this situation, but it was not a primary feature in the double bind. The concept of the double bind is used to describe cultural processes that simultaneously give two contradictory demands, in which the fulfillment of one forfeits the other (Bateson et al. 1956). While Bateson and his colleagues developed this concept to describe schizophrenia, a double bind was articulated in the moral economy of la zona without sex workers being in any way schizophrenic, medically or socially.[4]

A good (single) mother was not only expected to provide economically for her children but also to be respectable (as part of fulfilling her duty of moral care). For many sex workers, however, working in prostitution to support their families forfeited respectability for two reasons. First, a double standard held that men were inclined by nature to have multiple sexual partners (as described in chapter 1) while women should be chaste or monogamous. Furthermore, a sex worker mother was widely considered to provide inadequate "moral care" because she set a bad example to her children. This was exacerbated if the children grew up in la zona.

Material, emotional, and moral care were also important to the sex workers in Boystown. The potential for earning more money in prostitution made it possible for sex workers to provide economically for their children, fulfilling one of their necessary roles as mothers. Sex workers referred to what

Parreñas describes as emotional care as *cariño*. Migrant mothers have managed to provide these forms of care to their children transnationally (Ehrenreich and Hochschild 2003; Gamburd 2000; Parreñas 2001). When sex workers lived far from their families, family members provided some emotional and moral care. Furthermore, sex workers kept in touch with their children and provided emotional and moral care through phone calls, text messages, and visits several times a year. They felt guilt, regret, and grief for not providing these forms of care face-to-face.

Negotiating Double Lives

Some sex workers exercised agency in relation to the double bind through *la doble vida*, which included a spatial separation of "work" and "home"; lied to their families about what they did for a living; and kept information about their homes and real names from their colleagues in Boystown. Most of the sex workers I interviewed lived in small accessory rooms and sent money weekly to their families via money wiring services such as Western Union. They often went to great lengths to put geographical distance between themselves and their families in order to protect their families from the stigma of prostitution and bear the weight of the stigma themselves. Furthermore, this separation worked to protect sex workers from possible rejection by family members. Several sex workers explained to me that although they could have worked in prostitution close to their families, they moved to Reynosa precisely to be far from them. *La doble vida* was an important part of the moral economy of la zona because it was a strategy to both work in prostitution and still be seen as providing adequate moral care to their children. Those who juggled a double life criticized others who did not.

Rebecca, the woman who pretended to have a daughter, was the first to describe the *doble vida* to me. When I interviewed her in the room where she lived and worked in la zona, Rebecca explained how it made spending time with her family stressful:

> It is very difficult because, for example, my family doesn't know that I am in this line of work. So when I go back home, it is so difficult for me to talk with my family, merely to talk with them is so difficult because sometimes they ask me, "How are things going at work?" or "What have you been doing?" etc. So then I have to alter the story so that they don't figure it out. For example, my family thinks that I work in a snack shop . . . so if a client comes and tells me something funny, sometimes [when I'm with my family]

I remember something that the client told me, then there, back home, I have to say, "The other day a man came to buy something in the store, and he was telling me that so and so happened." That's how I have to adjust things to be able to tell them stories. It's truly a double life that one takes on. Because even the attitudes and everything [that one takes on in the different lives are different]. Back home I don't act the way I do here. So, yes, it is very difficult, because, for example, here you must use bad words, and back home I don't say bad words at all. There are a lot of things you learn to do in order to handle it [the double life] well.

Through this statement Rebecca also indexed her respectability in her other life; she used bad words in la zona because she "must." Rebecca told me on several occasions that when she was outside of la zona, she wore very little makeup and did not dress provocatively. Indeed, the first time that I arrived in la zona to pick Rebecca up for lunch with her and Ashley, I almost did not recognize her without her red lipstick, black eyeliner, and tight-fitting, skimpy clothes. Rebecca told me that she asked clients and other people who knew her from la zona not even to say hello to her if they saw her on the street. She explained that this was a way for her to protect herself from the stigma attached to prostitution.

Sex workers expressed that the double life complicated their lives both in la zona, where they felt like they could not "have real friendships," and with their families, to whom they were afraid to reveal information that would give away their occupation. Rebecca said,

If there is competition, there is no friendship. It's logical. Here, I think that we all have a double life, and I think that you cannot have friendships, because you're not a candid person; in reality, you are lying. To begin with, no one uses her real name. That's just for starters. Then there are the kinds of things you can talk about: you can't talk about your family because you cannot get your family mixed up in this place, or rather, you can't talk about problems that happen to you because they are problems that have nothing to do with your surroundings. Perhaps there are people with whom you get along better . . . but you can't be friends . . .

Lola also expressed the difficulty of not having friends: "I have always said that in this line of work, there are no friends. It is tiresome. You don't have a friend to listen to you or understand you. Here, I don't talk to anyone, just hello and whatnot, and that's it." Lola mentioned that she only had one friend in la zona who confided in her about personal problems, and while she listened and tried to give advice, when the friend asked her anything about herself, she changed the subject. Lola called this woman her friend, yet used her as an example to argue that friendship with coworkers is impossible for sex workers. While this notion that competition stands in the way of "real" friendships is common in other competitive environments, what is distinct here is the way in which sex workers saw this as a way to protect themselves *and* their families. The whore stigma could lead to rejection of a sex worker or her family members. This might have been one of the reasons that some sex workers seemed to appreciate spending time with missionaries. Considering them more neutral and trustworthy, sex workers were more likely to talk to missionaries about their families.

I was often surprised to see sex workers I thought were friends indicating distrust toward one another. Generally, sex workers would form alliances; for example, Rebecca and Alicia seemed to be good friends, as well as Eva and Sofía. They often ate together, spent time in each other's rooms and chatted, and asked each other to keep an eye on their rooms if one of them left town for a few days. Yet they also kept secrets from the person I thought to be one of their closest friends. Sofía's concern that Eva would find out that her son was using drugs is one example. On several occasions, Rebecca told the missionaries and me, "I am leaving town tomorrow, but don't tell Eva." Alicia, who would sometimes say that Rebecca was like a sister to her, once told us, "I am leaving tomorrow, but please don't tell Rebecca."

Sex workers with double lives went to great lengths to keep up their lies to their families. As Kelly writes, "a sex worker must lie frequently and can rarely let her guard down, even in, or especially in, her own home. There are few occupations, aside from international spy, mobster, and police informant, that require so much subterfuge" (Kelly 2008, 195). Eva told her family that she worked cleaning a house and caring for the child of a family in Reynosa. Sofía told her family that she worked in a second-hand store. Rebecca told her family that she worked in a snack shop. When I saw Rebecca after she had left la zona and moved to Mexico City, she showed me pictures of herself with some missionaries at a restaurant where she told her family she worked. Missionaries shared several other examples like this. Ashley told me that a sex worker asked her if they could take pictures on the streets of Reynosa to send to her family, because she rarely left Boystown and had no photographs of Reynosa. When Alicia visited the Holiday Inn with a client, she took photographs and told her family that she worked there. Rebecca once chastised me for writing her (work) name on a Christmas card I gave her. She told me, "It's better if you just write 'Dear friend,' because sometimes we want to show our family members what you sent us."

Double lives and double names provided some complications to sex workers and their intimates. Rebecca was one of the few sex workers that I socialized with regularly who never told me her given name while we both still lived in Reynosa. She said that if I were ever to visit her family in Puebla, she would tell me her name a month ahead of time so that I could practice calling her by it. Indeed, she finally revealed her given name when we met up in Mexico City a year and a half after I left Reynosa and a few months after she left Boystown. She wanted me to have time to practice in case I might meet her mother on my next visit. Eva, Rebecca, and Sofía told me that when they returned to their hometowns to visit their families, they found it challenging to answer to their baptismal names, and they did not always respond straightaway. This is not surprising, since they generally lived and worked in Boystown ten and a half months of the year and only spent about a month and a half with their families.

Although women without drug addictions were more likely to describe themselves as leading double lives, Cubana, a drug user, referred to a related splitting of the self. Cubana wrote in her memoir, *Abismo,*

> No one knows what Liliana Margarita López Cabrera is like. She is the other part of la Cubana. Liliana is elegant, cultured, respectful, humble, and simple. If someone wants a great friend, she [Liliana] will always be by your side. Liliana keeps sadness so deep inside of her so that no one close to her need experience her sadness.[5]

Cubana, like Rebecca, pointed to her other, respectable self. Her behavior as Cubana in la zona was far from what most of her colleagues defined as humble, elegant, cultured, or respectful: she chewed with her mouth open, cracked sexual jokes, stole from other sex workers, bragged about how she was the best whore in la zona, and walked around with her large breasts exposed. However, through this statement, Cubana indicated another part of herself that she hid from people in la zona.

I learned ten years later that Cubana had been hiding many parts of her life from other sex workers, missionaries, and me. By 2009 she had been in Reynosa for twenty years.[6] In face-to-face interactions and in her memoir, Cubana often mentioned that she had a bachelor's degree in physical education and had first traveled to Mexico from Cuba on a basketball scholarship. In later installments of her memoir that she wrote when she was sober, Cubana claimed that this origin story of her migration was a lie. She has been sober since 2011, and she gives credit to both God and to Jesus for her sobriety. Cubana eventually wrote five installments of her memoir between the years of 2006 and 2016, the second which she entrusted to me, and the other four to Abigail. Abigail later pursued a master's degree in Spanish, and she transcribed and translated Cubana's handwritten notebook and worked closely with her to decipher some of the text (Knobloch 2016). I learned from these later installments and from the thesis that Cubana had actually left Cuba in 1980 on the Mariel boatlifts. After arriving as a refugee, she stayed for two days at the Orange Bowl sports stadium in Miami, where she says the undesirables that Castro kicked out of the country were sent. From Miami she was sent to Wisconsin, then was sponsored by a Catholic priest in Ohio. She eventually moved to Chicago, where she had a daughter, worked as a prostitute, and was beaten by her abusive boyfriend, who was a gang leader. The FBI raided their house, where there were drugs and weapons, and she ended up in jail for two years, during which time her daughter was placed with a new family. She fled Chicago to Mexico and violated probation. She was very sad to leave her daughter, but believed that her daughter would have a beter life with new parents than with a drug addict as a mother.

Many people believe that sex workers' double lives are a psychological strategy to deal with "selling themselves." For example, Stacy suggested that the sex workers keep their given names a secret because "it's the one last piece of who they are that nobody can take." I suggest, rather, that double lives are a form of agency that allows sex workers to fulfill their obligations to family members; define themselves as respectable to themselves, other sex workers, and outsiders; and protect their families from the whore stigma. The double life was a way for sex workers to exercise agency in respect to the material/moral care double bind and provide both material and moral care to their children. The double life articulates values important to the moral economy of Boystown—that in order to fulfill one's obligations and protect one's family from the whore stigma, deception and secrecy were often necessary. This consciousness of multiple selves also exemplifies theories that defy the idea of a unified self (Anzaldúa 1987; Du Bois 1903; Sandoval 2000). Sex workers found ways to hold or synthesize categories and worldviews that many others saw as competing and mutually exclusive. Sex workers were able to keep a stable sense of self throughout the recognition of multiple, shifting subjectivities that were required by their maneuvering between different contexts or systems of value.

Familial Complications

Sometimes Eva wished she could move to central Mexico to live with her family. Once her toddler grandson's skin disorder was in such a flared and infected state that the doctors thought he might die. She wanted to take him to the *curandera* in Oaxaca who had cured Eva when she was very ill a few years before. She wished she could live with her grandson and help take care of him. However, even when business was bad, Eva could still make more money in Reynosa than where her family lived. She also held on to the hope that business would improve. Eva saw no choice but to stay in Reynosa.

While the three of us walked together to the tourist attraction in Mexico City that used to be the presidential palace, Sofía, Eva, and I talked about their relationships with their children. Marking the distinction between providing material support and face-to-face caring time, Sofía said, "I worked all of those years to give my son everything, but now he says that he didn't want everything; he just wanted to be with me." Eva told us that her children had the same complaints. Sofía then said: "maybe our children will complain no matter what we do." Eva agreed and said, "My youngest just turned eighteen. She complains that I wasn't around, but she's big now. She can fend for herself. I have done my part." Sex workers sometimes felt guilty for not being able to provide all forms of care. Yet Eva and Sofía recognized the logic of the double bind well enough to be at peace with their decisions: they realized that they had to give up something and that it was impossible to fulfill all of the necessary roles of motherhood in a way that would make everyone happy and avoid criticism.

Familial ties were not always positive or easy. Eva had no family in Mexico, except for her daughters and grandchildren, and she was not sure whether any of her family members had survived the civil war in El Salvador that she fled. Eva spoke about her lack of family with sadness, and, like Sofía, she cited it as a reason that she could not leave la zona: not only did she have children and grandchildren to support, but there were no other family members she could live with. At the time of our Mexico City reunion, Sofía had been retired from sex work for about two years, and she spent her time doing odd jobs and living rent-free with various family members, including her mother and sisters in Tampico and cousins and nieces and nephews in the state of Jalisco. Some of these relatives had also provided lodging for her son, Sergio. Sofía complained about various people in her family that she and her son had lived with, recounting the same four or five stories of people behaving rudely to Sofía. Finally, Eva said, "Maybe it's better not to have family. When my daughters moved to the State of Mexico, they had nothing. They slept on the floor of their tiny apartment. Now they have six beds and a television. They don't have much, but at least they don't have to deal with family members being rude to them." She encouraged Sofía to try to rent her own place and rid herself of the annoyance of the family members she complained about. In another instance of Sofía complaining about her family members, Eva suggested that Sofía dance with men for money to achieve some financial independence. She told Sofía, "You like to dance. Why don't you work as a *fichera*? You can make decent money." Thus, although Eva at times expressed sadness that she had "no family" (because many of her relatives in El Salvador were probably dead), she presented the possibility of a person without familial obligations, even one working as a sex worker, as a source of relative freedom. The interdependencies and nonsovereignties created by familial bonds could be both supportive and burdensome.

When the Two Lives Merge and Family Members Find Out

Lola started working as a sex worker when she was thirteen at La Merced, a neighborhood associated with prostitution in Mexico City. Lola, like many other sex workers, was inspired to enter sex work in order to shop: she started after asking one of her coworkers at a computer center how she was able to afford such pretty clothes.[7] After meeting a Colombian woman who showed her the ropes, Lola started traveling to the United States to work in *casas de cita*, clandestine brothels where clients could choose between three women, as well as *de libres*, which entailed making visits to men's homes. At *casas de cita*, clients payed roughly between sixty and two hundred dollars for an hour of services,[8] and Lola's earnings were on the higher end of that, perhaps because she had been both underage and conventionally attractive for most of her career. Her three years in the United States were spent in Las Vegas, San Francisco, Washington, DC, New York, New Jersey, and San Jose. Lola was able to make up to eight or nine thousand dollars a week in the United States, which is much more than anyone could make in la zona. Lola explained to me that while working in the United States involved being cooped up in a house for a week or two at a time and running the risk of deportation, she preferred it because she could earn substantially more. She explained that while she had to service twenty clients in Reynosa to earn two thousand pesos, in the United States she could easily earn a thousand US dollars a day with only five clients.

With the income, Lola bought a nice house for her whole family to live in, a truck her family used to sell vegetables, a Ford Lobo for her father for his birthday, and a Jetta for her brother for making good grades. She also put money in a bank account in her mother's name so that her mother could "take care of" it for her. But she explained that her mother took her money and spent it or loaned it to other family members without asking permission. Lola was upset that although she worked for the money and believed that it belonged to her, her mother divided the house and the money into an inheritance for each of Lola's brothers and sisters. When I interviewed her, Lola planned to start putting her earnings into her father's bank account instead, because she said that even when her paternal grandfather was dying, her father asked, "Could you loan me (*prestar*) this money?" whereas her mother would report, after the fact, "I took this money" (*agarrar*). Lola believed that by asking permission, her father demonstrated his respect that the money belonged to her and that she had the right to make decisions about it. Her mother, by taking Lola's money and only telling her after the fact, indicated a lack of respect and a sense of entitlement.

Lola told me, with tears in her eyes, that even though her whole family was living on her money, no one except her father respected her and her three-year-old daughter. Of her seven siblings, only the younger ones talked to her; "for the rest, I am the black sheep." Lola said that her daughter would ask her, "Why don't your siblings love us?" and that her brother would tell her daughter, "Get off of me, get off of me because you contaminate me." Once, when she was living with her family for two months, Lola said that she heard her nephew call her daughter a bastard. Lola was among the very few sex workers who told me that their families knew what they did for a living.

Obligations to Pimps and Clients

Sex workers' relations with clients and pimps were as varied as their relations to children, parents, and siblings and also contained elements both enabling and disabling. Pimps often became the family members of sex workers, as their partners and the fathers of their children. There was a specific kind of queerness in the relationship between pimps and sex workers, as their relationships were stigmatized and considered to be exploitative, and they often had to be hidden or lied about.

Although it is not necessary to have a pimp in Boystown, pimps brought many women to Reynosa. Based on my own observations and what other sex workers have told me, I estimate that about three-fourths of the women who worked in accessory rooms had pimps, but scholars researching other zonas in Chiapas and Tijuana have reported much lower numbers there.[9] In some parts of Mexico, women with pimps are called *obligadas* or "the obligated ones" (Kelly 2008). In Reynosa, they were more likely to be referred to as *padroteras*, or "the ones with pimps," but they were said to be obligated by their partners (*maridos*) to work, usually having an earnings quota. Most were in their late teens or early twenties and came from rural areas or small towns in central Mexico, many from Puebla, but also from Tabasco, Chiapas, and Veracruz.[10] They worked in accessory rooms in Boystown and lived in apartments outside of Boystown.

Women with pimps were usually highly mobile, working throughout Mexico in *zonas de tolerancia* as well as bars and clubs associated with prostitution in cities without zonas. Many also traveled to work in US cities for weeks at a time in *casas de cita*. While women with pimps had often worked all over the United States and Mexico, their mobility was said to be regulated by their pimps. Even when pimps were absent, I was told that sex workers with pimps often monitored and reported each other's behavior to pimps via text message. Sex workers' mutual surveillance was enabled by the panopticon-like structure of the prostitution zone (which Kelly [2008] has noted) with accessory rooms that face one another, as well as the fact that many of these women had pimps who knew each other.

For his master's thesis about the modus operandi of pimps in Tlaxcala, Óscar Montiel Torres provides an excellent account of pimps' perspectives and places these practices in a sociohistorical context (2009). However, while Montiel Torres uses the framework of trafficking and exploitation to analyze these relationships, I instead want to emphasize that pimps perform emotional and sexual labor. Many pimps have developed highly sophisticated techniques that draw upon spatial, psychological, and social factors to cultivate obligation and love.

Most of the pimps in Reynosa came from Tlaxcala, the smallest Mexican state, where people told me that they were born into powerful families who raised them from childhood to become pimps. Montiel Torres indicates that not all men come from families of pimps, and some go through training to become pimps to earn more money than they could otherwise. He notes that in families where the men are pimps, it is seen as "normal" that later generations would become pimps, but men who are the first pimps in their families sometimes face resistance and rejection from family members (2009, 101). A pimp would usually travel to another town[11] and court a woman in her hometown. He would convince her to leave town with him, and then would try to convince her to work in prostitution so that the couple could work toward building a house and a life together. Stories I heard in Boystown of women who were forced into prostitution by pimps or sold by their families were verified by Montiel Torres's ethnographic data. He writes that pimps' first technique was "*el verbo*," using words to convince women to work for them, and if this did not work, they would sometimes use more violent techniques such as kidnapping, rape, and other forms of physical abuse (2009, 31–32). Pimps who were more established would sometimes buy women from their families (2009, 32).

But many relations between pimps and sex workers defied clear distinctions between consent and coercion; some women with pimps expressed loving them and wanting to work for them. While he does not use the concept of emotional labor, Montiel Torres does describe some practices that could be interpreted as such. Part of a pimp's training involves learning how to have relationships with women that would lead to women falling in love without the pimp himself developing feelings for her. In Reynosa, several people told me that pimps' seduction of women involved performing oral sex upon them. One typically imagines a sex worker performing sex for money for a pimp. But this seduction story also suggests that a pimp performs sexual labor as part of a longer-term sex-for-money transaction. Sexual and emotional labor are merged, perhaps, through cunnilingus, as a technique intended to bring about pleasure and to help induce love and obligation that would lead to money from a future sex worker. Intense physical pleasure and romantic love are both forms of being out of control, or nonsovereignty.

Frida, who came from a small town outside of Mexico City, had a relationship with a pimp that followed a similar pattern to the one Montiel Torres outlines. From a young age, she traveled away from her parents' house to perform housework. At the age of sixteen she fell in love with Alejandro, who was twenty-one, and he invited her to go away with him for the week. Alejandro took Frida to San Luis Potosi, told her that he was in love with her, and asked her if she would be willing to work to help them build a life together. She agreed. Alejandro then showed her a magazine that told the story of a woman who worked in prostitution to support her boyfriend, and asked her if she would do this for him. Frida said that when she initially refused, Alejandro would not take her back home or let her call her parents. He then left Frida in a completely empty hotel room by herself and went out "to work" all day for several days. She explained that she was afraid, she had nothing to eat, she knew nobody in that town, and she did not know how to get to the bus station from the hotel. When Alejandro returned, Frida eventually agreed to sell sex, and she worked for several weeks.

Alejandro left town again, supposedly for a Mexican Catholic ritual celebrating *la Virgen*, but, in retrospect, Frida suspected he was visiting his other girlfriend, another sex worker. As Frida and others note, a pimp usually has several women working for him. While Alejandro was out of town, Frida had been working for fifteen days and had earned ten thousand pesos. She said that for her it was *muchísimo dinero*, because she had worked previously as a housecleaner and earned very little. Frida escaped by getting into a taxi and telling the driver to take her to the bus station. Terrified, she had no idea where she was or how to get to the bus stop. When she arrived at her parents' house, her mother cried in relief, having believed Frida had been murdered. Frida told me she felt ashamed that her family knew she had cohabitated with a man and was no longer a virgin. Because her family perceived her virtue as damaged, Frida never again felt comfortable around her family. She went to live with her sister, who was mean to her, and she worked at a sandwich shop. When her relationship with her sister got much worse, Frida left her sister's house to work as a housekeeper again and went to school. When Alejandro returned to her town a year later and she saw him at a dance club, Frida went away with him willingly. She describes her motivation to go back to Alejandro as a mixture of being in love with him and wanting to get away from her uncomfortable family situation. She worked for him and stayed in a relationship with him for several years, working in zonas throughout Mexico and in clandestine brothels in the United States before deciding to leave him and work independently. Even after Frida left Alejandro, she still felt like he exercised power over her and that he was using witchcraft to keep her from earning much money. She explained that Alejandro possessed some items of her clothing as well as a picture of her, which could be used for witchcraft.

A pimp's ability to create obligation and get access to a woman's labor depends in part upon sociocultural ideas about what a good woman is. As Montiel Torres notes, the long-standing and accepted Mesoamerican practice of the *robo de la novia*, the stealing of the bride to begin conjugal life in the region, was transformed into a strategy for pimps to recruit prostitutes (2009, 6). It arose as a strategy for young couples who wanted to get married but lacked either sufficient money or approval from the bride's parents. The boy would arrive at the girl's parents' house to pick her up, but she would not return home that evening. Sometimes, the couple would be hidden in the house of the boy's parents. Because the couple would be assumed to have had sex, arrangements would then be made for them to get married, and they would have a less expensive civil ceremony.[12] Frida told a similar story of the beginning of her relationship with Alejandro. While they did not get married, Frida's family's knowledge that she cohabitated with a man (and presumably lost her virginity) was, for Frida, an important factor in her future relationship with both Alejandro and her family.

Frida's entry into prostitution is a powerful example of how obligations of pimps and family members can function similarly and in conjunction.

While it was first a mixture of love and coercion that created her obligation to Alejandro, she ultimately returned to him not only because she loved him but also to escape the judgment of her family once she was marked with the whore stigma.

For women with "double lives," keeping one's occupation a secret from family members often entailed lying about one's geographical location. In the case of women who lived with pimps in well-known areas of prostitution, knowledge of the town that one lived in could indicate to the family both a sex worker's profession and the fact that her boyfriend was her procurer. Because several towns in Tlaxcala are well known for pimping, Frida told her family that she was living in Puebla. After the birth of her daughter, however, Frida's family arrived at a bus stop in Puebla to surprise her and meet her daughter. Frida then had to tell them where she really lived— a town so associated with prostitution and pimping that they immediately figured out what she did for a living.[13] Her *marido*/pimp got mad at Frida for telling her family where they lived, because he did not want her family to know.

A pimp's earning potential was achieved through a combination of purposeful manipulation (some of which involved space), the creation of social obligations, and the nonsovereignty-inducing capacities of love. Pimps learned that by turning sex workers into mothers, they could increase their long-term earning potential by creating a new obligation. Many sex workers in Boystown told me that when a pimp suspected that a woman might leave him, he would try to impregnate her. I was also told that the children conceived between sex workers and pimps were usually cared for by the pimp's mother.[14] This also happened to Frida. Like many women whose pimps/ boyfriends from Tlaxcala brought them to Reynosa to work in prostitution, Frida's daughter was sent, from the time she was a baby, to live with Alejandro's mother.

Frida explained that although she loved her daughter and wanted to provide for her, she did not feel very close to her because she did not raise her. At the time of our interview, even though she had broken up with Alejandro, his family continued to use her daughter to get money from her. Frida said that her daughter would call her to ask, "Why don't you send me money? Do you not love me?" Frida's experiences with her daughter and pimp demonstrate how intimate ties (of a partner/pimp or of a child) could be used to leverage financial obligations. It was hard for Frida to imagine that she would ever cohabitate with her daughter because she would not be able to afford to send her to the kinds of schools that her ex's family sent her to.

While Frida did not feel very close to the daughter that she did not raise, she felt much closer to her son, Miguelito, eighteen months old when I met him, who lived with her in Reynosa a few blocks away from the prostitution zone. Frida asked me to call her by her baptismal name when we spent time together because Miguelito was usually with us and she did not want him to be confused by her two names or to later figure out the reason for them.

Several sex workers who were separated from their children from birth denied the idea that mothers naturally and immediately bonded with their children. This seemed to surprise missionaries, who responded to such assertions with awkward silence. Sofía and Eva were in the room for part of my interview with Frida when she told me about her very different relationships with her son and her daughter. A year and a half after the interview, while I was eating breakfast with Eva and Sofía at a bed-and-breakfast in Mexico City, Sofía said to Eva, "When Sarah interviewed Frida, Frida said that she didn't love and miss her daughter as much as she loves Miguelito." They talked about this for a few minutes. "But it's logical," Eva decided. "Like they say, love is made, not born." Sofía agreed. This phrase is usually used to describe falling for a romantic partner gradually as opposed to love at first sight. But Eva and Sofía applied it to maternal love in a way that strips maternal love of its biological necessity.

I occasionally refer to sex workers who neither used drugs nor had pimps as "independent" because they called themselves independent relative to sex workers whose money went to crack or to pimps. "Independent" is not an analytical category, however. The ways in which "independent" women criticized other sex workers seem to invoke the idea that a "good" prostitute is something akin to a Western liberal subject: an autonomous, self-owning woman who works for herself and keeps the money she earns. But within the moral economy of Boystown, the most respectable kind of sex worker was not "independent" at all—rather, she worked to fulfill her familial obligations. These moral valuations can be understood as hierarchies of nonsovereignty—some ways of being in or out of control or more or less dependent were valued more than others.

Many women without pimps distinguished themselves from women with pimps, or *padroteras*, in ways that made the speaker sound more modern, independent, or intelligent. I often heard claims that *padroteras* were taken advantage of because they were brainwashed and uneducated. After hearing many stories about how pimps hit women, exploited them, and took their money, I started asking, "What is a pimp good for?" Most of the sex workers without pimps replied, with a hint of laughter, "To take away their money." Their other explanations for why sex workers have relationships with pimps included:

1. They are forced and exploited, like slaves, and are sometimes sold by their parents.
2. They are ignorant because they are uneducated.
3. They are brainwashed by the coercion of the pimp (*Les lavan el coco*).
3. They have low self-esteem, need to feel wanted by a man, and are afraid to be alone.
4. Their pimps are good in bed and seduce women through cunnilingus.
5. For those born into families of pimps, it is part of their culture to have a pimp.
6. As part of their rural upbringing, their mothers taught them that they must be loyal to their husbands.
7. They are in love with their pimp.
8. The pimps have nice bodies because they spend a lot of time at the gym.

Many of the discourses "independent" sex workers circulated about *padroteras* were combined with and informed by racializing discourses about rural *indias*, or indigenous peasants. Through their discourses about *padroteras*, other sex workers, many of whom were considered by outsiders to be veracruzanas, reproduced this category and distanced themselves from that of the racialized, rural, indigenous peasant. Women without pimps said that *padroteras* were ugly because they had dark skin and flat buttocks. In stories that chart the moral career of the *padroteras*, these *indias* became more modern and civilized both through cultural osmosis of urban and civilized Reynosa and through the education of the pimp. Some residents of Boystown claimed that pimps were sexually useful to the women or that they transformed *indias* into civilized urban women, but Cubana interestingly conflated these two discourses when she answered my question, "What are pimps good for?":

[Pimps are good] to fuck them [the *padroteras*]. All of the [women] give them money, ah, but they [the pimps] fuck well. The majority of women with pimps . . . before they were, indigenous, you know, they didn't know how to talk, nor dress themselves, nor walk well. Nothing. They had never experienced civilization like there is here, because they come from a farm. [The way that it happens is that] these men [the pimps] arrive at the farm and give money to the woman's father so that the parents can build a house. They get money to build a house, and in exchange [the pimp] takes the girl to Mexico and the United States [to work in prostitution]. [They find the women] in rural areas, like in Veracruz, (in English) *you know*, so the man takes these girls, and they never in their life have had sex, eh, it's their first time, they are going to (English) *suck their pussies, you know,* (unintelligible) (English) *crazy.* Yes, they are going to make love to them crazy like the girls tell them to. So later they are going to show them how to talk well, how to dress well, to walk well, and the girls are like, "Wow, what a change from the *india* I was before." Then they are madly in love with the men, who are able to convince them to work in prostitution. The pimp stays with the woman for six or seven months. Yes, for sex. So then the girls fall in love with the man, who does not hit her or anything. He gives her everything that she wants, including money, during this period, but he is giving her the money that another idiot is giving him.

Rebecca also told me that pimps went to little towns to look for "little indians" and that while they acted like *indias* when they first arrived in la zona, a month later,

> ... they start to act differently, and when they later start to earn more money, they look very modern, they have their hair dyed, even they start to get piercings. They arrive not knowing how to talk, and later they have name-brand boots. It's really funny.

Cubana and Rebecca were among the many both inside and outside of la zona who referred to these girls as *indias* or indigenous when they first arrived, and mentioned that they did not know how to properly walk (in heels), to talk, or to dress. In these discourses, Reynosa is seen as more "modern," more "civilized," and it is through either the education of the pimp or of the urbanity of Reynosa that they cast off their supposed indigenous lack of civilization. Positing "*indias*" as not knowing how to walk, talk, or dress properly was a way for sex workers without pimps to present themselves as modern and urbanized because they did not need, or had long ago undergone, this bodily training. For Cubana, the pimp educates his woman by sharing sexual and cultural knowledge with her. In this Pygmalion-like story, his power comes through his act of cultural translation, his modernization of a woman who does not know how to walk, talk, or dress. It is a cultural trope often repeated and even turned Hollywood fairy tale: like Richard Gere's character in the movie *Pretty Woman*, although instead of the john turning the uncivilized prostitute into a respectable lady, the pimp turns an uncivilized *india* into a civilized prostitute.

Cubana is one of several people who suggested that a pimp's power in part came from his remarkable cunnilingual abilities that caused women to fall in love with him and give up their money. Although Cubana's tale is surely a simplified and exaggerated version of the story, plenty of pimps did convince women to fall in love with them and give them money.

Eva and Sofía also posited *padroteras* as victims of the gender roles of a rural, antiquated culture that is passed on by mothers. They said these women came from a "culture of the past," in which a mother would teach her daughter, "if your husband wants to live under a tree, you have to follow him, you have to always support him." Eva told me, "Here in Mexico, out in the country, they get married for life. They think of divorce as a sin. They think that a divorced woman has no value." Eva also referenced maternal culpability, even implicating herself, saying, "We, the mothers, are to blame as well, because we tell our daughters that they have to stay with their husbands no matter what." Eva's mother, who was from a rural area of El Salvador, also told her this when she was young.

Sex workers in la zona reproduced racializing ideologies surrounding backward indigenous peasants in ways reminiscent of the way that locals talked about veracruzanas. Indeed, discourses about *padroteras* are a fractalization of the veracruzana category among sex workers and a way that sex workers associated pimped women with the category of the *india*. *Padroteras*, like veracruzanas, were considered to be indigenous, rural, dark, ugly, and less modern and "cultured" than other people in the city of Reynosa. However, I would like to point out three important differences between the way that middle-class *reynosenses* discussed veracruzanas and that the sex workers in Boystown (who would be considered veracruzanas) reproduced these to discuss women with pimps. First, while it was possibly in part veracruzanas' financial independence and residence outside the patriarchal family that made them suspect for middle-class *reynosenses*, sex workers saw *padroteras* as victims of patriarchy and less independent than they should be. Second, while *reynosenses* saw veracruzanas as tainting Reynosa's culture with their backwards indigeneity, sex workers did not naturalize *padroteras'* peasantness (see Chu 2010)—sex workers believed that Reynosa's influence could modernize *padroteras*. Third, while Reynosa locals criticized veracruzanas for earning easy money through maquiladora work or transactional sex, "independent" sex workers pointed to the ways in which *padroteras* had to work harder for the money they earned than "independent" women. Because *padroteras* were obligated by their pimps to work and had to reach a sales quota set by their pimps, Eva and Sofía told me, they charged the same amount of money as "independent" sex workers but were more likely to engage in acts that most sex workers preferred not to perform, like anal sex or sex without a condom. Eva said, for example, that she would have sex for one hundred pesos, but she would not include oral or anal sex at that price.

While she could tell a man not to kiss her breasts, or make him get off of her if she got tired of the sex act, *padroteras* did not have this luxury because they had to meet their quotas. Eva mentioned, as an example, that when she had visited Marisela's room earlier in the day, she saw feces everywhere, so she assumed that Marisela had engaged in anal sex with a client to meet her pimp's earnings quota. Sex workers in Boystown used the foil of the *padrotera* to distance themselves from racialized indigeneity and rural associations, and to present themselves as more modern, intelligent, and independent.

Many sex workers recounted what we might call the moral career of the *padrotera*. Cubana told me a version of the end of this story—that the pimp would eventually leave the woman, she would start to work for herself, but by then she would be all used up. She would start using drugs, get addicted to crack, and then she would die in la zona. Cubana told me that her relationship with a woman she worked to support was "the same" as the relationships of sex workers to their male pimps. After working to support Jessica, her partner and *madrota* (female pimp) for eighteen years, Jessica left one day with all of Cubana's money, as Cubana explained, just like the male pimps do.

Frida used the verb *obligar* only once to refer to a sexual act with her boyfriend, who was also her pimp. Although Frida alluded to times in which she enjoyed and wanted sex with her pimp/boyfriend, whom she was in love with for several years, she also mentioned times, especially at the beginning of the relationship when she was a virgin, when she didn't want to have sex with Alejandro and "*me obligaba*." She differentiated this act of obligation from rape. She described a time in which he was very drunk and he raped her, and did things to her that were "horrible" and "worse than being with a client." When discussing sex, Frida used *obligar* to describe acts in the gray area between enthusiastic consent and rape. *Obligar* was usually used to refer to coercion by social rather than physical force. But pimps and sometimes clients would create obligations by manipulating the relationship between their bodies, sex workers' bodies, and space. These become relevant in the prostitution zone, where sexual acts were verbally agreed upon between clients and sex workers before the encounter, in terms of how much money would be paid and which positions would be included in the price. Both clients and sex workers often became upset when events did not occur as they were previously negotiated.

Both sex workers and clients accused each other of trying to get something extra out of the transaction. Clients complained about sex workers' boundaries regarding where they could be touched, and they also complained about sex workers' rules for regulating the temporal limits of the sex act. Clients complained that sex workers did not perform previously agreed-upon acts, or that they claimed twenty minutes passed when it had been only five. Sex workers complained that clients would agree on a price for certain acts and then would try to get extra positions, or would try after the encounter to pay less than had been agreed.

Several sex workers told me that I shouldn't talk to David, a frequent white American client, because he did not respect them. Some sex workers reported having overheard him saying that they were trashy, ugly *indias*, and they claimed that David would tell his American friends to pay them less than the prices they asked for because they were not worth more. Rebecca told a story of David taking one sex worker back to his house and forcing himself upon her without a condom. The woman went to the police station in la zona to report him to the authorities. Such stories may confound David with several of his white American friends. The story about the condom seems likely to have been about Chuck, David's friend, who talked very candidly to me about his sexual desires and experiences while sitting on a bench outside of a chain bookstore on the Texas side of the border. Chuck was interested in what he called the "girlfriend experience"—he only wanted to have sex with women who would kiss him, exchange massages, and have sex without a condom. Chuck told me that he received no pleasure from sex if he wore a condom, and he shared his strategies with me to convince women to have sex with him without one. He told me that although most of the "girls" who worked in la zona demand condom use, many of those who worked in *fichera* bars (where women drink with and talk to clients) were also often addicted to crack-cocaine and could be "coaxed into sex without a condom." Sometimes sex without a condom could be arranged by offering additional money. Chuck told me, however, that he and his friends figured out over the years that if you can get a woman to leave la zona with you and "onto your turf," that is, the man's apartment, "they are way, way more willing to agree to whatever you want." He said that he would never force a woman to have sex without a condom but would tell her, once she was in his apartment, that he was unwilling to have sex *with* a condom. Chuck said that within Boystown or other places of prostitution, a bar owner or pimp could knock on the door after thirty minutes to tell the client that his time was up, or a woman could turn a client into la zona police if he didn't pay her. However, Chuck said, if "she's on your turf, you can set the time limits, and the woman knows you're not going to pay her unless you're satisfied."

Invoking ideas of contested gang territory and competitive sports, Chuck's strategy to get women on his turf was clearly coercive. When I asked him why he thought women were more likely to agree to sex without a condom "on his turf," he said that at that point they realized he had invested a lot of time in the transaction. We can see three parallels between the case of the pimp who tried to get a woman to work in prostitution and the client who tried to get extra services out of a sex worker. First, they both begin with a plan to get someone to do something they know the person might not want to do. Second, part of enacting that plan has to do with manipulating space, taking a woman to a space in which she might feel more vulnerable to violence. The pimp separates a future prostitute from her family in order to convince her to engage in sex work and to make it more difficult for her to go back home. By making her a mother, the pimp cultivates further obligation, having his mother raise the child, who will always need to be sent money. The pimp uses both spatial and social knowledge to his advantage. A client knows that a woman's obligation to her pimp or her family is not usually enough to get her to have sex without a condom, but women with crack addictions are more likely to agree. Like the pimp, the client knows that if he separates a sex worker from the space of la zona, he is more likely to get her to do things she might not normally consent to. Both pimps and clients likely know that the surveillance of her family or the structure of la zona can provide protection for women. In contrast, taking a woman off of her "turf," which both Alejandro and Chuck did, may reduce her sense of security and make her more compliant.

It is important to note that these stories do not represent all relations between sex workers and their clients and pimps. Sex workers also told me many other stories of clients giving them presents. I witnessed warm interactions between clients and sex workers occasionally and watched clients bring sex workers gifts after trips out of town. When Eva was very ill and could not work for many months, some of her frequent clients gave her money and food. An American client helped Alicia to leave Reynosa so that she could return to Puebla to live with her six-month-old son and no longer have to work in Boystown. Rebecca, Alicia's "best friend" in la zona, said that Alicia "lucked out with this gringo," who also gave her a truck to drive to Puebla, but added that he was really ugly and old.

Relationships between sex workers and pimps were also more varied. Marisela told me that she chose her pimp and wanted him to be her pimp, and I heard stories of other women who chose to have pimps rather than being coerced into those relations. It is also important to note that not all pimps were "raised to be pimps" like the men in Tlaxcala are. I interviewed two men who claimed to have accidentally become pimps for short periods of time because of their relationships with sex workers. As discussed in chapter 1, Diego's relationship with a sex worker in la zona led to him becoming, temporarily, the pimp of several women. He told the story as if it was the role he was expected to inhabit as the boyfriend of a sex worker/madame. Jimmy, a bilingual man who was born in Chicago and worked as a tour guide for visitors to Boystown, explained to me that he became a pimp unintentionally after beginning a relationship with a sex worker. He also worked in the prostitution zone and started his relationship with her as a client. In his self-aggrandizing story of the beginning of the relationship, he explained that he paid her three times more than her asking price so that she would let him do "anything he wanted," and he explained that he pleased her so well (in great part through oral sex) that she wanted him to be her pimp and her boyfriend. He then took on money management responsibilities. While the story sounded a bit far-fetched to me, Jimmy was not the only person who suggested that sex workers keep their pimps around in part because of their cunnilingual abilities.

After Cubana told me the story of her *madrota* leaving with all of the money she had earned, she lamented, "They [the sex workers with pimps] can choose freedom, but to work for someone becomes a habit (*costumbre*), to have someone who fucks you nicely becomes a habit, and many times the relationship between partners is not because you love each other; it is habit." Cubana used the Spanish word *costumbre*, which can mean either habit (at the level of individual) or custom (at the level of a culture). This is the same word that women have used to describe to me their difficulty leaving Boystown because they grew accustomed to making money. Cubana's invocation of habit/custom highlights the convergence of structural (cultural) conditions and the individual biography involved in the situations she described. Cubana was also addicted to crack cocaine, another habit that kept women in la zona. Many women claimed to love the pimps or children they worked for, and, as Lauren Berlant notes, love entails nonsovereignty (Berlant and Hardt 2011). Cunnilingus, romantic love, and maternal love were all factors that led to sex workers' nonsovereignty. These forms of nonsovereign love often led to financial obligations that women fulfilled through sex work. Thus, relationships with pimps and clients sometimes included coercion, intimacy, love, and a number of different kinds of configurations of financial and sexual ties.

Conclusion

David's comment at the beginning of this chapter was that pimps and families both pimped out sex workers, and he argued for the sex worker keeping her money for herself. Like much of Western liberal theory, this assumes a sovereign, atomistic, self-owning subject and a dichotomy between force and choice. Sex workers' relationships with the people they labored for, I argue, can be better understood through an expansion of sex workers' emic conception of *obligar* to encompass many kinds of relations that are both burdensome and desirable. These are relations that have nonsovereign qualities. Sex workers' relationships with people like pimps, children, and other family members sometimes influenced their lives in ways they could not control. Furthermore, the whore stigma was an important element that shaped sex workers' relationships to each other and their obligations to their families.

While David did not understand why sex workers did not "just work for themselves," I suggest an answer: a completely sovereign, autonomous subject was morally untenable in Boystown, as we can see from the case of Rebecca pretending to need to work in la zona to support a fake child. While obligations to family members that fostered nonsovereignty were valued, however, there was a hierarchy of nonsovereignty and interdependency. On the one hand, sex workers with pimps were not criticized on moral grounds, but their pimps were seen as having too much control over them. Sex workers with drug addictions, on the other hand, were considered to be low in the hierarchy of nonsovereignty, as they had too little control over their lives and did not fulfill obligations.

Sex workers who worked for obligations to their family members (especially children) were at the top of a hierarchy in la zona. Other sex workers did not criticize women with pimps on moral grounds because they were seen as victims of men and of their rural and indigenous "culture of the past" that taught them to be subservient to men. Through discourses circulating within Boystown about *padroteras*, we can see the way their moral careers were imagined. While this chapter demonstrates how sex workers without pimps posited themselves as more modern and independent than sex workers with pimps, they still did not value individual autonomy. The only woman I met who (much later) admitted to working for herself felt the need to pretend to have a daughter while she was in Boystown. Creating value through sexual labor was not just a matter of performing sexual acts in exchange for money. It required a good deal of work to posit one's labor in relation to ideas about motherhood and agency.

CHAPTER 4

"Sometimes We, as Mothers, Are to Blame": Drug-Addicted Sex Workers and the Politics of Blame

Sometimes we, as mothers, are to blame. Once, I was talking to my child on the pay phone, and the son of [a drug-addicted sex worker] said to me that he wished he had a mother like me. It must be difficult for them.
EVA

Eva spoke these words sadly and earnestly as we sat facing one another on her bed in the small room where she lived and worked in la zona. Eva had spent the morning preparing chicken soup for a small celebration she was hosting in her room for Stacy's birthday. But as a few missionaries and I were getting dressed for the party, the celebratory spirit ended with terrible news. María, a former sex worker known for her heavy crack cocaine and alcohol abuse, discovered the body of her sixteen-year-old daughter, Estrella, dangling from a bedsheet-turned-noose in their home, a dilapidated former bar in Boystown. The party was canceled, and missionaries and I took shifts grieving with Estrella's friends and family members, with breaks to eat soup in Eva's room. When Eva said, "Sometimes we, as mothers, are to blame," she was indirectly blaming María for the suicide of her sixteen-year-old daughter. By telling a story about the child of a drug-addicted sex worker who wished he had a mother like Eva, she also pointed to her own mothering as a positive example. Eva distinguished herself as a better mother than María, perhaps for not using drugs as well as for protecting her children from the prostitution zone by employing the double life strategy. While Eva was born in El Salvador, her family lived in central Mexico and believed that she worked as a housekeeper and child care provider for a wealthy family in Reynosa.

Sex workers were entangled in a web of obligations, not only to provide moral, emotional, and economic care to their children, but also to demonstrate to other sex workers (and perhaps to missionaries, anthropologists, and themselves) that they were good mothers. As the last chapter showed, sex workers exercised agency in relation to the whore stigma by casting themselves as respectable prostitutes working out of maternal obligation. This chapter examines how sex workers established themselves as good mothers by criticizing bad mothers. Women with drug addictions, like María, were especially likely to be the targets of criticism. The children of sex workers with drug addictions were frequently a topic of conversation and gossip in la zona. Sex workers and missionaries alike were concerned with the futures of the children of Boystown. Sex workers criticized drug-addicted mothers, and both missionaries and sex workers invested in futures where their children would not become sex workers. Both critique and investment reproduced the whore stigma. Patricia Hill Collins (2004) has shown how the "controlling image" of the crack-addicted single black mother and the "welfare queen" demonized and criminalized low-income black mothers who were already seen to have excessive fertility and non-normative sexuality. These discourses not only blamed black mothers for social problems but also justified the gutting of public assistance programs and fueled Reagan's war on drugs. Social scientists such as Oscar Lewis and Daniel Patrick Moynihan helped to produce some of these discourses that blame racially marked mothers for poverty and social problems (Briggs 2002). This chapter examines the way that some sex workers themselves reproduce the whore stigma through a politics of respectability that uses the image of a crack-addicted sex worker to create positive images of themselves as mothers.

The stories that some sex workers in la zona tell of other, "bad," sex workers highlight their own values. Their denouncements were a way to present themselves as morally superior and shed light on the moral economy of Boystown. I argue that drug addiction embodied the ways in which Boystown could make life worse instead of better for sex workers and their family members. Sex workers initially hoped that la zona would change their lives and those of their children for the better. Crack cocaine–addicted women and their children served as evidence that the relations fostered in Boystown could become obstacles to this aspirational economic opportunity. As such, their lives provided one possible cautionary tale for how the moral career of a sex worker might end very badly for herself as well as for her family.

First, I discuss the moral career of the drug-using sex worker in la zona. Much of the data in this chapter comes from observations and interviews surrounding two children of drug-addicted sex workers who spent part of their childhoods in the prostitution zone. I first focus upon the politics of blame around sixteen-year-old Estrella's suicide. I then turn to Lucía's narration of how drug addiction and prostitution influenced her relations with her children. I end with discourses of blame and concern surrounding the fate of Lucía's eight-year-old granddaughter.

Moral Careers of Drug-Using Sex Workers

The rhyming adage that stated that those who were born in Aquiles Serdán, the neighborhood of la zona, would never leave was perhaps especially true for people with crack cocaine addictions. While most sex workers in Boystown worked for a period of a few months to a few years before leaving, the crack cocaine users tended to stay, sometimes for twenty to thirty years, and sometimes had children and grandchildren who lived or worked part of their lives in the same community.

Other sex workers claimed that drug-addicted sex workers had many children, speculating that women with addictions were more likely to have sex without a condom because their desperation for drugs made them more willing to engage in risky acts. I heard rumors of some women being impregnated by clients, but at least two of the drug-addicted women in la zona had children with current or former partners. When I was in Reynosa, three of the women with crack cocaine addictions had at least one child who lived or worked in the prostitution zone. In Boystown, a child born into the prostitution zone was referred to as *un niño de la zona*.[1] I never met a woman in la zona who claimed to be *from* Reynosa except for two children of drug-addicted sex workers. It was because of the stigma attached to sex work that most women migrated elsewhere, away from their families, to work.

Many sex workers in la zona were addicted to crack cocaine and alcohol, and they were living examples of the way that the drug trade has changed the landscape of Reynosa over the past several decades. Sex workers with drug addictions not only were the least mobile and the most likely to stay in Boystown for the rest of their lives, but also appeared to be the least affected by the drug war, as they spoke less about being afraid of drug violence.

While drug use in Mexico is much less of a social problem than it is in the United States, it has increased since the late 1990s and early 2000s (Aguilar and Castañeda 2009, cited in Diaz-Cayeros et al. 2011), with cocaine use in Mexico doubling between 2002 and 2008 (Guerrero Gutiérrez 2010, 83). Campbell says that beginning in the late 1980s or early 1990s, Mexican cartels started to sell their excess supply within Mexico, setting up drug-selling outlets called *tienditas* throughout the country (Campbell 2009, 97). Other researchers have suggested that drug consumption in Mexico increased when wholesale drug importers started to make payments to their employ-

ees in drugs, and that consumption is higher in areas where drugs are produced or transported (Aguilar and Castañeda 2009; Guerrero Gutierrez
2010, cited in Diaz-Cayeros 2011). Aquiles Serdán was full of *tienditas*, facilitating the crack cocaine use that was common both within the prostitution
zone and in the neighborhood surrounding it.

Cubana explained to me how crack affected her life and other sex workers' lives. Both in her unpublished, handwritten memoir and in interviews,
Cubana emphasized her education and the fact that she had taught less-
educated sex workers in la zona to read. Cubana said that she got stuck in
Reynosa because she started using drugs, including cocaine, mushrooms,
peyote, acid, pills, and crack. She explained that once a woman begins using drugs, she works not for herself, her pimp, or her family, but only for the
drugs. She said,

> If you have one hundred pesos and the drug costs one hundred pesos, you're
> not going to buy a dress—no, drugs are better! The drugs are most impor-
> tant, and then everything else. That's why many of the women are really
> skinny. They don't have money for food because they spend it on drugs.

Cubana discussed her own drug use, which was ongoing, in the past
tense: "if I had fifty pesos to eat, nah, I went to buy drugs. I preferred drugs
to food." She explained that a rock of crack cost one hundred pesos and that
its effect lasted fifteen to thirty minutes. While one could occasionally make
enough money to buy a hit by having sex with a client, Cubana explained, it
had recently become very difficult to find clients.

As women with drug addictions grew older, they tended to retire from
prostitution and run errands for sex workers. Cubana, for example, washed
the work clothes of younger women for pay or walked to a convenience
store directly outside of la zona to buy them snacks in exchange for money.
Lucía said that when she retired from sex work, she began to clean younger
women's rooms to survive, or, rather, to buy drugs. Retired drug-using sex
workers were also well known for asking for money from their own children, other people who lived or worked in la zona, and missionaries.

The moral career of a drug-addicted sex worker included expectations
about her death and her posthumous reputation. Although Cubana continued to use drugs and alcohol, she emphasized to me that drug users "become skinny and like idiots, they fuck up their lives." She continued:

> Crack is the worst drug of the century. It kills. Some die from an overdose,
> or they get desperate and kill themselves, and others get killed. They get

killed because they want a rock of crack . . . and they all go to a *fosa común* [common grave].

Her former partner, a "small, beautiful woman with light-colored eyes named Heidi," was killed by the people from whom she stole to support her crack addiction.

In her memoir, *Abismo*, Cubana told the story of four other sex workers who had died: two of tuberculosis, one in an accident, and another who was killed for stealing. After telling the story of each death, Cubana described what happened to each woman's body after she died. In two cases, the woman was sent to the *fosa común*, where people who were unidentified or unclaimed were buried. In two other cases, the women "were luckier" in that their families traveled to Reynosa to claim their bodies. Abigail told me that several of her friends in Boystown were afraid of ending up in the common grave and asked her to ensure that they would not end up there when they died. Sex workers feared that with their corpses buried in unmarked graves, the whore stigma would haunt them after death.

Discourses of Blame about Estrella's Death

Although Estrella's parents were both to some degree a continued part of her life, I only heard people blame her mother, and not her father, for her death. María had medium-brown skin, a somewhat weathered face, and very short gray hair. She often wore cut-off denim shorts with a T-shirt or a one-piece bathing suit and either white sneakers or lace-up boots made of ostrich skin that were a gift from one of her boyfriends. María said that she had two *mascotas*, or pets, referring to the penises of her two boyfriends. Penises are not typically referred to as *mascotas* in Mexican Spanish—this is an inside joke between María, Lucía, and Stacy. One day, when Stacy was hanging out with María and Lucía in Boystown, she said, in Spanish, "I want a pet about this size," holding her hands about a foot apart. María, the story goes, started laughing and saying she wanted a *mascota* of that size as well, indicating the sizes of the *mascotas* she already had, of her two boyfriends. Sex workers in la zona tended to make many sexual jokes together, often when I was around. They would occasionally try to bring missionaries into the joke, but the missionaries usually engaged just enough to be polite.

One of María's boyfriends, El Teacher, lived in Reynosa. Her second boyfriend, Don Lopez, the father of several of her children, was originally from a town near Reynosa but lived on the US side of the border with his legitimate family. He visited María once a week. He was Estrella's father and the owner of the (no longer operating) bar where Estrella and her mother lived. He was about thirty years older than María and had just turned seventy-nine when I met him. He moved slowly, had white hair, and was very thin, with the exception of a small belly that bulged above his high-waisted, belted khakis. Eva said she felt great pity for Don Lopez because he had to mourn the loss of his daughter, Estrella, while hiding his pain from his legitimate family members on the US side of the border who did not know about Estrella or María.

Eva told us that María had a son who was the age of Luz (Lucía's granddaughter) and when both children were about four years old, they would run around la zona together at night unsupervised, asking for food and money from Eva and other sex workers whom they called their "aunts." Eva told us that social services workers took María's son away because María didn't care about him and didn't properly take care of him. Eva postulated that María's son must be adopted by now, and she emphasized that María never fought to get him back.

Eva's denouncement of María was perhaps a way to assuage some of her own guilt about motherhood, by presenting herself as morally superior. It also evidences the moral value placed upon motherhood in Boystown. One way that sex workers created value despite their stigmatized labor was through the denouncement of other sex workers. Sex workers who were not drug users could recast prostitution as less negative by showing that they did it to fulfill obligations, whereas drug workers could not use this strategy. Drug-using sex workers were sometimes called *egoístas* because they were unlikely to fulfill economic and other obligations to family members and sometimes because they did not reciprocate favors to other sex workers (Castillo, Rangel Gómez, and Delgado [1999] also found that drug-using sex workers were called egotistical in Tijuana). Non-drug-using sex workers complained that they gave drug users money or food when they needed it, but this kindness was never reciprocated. They said that drug users only used their money for drugs and alcohol, engaging in one "vice" to feed another. The drug-addicted woman's thinness was an outward sign of her vice, and of her investment of morally suspect sex for money in self-gratification and self-harm, instead of in reproduction of intimate ties.

Eva further told us that Lucía also had a son, whom she "sold." Eva said, "Who knows for what, but she sold him to someone from the other side [of the border]. Perhaps someone wanted to adopt him, but maybe they bought him to sell his organs, because that happens, right?" Eva's comments about the possibility of Lucía's child being sold to Americans for organs echoes many other Boystown rumors of the children of drug-addicted sex workers. Missionaries told me that when they spent time with pregnant women and encouraged them to seek prenatal care, people in Boystown believed that the missionaries were planning to buy or adopt the babies of pregnant sex workers. In all of these stories, sex workers' children were commodified, and the assumption was that the sex workers then used the money to buy drugs and alcohol. The stories express anxieties about the value of Mexican bodies in relation to US dollars, and the values of Mexican bodies (especially those of abject, poor, drug-using Mexican sex workers) in relation to American bodies.

This anxiety surrounding the value of the US dollar could be seen as the flip side of the hopes surrounding it. Some sex workers hoped that gringos and their dollars would again be plentiful in la zona, and others hoped they would one day cross the border to work in the United States and save money to buy property in Mexico. Boystown, for most of these women, was initially a site of optimistic attachment—an attachment to a belief in some kind of flourishing that is tied to a notion of the "good life" (Berlant 2011a). The drug-addicted sex worker embodied negative value in Boystown not only because she was seen as egoistic and a bad mother, but also because she was a threat to the optimistic view of Boystown. The thin crack-addicted sex worker wearing tattered clothing, whose face showed wear and deterioration beyond her years, was a sign of how the life of a woman and her family could become worse instead of better. Limping along the streets of Boystown, she would use the money earned from sex to buy drugs instead of to support her family, violating the moral economy of Boystown. The prostitution zone always had the potential to entail cruel optimism, whereby the thing a person desires becomes "an obstacle to flourishing" that "impedes the aim that brought you to it initially" (Berlant 2011a, 1). But instead of serving as a reality check, the obstacle gets woven into the positive values of the practice that animates it. Berlant writes, "The very pleasures of being inside a relation have become sustaining regardless of the content of the relation, such that a person or a world finds itself bound to a situation of profound threat that is, at the same time, profoundly confirming" (2011a, 2).

Many of the dynamics in sex workers' lives in Boystown could be described as cruelly optimistic. Pimps were difficult to leave, even when they were abusive. And the prostitution zone felt safer and more comfortable than the outside world, despite its debilitating qualities. Family members could function similarly. Relations among sex workers also became like kinship: several sex workers described themselves as "like sisters." When Lucía tried to leave la zona before her miracle, she always found herself going back, in part because her daughter and best friends lived there. La zona fostered relations that were, following Berlant, both confirming and threatening.

Because women with drug addictions were thought to be irresponsible mothers, non-drug-using sex workers often commented, "When the doctor is delivering the baby, why doesn't he just sterilize them?" I knew of one case in which this supposedly did occur. When a thirteen-year-old who was addicted to crack gave birth, the doctor sterilized her because he said he did not want to deliver a new baby from her each year. Although I doubt this story was common knowledge, sex workers frequently made comments about how sad it was that these drug-addicted women kept giving birth to children that they did not care for.

The second instance of blaming María for her daughter's suicide occurred in the bar where Estrella and María lived, when friends and family gathered in mourning just hours after Estrella's death. I walked the block from Eva's room to María's bar with Stacy, Ashley, and a teenager visiting from England who thought she might want to join Stacy's team. The bar had been closed for years by that time. A sign indicating the name of the bar still hung in front, a Santa Claus was painted on the left wall with "Feliz Año 2006–2007," and Estrella's name was scratched into the paint. Across from the Santa Claus painting, on the right side of the room, was the bar where drinks used to be served to customers. When I was there it was usually filled with empty beer bottles. The inside of the bar was dark, enclosed in a crumbling ceiling and plywood walls full of holes. María's bed sat in the back of the room in front of a television where she watched soap operas. Above her bed was a painting (figure 8) depicting a semi-nude blonde woman in front of high-rise hotels and a lush jungle, with the sand and ocean in front of her. She sat on her knees, perky breasts exposed, holding a white kite with one hand while removing her bikini bottom with the other. To the left of the painting was a men's bathroom, with a sign in English. It smelled as if the toilet had been broken for months but had continued being used. The physical space of María's bar evidenced the days when la zona was booming with life and spilling with dollars, and also the signs of dilapidation from the era of decline in the prostitution zone.

When we arrived after hearing the news of Estrella's suicide, several people were crying outside of the bar. Inside, María was sobbing in a white plastic lawn chair. When Jorge, Estrella's boyfriend, whom I had been told was a drug runner and drug addict, stormed into the room, he exploded with grief. He screamed to María, "Where is Estrella? Where *is she*?!" María responded that Estrella was dead. He yelled, "No! Where *is she*?!!!" and his voice cracked in between tears. María repeated that Estrella was dead. Someone walked toward him to offer him a plastic chair and he kicked it over. At the corner of the bar, near the block of light entering through the door, Jorge threw himself on the ground, kicking, and screaming "Nooooooooo!" A long string of yellow-green snot spilled out of his nose while he sobbed and yelled at María, with his voice cracking again, "It is your fault. *WHY DIDN'T YOU TAKE CARE OF HER*?!" María replied, between sobs, "She was with me. I was here. I am the one who found her."

These accusations pointed to the way that María's drug addiction made her unable to fulfill obligations to her daughter. At this event, María was also threatened by one of her closest friends, Chilango,[2] who said that Estrella would not go to heaven if María did not stop drinking. This perhaps fueled María's sobs into Stacy's chest. Chilango was preaching about God's will, saying that God is the one who gives us things and God is the one that takes them away, yelling that it was God's time for Estrella to go, and arguing that we shouldn't question that. While María continued to cry, Chilango yelled at María that it was God's time to take Estrella and told her that she needed to stop crying if she wanted Estrella to go with God. María finally rested her head on Stacy's chest and caught her breath while Ashley caressed her back. Several people, including one missionary, told Chilango to be quiet. At one point, while Stacy was squatting at María's knees and holding her hand, María asked Stacy, "Please say a prayer for her so that she will go with God." This was one of the many instances in which missionaries were seen as mediators of relations between sex workers and God.

Inside Boystown, people generally blamed María for Estrella's suicide. However, media coverage surrounding Estrella's death, which was in part based upon her suicide note, blamed the social space of la zona. The next day, when I talked to Eva, she sadly told me that the newspapers reported that Estrella killed herself "because she didn't want to be around people like us anymore. She wanted to be around different kinds of people." Eva had blamed María just the day before, but she wavered now that media reports implicated her in the supposedly contaminated social world that brought Estrella to kill herself. I finished my meal with Eva and then went to the 7–11 convenience store across from Boystown to buy the newspaper so that I could see for myself what Eva was referring to.

In the June 11, 2009, issue of *La Tarde de Reynosa* a headline reads, "Without Options: Fed up with life, adolescent hangs herself. Born and raised in the tolerance zone, there she contemplated her uncertain future" (Ramirez 2009). According to the article, Estrella was not a sex worker but killed herself in a room that used to be in a nightclub of "vice." Several sex workers and missionaries contradicted this account and told me that Estrella worked in prostitution outside of la zona. The article mentions the relationship between her parents, claiming that Estrella was "made by a couple that was, in some way, associated with the oldest profession in the world."[3] The tone of the article was somewhat warm, referring to Estrella as a "little young lady" and making reference to her "short existence" (Ramirez 2009).

The article included three photographs. In the first, Estrella's head is at the bottom center of the frame, with a man bending down toward her body, which is partially visible. A second photo shows the sheet that she used, still hanging from the ceiling. The third is close-up of her diary entry, which the article claims was written minutes before she killed herself. In the photograph published in the newspaper, it is possible to read her suicide note written in fat purple handwriting that looks like that of a teenage girl:

> I think that in the first place I should not live here (in la zona). I've had
> enough of it. Second, what I would have to do would be to meet new people,
> spend time with normal people that would make me feel good, although if I
> really think about it, I would have to distance myself from everyone I have
> known up until now.[4]

For Estrella, it seems, ending her life was a more viable option than distancing herself from all of the people she already knew and starting a new life outside of the prostitution zone. Her note is a commentary on the disabling and negative aspects of kinship bonds that often accompany their enabling and desirable ones: these bonds are not easily severed, regardless of their quality.

This is the passage that Eva likely referred to when she implicated herself in the suicide of Estrella by saying, with solemnity and sadness, "She didn't want to be around people like us anymore. She wanted to meet new people." While Eva distanced herself from mothers whose drug use subjected their children to the prostitution zone and made them unable to fulfill their obligations, her reference to "people like us" included herself as part of the reason that Estrella killed herself.

Several of María's friends, both sex workers and missionaries, hoped that Estrella's death would be such a shock to María that it would convince her to stop using drugs and alcohol. Although she did seem more sober for the first few weeks, María eventually started drinking again. A couple of weeks after Estrella's death, I took some pasta to María and two of her friends, Bookie and Gloria, and we ate in plastic chairs in front of María's bar. María and Bookie also drank *huachi* out of the bottom half of a gallon milk jug filled with ice. They offered me some, as usual, and I declined. After making small talk, María told me that Magdalena was going to give her one of her triplets if one was a girl. Magdalena was a thin drug user with lovely curly hair and a huge pregnant belly whom I occasionally spotted on hot days walking around la zona completely naked with the exception of flip flops. Gloria also said that Magdalena was going to give her one of the triplets. Rumors about the fates of sex workers' babies, especially those of drug users, constantly circulated through la zona.

María decided that she wanted to show me her patio where Stacy and other American missionaries had built a garden. We walked through her bar, past her bedroom and bed, and through a door into the patio area behind the bar, which opened up to a courtyard lined by abandoned accessory rooms. The air was damp and smelled of sewage, clothes were strewn about the bright green grassy area, and a mattress sat decaying in the grass. The courtyard was once the project of Stacy and a short-term team, who planted a garden and repainted some of the buildings as well as created a sculpture out of bicycle tires that they spray-painted pink. Symbolic of failed efforts to help, the pink bicycle tire sculpture hiding in the overgrown garden was now the only remnant of the work that the missionaries had done. We sat together on the sidewalk, in front of a row of empty rooms.

Once we were alone together, María cried, apologizing for her tears. She pointed upstairs to what had been Estrella's room, explaining that it was boarded up after she died. By this time, she was sufficiently drunk on *huachi*, and her slurred speech made her unintelligible. Perhaps in reaction to those who embrace the double life and reject the cohabitation between sex workers and their children, María pointed to her physical proximity to Estrella as evidence of her care. "That was her room," she said, pointing again, "but she usually slept with me. She would come into my bed at night because she was afraid to sleep alone." María and I cried together until one of her drug-using friends arrived with a pipe and a rock of crack that he had scored. María said, "*con permiso*," a very cordial request of permission before she started smoking the crack with her friend, and I invented a reason to leave.

A later account of Estrella's suicide, given by another crack cocaine user, was another example of how the politics of blame helped sex workers to position themselves morally vis-à-vis María and highlight negative values of Boystown. A month later, while eating roasted chicken and tortillas with Ashley just outside of la zona, Cubana told us that María didn't even cry over Estrella. Cubana retold the story of Estrella's suicide, beginning with a new detail: María asking Estrella for ten pesos for crack on the day of Estrella's death. Cubana took this opportunity to explain that a rock of crack costs one hundred pesos. She tore a tiny piece of a tortilla to represent the physical quantity of crack obtained for that price, put it on Ashley's plate, and said, "that's what you get for one hundred pesos." Cubana then started telling the story again, saying that on the day of Estrella's death, María demanded of Estrella, "Give me ten pesos," because she wanted to buy crack. Estrella refused, and María replied, "Go to hell" ("*Vete a la verga*," literally, "go to the penis," a common saying in Mexico), cursed at her and left. According to Cubana, by the time María returned to their home, Estrella had hanged herself, but was not yet dead and had just broken part of her spine. Cubana illustrated this by pointing to a bone on the back of her own neck. She told us that Estrella cried, "Take me down and untie me, Mama," and then María untied her and took her down, and tried to give her mouth-to-mouth resuscitation. But Estrella died in her arms. Cubana said again that María never cried.

I knew that Cubana's account was not accurate because, in addition to my suspicion of its *telenovela*-like elements, I had witnessed María's tears. However, it is noteworthy that this version of the suicide of Estrella indirectly blames María for Estrella's death, by way of her crack addiction; involves not only money, as in other stories of blame, but the exact same ten peso amount that María blamed the rosary-wearing woman for not giving Estrella; and alludes to María asking her child for money, which I knew that Cubana herself did with her own son.

This story of Estrella's suicide is another commentary about the relationship between drug-addicted sex workers and their children, a commentary in which Cubana implicates herself. We can see parallels between elements of her story and her own relationship with her son, which shed light upon Cubana's moral values. Cubana wrote in her memoir that crack made her stop taking care of her son when he was a baby, because it made her not think about him. Because of her drug addiction, Cubana explained, she could not devote the time and care to him that he wanted and needed. She often let her girlfriends take care of him. If they refused, she left him with other people. While some of his caretakers taught him how to add and multiply, others mistreated him, which made her feel terrible in retrospect. Cubana said that when she would tell her son that she needed him, he would respond, "When I needed you, you weren't there." Cubana's expressions of guilt and regret and sadness for not providing emotional and moral care to her child—for not being present—echo those of non-drug-addicted sex workers with double lives. María's choice to keep her daughter close resulted in her being blamed by her colleagues for failing to provide both moral care and economic provisions by exposing her to la zona and spending the money she earned on drugs.

Cubana's version of the story about Estrella's suicide reveals the moral values of Boystown: María's demand for drug money from her daughter was believed to lead to Estrella's death. In the moral economy of la zona, María asking for money violated the expected circulation of money between a sex worker and her child. A mother was supposed to give money to her children, not take money from them. Furthermore, although Cubana did not allude to this directly, many sex workers in Boystown believed that sex workers should protect their families from the stigma of prostitution and exposure to "vice" by keeping them away from la zona. As Estrella was rumored to be a second-generation sex worker, being born in la zona likely influenced her occupational career. Drug use was believed to make sex workers unable to fulfill their obligations to their family members, whom they instead pressured to give them money to buy drugs. These factors combine to form a complete inversion of the positive moral values of Boystown.

Reciprocity was an important moral value for all sex workers in Boystown. Just as much as nonaddicted people judged addicts for misusing their gifts or money, women with drug addictions judged people as "good" or "bad" depending upon whether or not they gave them money, or shared drugs or food. I observed from my interactions with Cubana that her relationship with her son was in constant flux. Almost every time I saw her, she gave me an update about the status of their relationship. When Cubana described her son as "good," she was often living with him or he was paying her rent in an apartment outside of la zona. Even then, Cubana complained that her son would earn two thousand pesos and only give her one hundred. In the periods in which Cubana's son was not giving her money, she described him as "bad," and Cubana was more likely to live and work in la zona then, cleaning rooms in exchange for rent in addition to cleaning women's clothes and doing odd jobs in exchange for money that she used for drugs, alcohol, and food. In April 2009 she told me that her son worked at a nearby restaurant and that he helped support her. In fact, she was living with him, and he gave her money for food but never drugs. I knew from other people, and Cubana confirmed this in a later interview, that her son actually worked in la zona selling drugs.

Cubana's relationship with her son soon became more complicated. A few months after Estrella's suicide, Ashley and I were walking in Boystown and heard someone yelling for our attention. We turned around to see Cubana walking strangely and slowly, limping along the dirt road in her flip-flops. She told us that she had a lot of pain in her feet. We asked her if she was now living in la zona and she said yes, and when we asked her why she started crying, saying my son, *mi hijo*, switching from Spanish to English as she often did. We stood in the scorching sun right by a taco cart and talked to Cubana while she wept. "He used to be good to me, he was always good to me, but now he is bad." Cubana explained that her son had married Jorge's mother (Jorge was the boyfriend of Estrella), whom Cubana described as "a little old woman, even older than I am." She added that the *vieja* was sixty years old and her son was only twenty-one. I asked Cubana why her son married the woman. She made a gesture of several inches of thickness with her fingers, to indicate a large wad of cash, and said, "for money." She explained that Jorge's mother was a prostitute and that her son had taken the role of his new wife's pimp. A few days later, when I saw Cubana again, she told me that her son had broken up with that woman and her relationship with her son was now better.

Cubana complained to me at one point that she was paying ten thousand pesos per month so that her son could learn to be an airplane pilot, but that he still decided to work for the narcos selling drugs. She explained that although she preferred for him to work for the military or the federal police, he preferred to work for the narcos because he could make more money that way. Cubana said that her son did not understand that he could go to jail for up to twenty years for selling drugs.

As we can see from Cubana's relationship with her son as well as some of the discourses surrounding Estrella's suicide, the intimate and economic ties between drug-using sex workers and their children were sometimes the inverse of those of non-drug-using sex workers. Non-drug-using sex workers were likely to provide money to their children, but they could not offer them daily, face-to-face emotional and moral care, because they lived far away. Drug-using sex workers were more likely to be physically present and spend time with at least some of their children, as María emphasized. However, they usually used most of their money on drugs and ended up asking their children for money, which violated one of the moral values of Boystown. Furthermore, other sex workers criticized drug-addicted women for failing to protect their children from la zona, and thus failing to provide moral care.

Lucía and Her Children

Lucía's intimate and economic relationships to her family and drugs changed somewhat once she stopped using drugs. Like most of the women in Boystown, Lucía believed that if a woman was working in prostitution, it should be for her familial obligations. But like Cubana, she told of how addiction kept her from fulfilling these obligations and shaped the lives of her children. Lucía is originally from Chihuahua City, Chihuahua. She was fifty-seven when I met her in 2008, and at that point she had lived in Reynosa for thirty-four years. She moved to Reynosa in 1974 to try to earn more money for her family, leaving her children in Torreon. For the first six years, she sent money to her family and drank only when she had to in order to solicit clients in bars in la zona. But Lucía said, foreshadowing her later addiction, "Unfortunately, every day, I got more into drugs and alcohol." She described how she started to use drugs including paint thinner, spray paint, marijuana, pills, cocaine, crack, and beer. She said, "I was drinking every brand of wine until I reached the ultimate in alcohol, *guachacol*, the highest proof at the lowest price."

Lucía described her relationship with her children changing due to her increasing alcohol and drug use:

> For me, truthfully, I didn't want to continue using [drugs and alcohol] but believe me, the damn vice made me want, each day, a larger quantity of drugs, and after these six years I never again sent money to my children and I forgot about them because of prostitution, and the vice of drugs and alcohol, which worsened by the day.

Lucía's framing of her sex work, drinking, and drug addiction as "vice" reflects the way these activities were seen as sin. She also criticized her own performance as a mother. Lucía had three daughters. Two were married and had families, lived in other cities, and refused to see Lucía while she was using drugs. Once she had been sober for several months, Lucía happily told me that she was going to see these two daughters for the first time in several years. However, when she spoke of her third daughter, Ana, Lucía still blamed herself. Ana had lived in la zona all of her life. She got pregnant when she was thirteen and had a daughter, Luz, whom Lucía raised inside of the prostitution zone for the first four years of her life, until another sex worker called social services and had her taken away. Luz lived with her paternal grandparents[5] for some time before Lucía was able to get custody. While I was in Reynosa, Lucía took Luz to live with her at the shelter and eventually in a small house near the periphery of Boystown. Meanwhile, Ana became addicted to crack cocaine at a young age, and she suffered from health and developmental problems that people suspected were caused by her drug use, and perhaps Lucía's. Lucía thanked "God that Luz turned out okay."

Lucía continued to enter Boystown every day to visit Ana and her best friend, María. She proudly reported that she did not succumb to the drugs and alcohol offered to her there: "Truthfully, I am not tempted. Yes, they offer me drugs, but I'm not tempted." She pointed to the fat on her belly, indicating that she had gained weight. In la zona, body fat was an index of drug dependence—drug users who gained weight often pointed to their fat as evidence that they quit drugs or reduced their drug use. Lucía also told us that her daughter, Ana, nicknamed *La Gorda* (the Fat Lady) in irony, was finally beginning to embody her name—she had gained weight because she was now only using crack occasionally. Linking bodily redemption with a spiritual one, she also mentioned that *La Gorda* was attending the Good Samaritan Church in la zona every week and told me that she thought it was helping her daughter.

Lucía told me that although her life was more difficult with Luz, her granddaughter's presence kept her from *cayendo*, or falling, back into her former life. While we were waiting for Luz to come out of school one afternoon, Lucía told me that she had three prayers, the first two of which had already been answered: 1) to be free of drugs and alcohol, 2) to get Luz back, and 3) for Ana to stop using drugs and alcohol in order to take responsibility for Luz. Lucía added that Ana didn't have a good maternal example because she herself was a prostitute and Ana grew up around vice. She said, however, that at least she could now set a good example for her daughter and granddaughter. She needed to give her daughter time, because she was very young, but "one day, I'm going to die, and she's going to have to care for Luz."

Concern for Luz was widespread. Once I was sitting in Eva's room with her and Sofía when the two of them started talking about Luz living in the rehabilitation center with Lucía.

Eva: Why doesn't social services take Luz away? Why did they give Luz to Lucía? To me, it does not seem good that the girl is growing up among those women.
Sofía: No, no.
Eva: Because they are all women in rehabilitation. What can they talk about? What kinds of things can the girl learn there?
Sofía: Only how to talk about drugs.
Eva: (To me) What do you think?
Me: The truth is, I don't know, because I don't know what it is like to live there.
Sofía: It is full of drug addicts.
Eva: It's rehabilitation. Veronica is there, Lucía is there . . . a ton of old women who . . . who are lost souls (*perdidas*).
Sofía: And, further, prostitutes are there who are not educated. They can't

keep their mouths shut, and they say things that they shouldn't. The girl needs a family atmosphere.

They both repeat together: Family.

Eva: There, there is no family.

Sofía and Eva then argued that Luz would be better off at an orphanage, where she would be around other children, receive *cariño* (affection) and be taught "good things," indicating moral care. They mentioned that Lucía hid Luz from social services when she was young, as María had done to her son, and both children grew up in la zona since birth. Eva explained that while social services workers eventually took María's son away to an orphanage, Lucía had someone with drug cartel power make a phone call that would allow Luz to be cared for by her paternal grandparents.[6] Once Lucía was sober, she took responsibility for Luz again.

Sofía: But I say that it's Lucía's selfishness.

Eva: Yes, it's selfishness. She says that it's out of love, but I tell her, why don't you give the girl to one of your daughters, and you could go visit her every day?

Although most sex workers, including Sofía and Eva, saw providing for and spending time with one's children as an important part of parenting, they interpreted Lucía's decision to cohabitate with Luz as driven by self-interest rather than love. It was fairly common for sex workers to accuse current or former drug users of being selfish or doing things out of self-interest. The subtext was that if Lucía *really* loved Luz, she should not cohabitate with her.

The many conversations about Luz's well-being were also expressions of concern about children living near the prostitution zone or with sex workers. By telling these stories, the speakers distanced themselves from a maternal figure they assessed to be underperforming. Sofía either assumed that prostitutes were not educated or well behaved, or at least she distinguished herself from other, less well-behaved sex workers.[7] Lucía exposed Luz to drug addicts and uneducated "prostitutes . . . who cannot keep their mouths shut." The only way to be a "respectable prostitute," according to the moral economy represented by Eva and Sofía, is to take the whore stigma and the disorderly, vice-filled conditions of the prostitution zone upon oneself, while protecting one's family through geographical distance and lies. Cohabitation of children with sex workers was a failure of the provisions of moral care, because exposing them to the "vice" of the prostitution zone was seen to contaminate them. In this case, the idea of a "family" environment was stripped of all necessities of biological kinship: an orphanage, because it is not full of vice and sin, was seen as more family-like than a house with biological kin. A family environment was seen as a place where children receive moral and emotional care, untainted by vice and stigma.

As in discourses surrounding Estrella's death, sex workers suggested that their company contaminated children and interfered with their moral care. But Lucía, María, and Cubana, although they at times blamed themselves for their behaviors as mothers, also provided moments of defiance by choosing to live with their children.

Eva also criticized Lucía for failing to provide Luz with adequate material care. One day, while Ashley and I sat in Eva's room, Eva told us that Lucía often visited to ask her for a taco or for money to buy food for Luz's breakfast. She told us that when Lucía lived at Hermano Domingo's shelter, he gave her a lot of food and she was able to sell some of it. She got by well, but now she didn't live there anymore. It made Eva sad to think about the life Luz had lived, in poverty, and that she would not have a "normal" life. Eva speculated, "Perhaps she has never even had a doll or a birthday party." She continued, with her eyes slightly tearing, "I was the same, when I was young. We were poor. I didn't have a single doll. The only one that I had was a long squash, and I used charcoal to draw a face on it, and I made a dress for it out of a rag that my mother no longer needed." Eva told us that when she was a child, she didn't know any better. Now that she was older, it saddened her that she never had a doll or a party. She said that Luz's life would be the same. Eva asked, "What kind of life is it for her, to live first here, in la zona, and then with her grandparents who didn't treat her well, and now with Lucía, who doesn't even have enough money to feed her?"

Both sex workers and missionaries expressed fear that Luz might end up working in the prostitution zone. Eva asked us with a frown, "What is going to happen to Luz when Lucía dies? She's going to come to la zona to look for her mother. Her mother isn't going to want her, and she's going to work in this [prostitution]. She's going to stay here." The three of us looked at each other, eyes wide with concern. Eva asked Ashley and me, "Why don't you cross her to the United States?" I replied, "But it's really difficult for gringos to adopt Mexicans." Eva answered, "Who cares if she has papers, as long as she's safe, as long as she's away from here."

Missionaries shared the same concerns. Later Ashley told me that she and Stacy have always worried that Luz would end up in la zona like her mom and grandmother if she were not to get an education. For this reason, Ashley explained, Stacy and her new husband, Ken, planned to take some responsibility for Luz once their house was complete, and, if necessary, they would pay for Luz to attend school. Ashley added, "Because Luz didn't choose this. She didn't choose any of it. She didn't choose to be born in Boystown. And Estrella also didn't choose that life, at least not at first." In this instance, missionaries implied that those who were born into the prostitution zone, instead of "choosing" to work there, were the most deserving of aid. Luz and Estrella became symbolically important in la zona because their fates were thought to be determined by not only the conditions of the prostitution zone, but also inadequate mothers and grandmothers.

Conclusion

While working for one's familial obligations could recast sex work as relatively respectable, drug use remained merely vice because it made drug users unable to fulfill obligations to their children and family members as well as to colleagues and friends. Non-drug-using sex workers critiqued drug users for being bad mothers and for cohabitating with their children. These critiques were a way for non-drug-using sex workers with double lives to define themselves as good mothers and respectable prostitutes, and to reinforce their decisions to live far from their children to protect them from the stigma of prostitution. Fractally reproducing the Respectable Mother/ Disreputable Prostitute distinction through a critique of other mothers was a way for some sex workers to create value, exercise agency in relation to the whore stigma, and define themselves as respectable. It also deployed the whore stigma against other sex workers. Crack cocaine–addicted sex workers embodied negative value in the moral economy of Boystown. They were criticized for being selfish, bad mothers because they worked to fulfill their bodily desires instead of making money to reproduce their families and nurture their intimate ties. Drug-using sex workers also embodied negative value because while most sex workers saw Boystown as a site of hope, the lives of drug-using sex workers evidenced the ways in which la zona sometimes lead to abject poverty and bodily degradation.

PART III

MISSIONARY PROJECTS IN BOYSTOWN

CHAPTER 5

The Love Triad between Sex Workers, Missionaries, and God

David and Stacy are both Americans who each moved within blocks of a prostitution zone in the Mexican border city of Reynosa in order to facilitate their respective relationships with Mexican sex workers. David visited the prostitution zone as a client and chose this location for the "cheap rent, cheap food, and the abundance of pussy." Stacy, in contrast, was a missionary who aspired to build relationships with sex workers that might erase and replace sex worker-client relations. Stacy felt compassion for drug dealers and pimps such as Kilo, who was the means through which she gained access to Boystown and whom she called her friend. Still, her missionary team's "relationship building" was not targeted at clients. Stacy wrote on her blog about averting her gaze, perhaps in disgust, when clients drove by, and this is the kind of missionary reaction I usually observed in relation to clients. Stacy noted on her blog that it was hard for her to feel compassion for the American clients she saw "using" her friends. Missionaries believed that relations between clients and sex workers were instrumentalizing, or using a person as a means to an end.

Although Stacy perceived herself in opposition to David and other clients, their projects did contain some parallels. Stacy's and David's presence in Boystown and easy circulation in and out of Reynosa have been enabled by the same asymmetries structuring the US-Mexico relationship. And while most American sex tourists and missionaries who visited Reynosa crossed the border for short trips to buy less expensive beer, medicine, and sex or to build houses with their church youth groups, Stacy and David moved there with the intention to stay.

David himself grew up as a "missionary kid" and lived in Mexico with his American missionary parents from the age of three to thirteen. When he was in his forties, he moved to Reynosa from the American Midwest because he "needed a change" after he divorced his wife, lost his business, and lost his mother to cancer. Stacy also grew up "in the church." She was in her late twenties when God told her to love the men and women of Boystown. Then her ten-year-old nephew shot and killed her brother. Ten days later, she left for Texas.

Both David and Stacy moved to Reynosa in the wake of traumatic events and chose to live mere blocks away from Reynosa's prostitution zone. They also inspired or convinced other white English speakers to join them.[1] In Stacy's case, young people from the United States, England, and South Africa whom she met through her extended Christian networks felt led by God to join her project to love sex workers. David convinced several other single, often divorced men around his age to move to Reynosa, where he helped them rent apartments in his building and showed them around Boystown, instructing them how much to pay sex workers and cluing them in about which women provided good service.

A number of circumstances facilitated by the US-Mexico border worked to their advantage. Both David and Stacy benefited from being able to legally acquire US dollars yet live with lower costs in Mexico. David commuted to the US side of the border every day to work for a security company. When I met him, he had lived for nine years in the same apartment in Reynosa, where his living expenses were much lower than they would be on the US side of the border. With exchange rates in his favor, David's job paid him in dollars, but he paid for rent and food and sex in pesos. While Stacy did not move to Reynosa as a moneymaking venture, like most missionaries, she was financially supported by American members of church congregations. Her project was financially tenable because it was well publicized: Stacy was featured in several videos available on the Internet, and she received donations for her mission from members of her congregation in Tulsa and (more occasionally) from other congregations she visited in the United States. Like Stacy and David, many Mexican residents throughout Mexico also lived on US dollars their migrant family members sent as remittances. Unlike Stacy's and David's fluid movement between currencies and countries, however, many of these migrants paid dearly for the favorable exchange rates with border crossings that were neither easy, safe, nor frequent: many paid thousands of dollars to be crossed by a coyote, while also risking being deported and even losing their lives. Both David and Stacy could use their US passports to return to the United States, and once the violence in Reynosa reached a level that was no longer tolerable, they took that option.

While the client/sex worker relationship is much more likely to be seen as erotic than the relationship between missionaries and the populations they target, this chapter examines the erotics of the relationships between missionaries and sex workers. In line with missionaries' conceptions, I construct celibacy as a form of sexuality rather than an avoidance or absence of sexuality. I develop a queer reading of missionary relations with sex workers by arguing that missionaries sought to form what I call love triads between themselves, sex workers, and God, which they imagined would bring each party closer to the other two. They hoped that these relations could replace sex workers' relationships with clients. Forging and nurturing love triads was a form of gendered and gendering intimate labor. Nonsovereignty was an important part of this love triad. Missionaries believed that God made them fall in love with Boystown in ways that extended beyond their control, and they believed that their relations with sex workers would lead to relations with God that would similarly change their lives. This chapter explores the cultural logics of the missionary perspective and how they created value[2] through their actions. Sex workers' reactions to missionary projects will be addressed in the next chapter. The data that I use in this chapter is primarily from ethnographic observations and interviews as well as blogs and websites written by missionaries and their publics.

I first place Team Boystown's project within the context of an Emerging Evangelical movement, which constitutes a distinctly social and intersubjective form of Christianity. I compare the desire for authenticity that both Christians and clients of sex workers harbor. I then explain the framework behind my concept of love triads, which builds upon 1) Nancy Munn's theories of value transformation in Gawa, 2) a Peircean analysis of signs, and 3) frameworks that polyamorous communities have developed to describe triadic relationships. The remainder of the chapter unfolds how Team Boystown put love into action, forged love triads, and intervened in spatial, social, material, and spiritual worlds through building relationships with sex workers. Missionaries collected and circulated sex workers' stories to a wider (mostly Christian and English-speaking) audience, which increased intimacy with God and expanded his influence not only within the original love triads but also through and beyond them.

Team Boystown, Authenticity, and the Girlfriend Experience

It was like God took a branding iron and put [Boystown] in my heart and at that moment I knew, like I knew my own name, that Jesus wanted me to follow him here, and I've never known anything so clearly in my life, and I probably won't ever know anything that clearly ever again. I kind of hope I don't, actually, it was kind of a frightening moment.
STACY WHITE

During my first formal interview with Stacy in 2008, she described her first trip to Reynosa, in which she facilitated a short-term Spring Break trip for a group of ninth- and tenth-graders from a church in Tulsa. When Stacy learned of the existence of Boystown, she prayed that God would send "someone," presumably a missionary, there. Stacy refers to that prayer as "sneaky" and "dangerous"—sneaky because she said it in passing, and dangerous because God told her the next day that she was the one to go to Boystown. Stacy's narration of the "frightening moment" of perceiving God's voice and knowing his will for her can be seen as a narration of nonsovereignty. Far from an autonomous individual in complete control of her actions, she became an agent of God's will. God's desires for Stacy became her own: a desire to know, be known by, and love the sex workers of Boystown. This desire would make a love triad between sex workers, missionaries, and God the basis of her mission.

Several of Stacy's team members also point to intense moments of emotion and certainty that they interpreted as signs of God's will for them to go to Boystown. Some even talked about "falling in love with Boystown." Invoking a nonsovereign divine intervention rather than a notion of individual will and choice, missionaries working in Reynosa often explained that they wished God had sent them to a more beautiful or less dangerous place. God told Ashley, a Tulsa-based college student, that she was supposed to return to Reynosa while she was on her hands and knees scrubbing the floor for a sex worker during a short-term mission trip to Reynosa with her church during Spring Break. Eleanor, a South African woman in her mid-twenties, had an emotionally intense response to hearing about sex workers' stories and Stacy's project at a 24-7 Prayer conference in London, and God told her through dreams that she should go to Boystown. Ken, who would eventually become Stacy's husband, became close to her when he accompanied his church as part of a short-term team to construct the "modern-day monastery" that was to serve as transitional housing for sex workers. Stacy and Ken also planned to live in this house, and some of the young people who volunteered their labor in short-term teams used to joke, during Ken and Stacy's courtship, that Ken was building his own house. Ken became a part of Team Boystown but focused on prayer and construction rather than on building relationships with sex workers—he spoke little Spanish and only entered the prostitution zone on a few occasions. While I was doing fieldwork, Ken proposed to Stacy, they got married, and less than a year later they had a baby.[3] Ken's involvement with Boystown had more to do with falling in love with Stacy than falling in love with Boystown. Missionaries were involved in multiple triadic relationships, and Stacy's relationship with

Ken and God changed her own relationship with Boystown in ways that will be explored below.

Although they did not self-identify as such, Team Boystown shares similarities with many in the Emerging Evangelical movement, which rejects several tenants of evangelical subculture and places great weight upon notions of authenticity (Bielo 2011). Emerging Evangelicals tend to be critical of the materialism, consumerism, and commodified nature of suburban evangelical megachurch culture and seek more "authentic" relationships with Christ, in part through striving to be "missional" in their own societies (Bielo 2011, 11). I saw Stacy and her team similarly distancing themselves from suburban evangelical megachurch culture as well as the kinds of short-term mission projects they usually finance, but Stacy's project also relied on labor and money from people in these congregations. Stacy and her team members also did not like typical mission programs because they said that such programs "turned people into numbers" and thus failed to properly attend to the populations they targeted. (Indeed, most missions measure their success quantitatively, for example in numbers of converts.) But Team Boystown shares with Emerging Evangelicals the prioritization of what Bielo calls "cultivating relationships—not before or after conversion attempts, but in place of them" (Bielo 2011, 12). Stacy and her team members referred to their project not as focused on conversion but rather as "relational" or focused upon building long-term relationships with people. Although Stacy called herself a missionary to make it easier to describe her project, she expressed discomfort with the term. She believed that "Jesus, in calling us to follow him, called us to love our neighbors." According to Stacy, God asked her to move near Boystown so that her neighbors would be prostitutes, drug dealers, and drug addicts. God told Stacy "to love them," to establish friendships with them, and "to share life with them and engage in life with them."

Emerging Evangelicals typically seek out an authentic relationship with Jesus by becoming missionaries in their own societies in US urban areas through loving their neighbors there (Bielo 2011). Team Boystown did something similar but made poor Mexican sex workers their neighbors by moving to Reynosa. Both Team Boystown missionaries and Emerging Evangelicals find that suburban megachurch culture is not conducive to an authentic relationship with Christ. They seek closeness to him by spending time with the kinds of people Jesus spent time with. Scholars of both Emerging Evangelicals and of clients of sex workers show how this pursuit of authenticity is a response to larger economic and social transformations. Bielo shows how Emerging Evangelicals' rejection of evangelical culture is a reaction to both modernity and postmodernity. Elizabeth Bernstein shows how postindustrial forms of sexual commerce have shaped the organization of sex work transactions to provide a great deal of emotional labor in addition to sexual labor (Bernstein 2007). She draws on Katherine Frank's research, which shows that in order for strippers to sustain the interest of regulars, they had to perform authenticity and realness. For example, clients wanted to learn strippers' "real names," but preferred to learn them as an indication of intimacy instead of their being told from the start (Frank 2002). Bernstein builds upon some of Frank's work as well as her own research among high-end sex workers in the Silicon Valley to discuss the emotional labor and performance of what she calls "bounded authenticity" that she argues has increasingly become part of the sexual exchange in the postindustrial context (Bernstein 2007). Clients seek out the "girlfriend experience," with sex workers going on dates with them, simulating or developing an emotional connection, and performing many of the tasks that girlfriends perform. Bernstein argues that these clients don't see sex workers as a "poor substitute" to a regular girlfriend. They appreciate the bounded aspect of the encounter and do not want all of the obligations required of a traditional relationship.

We could draw a parallel between the short-term sex-for-money transaction and the short-term missionary trips, distinguishing both from the kinds of long-term relations that Team Boystown and many Emerging Evangelicals seek to establish. What Team Boystown missionaries tried to forge with sex workers is more akin to the girlfriend experience. Rather than short-term relations with conversion in mind, they sought to build more long-term relations that required, on both sides, a degree of emotional work. But to what extent is Team Boystown's pursuit of the girlfriend experience "bounded authenticity?" On the one hand, they claimed to want real friendships with sex workers. Much like clients of many sex workers, missionaries hoped to learn their "real" names and their stories. And like clients, they saw this as a special form of information that indexed intimacy and trust. But on the other hand, Team Boystown missionaries arguably sought a more reciprocal relationship with sex workers with a wider range of obligations than most clients of sex workers seek out. And many of the sex workers also wanted to have reciprocal friendships with missionaries. As Schneider says, "New monastics emphasize the importance of deep, committed, authentic, relationships—friendships—as the primary means of surmounting race and class divides" (Schneider 2018, 183).

Perhaps the part of the relationship more aptly described as "bounded authenticity" is that missionaries, for the most part, did not want to know details about sex or interactions with clients. Missionaries told me that they learned more of these details from me, because of the conversations that

I had with sex workers. Missionaries focused instead on sex workers' lives prior to moving to the prostitution zone and on their relations with their children. Because missionaries sought to avoid discussions about sex, which was clearly a big part of sex workers' lives, it would be apt to call what they sought a form of "bounded authenticity," but with different boundaries than the relations clients seek with sex workers.

Team Boystown enacted a model of Christianity that distinctly valued intersubjectivity, relationality, and connections between the spiritual and social worlds. Bielo argues that Emerging Evangelicals develop a "highly relational religiosity, a ritual life in which human–human connections are a precondition for human–divine relations to flourish" (Bielo 2011, 258). Because evangelical Christians place great emphasis upon the internal relationship between individuals and God, they have been assumed to be morally individualistic. Omri Elisha agrees that the evangelical belief in forging direct personal relationships with Jesus Christ "is essentially individuating," but he also argues that evangelicals recognize the social and intersubjective elements that are important to their beliefs (Elisha 2008). The socially engaged evangelicals Elisha studied in Knoxville, Tennessee, built relationships with others that "complicated the preeminence of moral individualism as a cultural paradigm without ever going so far as to subvert or reject it" (2008, 22). Team Boystown missionaries similarly complicated moral individualism by creating relationships with many significant others vis-à-vis God.

Love Triads

Let me begin by briefly explaining why I opt to speak of love triads rather than love triangles when it comes to the relations between missionaries, God, and sex workers. Love triangles typically do not involve relations between all parties, whereas in a polyamorous triad, all parties are romantically or sexually involved with each other. The plot of plenty of romantic comedies and dramas, a love triangle implies competition between two parties over the attention of a third. Shaped by hegemonic discourses of compulsory monogamy, a love triangle typically implies a structural conflict caused by jealousy or betrayal. Usually, in movies and books, it is two cis heterosexual men who compete for the love or affection of a cis woman. There was no similar structural conflict in the relationships I describe. Team Boystown's project aspires to a nonjealous reciprocity, so the concept of the triad is more apt to describe them. While jealousy is a key feature in love triangles, the love triads I examine are instead marked by comper-sion,[4] a concept used by polyamorous communities that is often considered the "opposite of jealousy" (Anapol 1997). Compersion describes the feel-ings of empathetic joy and happiness and emotional or erotic pleasure de-rived from one's romantic partner experiencing joy or pleasure from an out-side source, most commonly another romantic or sexual partner. I highlight ways in which missionaries used romantic and sexual idioms to describe these relationships, but it is important to note that these love triads were only "romantic" or "sexual" in the social-spiritual sense, not in the physi-cal one. Compersion, in this case, occurred when missionaries felt joy and pleasure when they saw evidence of a sex worker and God getting closer. It is also important to note that while compersion is said to be the opposite of jealousy, both can coexist. Compersion is often hoped for and sometimes achieved in polyamorous relationships, of which triads are only one vari-ant, but this does not mean that polyamorous people don't sometimes expe-rience jealousy. Across the multiple triadic relationships that missionaries were involved in, there were sometimes jealousies—for example, when sex workers became jealous of one another or of Stacy's boyfriend.

Missionaries saw themselves involved in several kinds of triadic relation-ships with God and sex workers, and an intermediation of signs was at play in these relationships. Pragmatist Charles Sanders Peirce argued that mean-ing is made through the process of semiosis, which entails a triadic rela-tion between signs, objects, and interpretants. A sign stands for, or points to, an object from a particular perspective (which is an interpretant). The interpretant—which is some kind of mental representation—links the sign and the object. For example, smoke is a sign of fire (an object) in many peo-ple's minds. While this example is nearly universal, most sign relationships are more slippery and involve different potential ways to interpret meaning. Paul Kockelman[5] describes the relationship between a sign, object, and in-terpretant as "a relation between two relations."

In this love triad, speech and other acts by sex workers and missionar-ies became, at different moments, signs of God. In the first triadic config-uration, interactions with sex workers became signs of God (the object) to missionaries. Sex workers were like the smoke signaling the fire of God. Sex workers could be said to have an indexical relationship to Jesus be-cause they were in proximity to him; missionaries highlighted that Jesus chose to spend his time with "poor and forgotten" people like prostitutes. Stacy also indicated an iconic relationship, or shared likeness, between Je-sus and sex workers. For example, Stacy sometimes quoted Mother Teresa, writing that the people in Boystown, many of whom were addicted to crack cocaine, were "Jesus in his most distressing disguises." Missionaries' ideas and actions were the interpretants making a connection between the sign (sex workers) and object (Jesus or God). Stacy and her other team members referred to "seeing Jesus" or "finding Jesus" in Boystown through its sex workers—whom they called their friends. Team Boystown missionaries sometimes said that Boystown was their church, because they saw Jesus there more than they did in official churches. Stacy wrote that her project was "not about [Boystown] or Mexico, but about loving the people he loved." Coming to know and love sex workers allowed missionaries to better know and better love Jesus. Furthermore, in spending time with sex workers and getting to know them, missionaries had the opportunity to become more like Jesus by mimicking his path: doing the things that he had, and expressing Christ-like love toward prostitutes. By loving sex workers, the missionaries not only loved God more. They also loved more *like* God.

In the second kind of triadic configuration, missionaries imagined their acts to become signs and mediators of their relationships with God (the object) and with sex workers (whose corresponding ideas and actions were interpretants). Missionaries understood that God already loved both sex workers and missionaries before he spoke to missionaries and filled them with love and desire for Boystown. At that point, the triad would be described by polyamorous communities as a vee or V—a triangulation in which A has a relationship with B (missionaries and God love each other), and B has a relationship with C (God loves sex workers), but A and C (missionaries and sex workers) do not have a relationship. Missionaries sought to turn the V into a triad, by seeking out direct relationships with sex workers and attempting to strengthen the relationships between sex workers and God.

While God's love of sex workers was presumed to be a given, missionaries saw it as part of their duty to provide sex workers with the knowledge that God loved them, making themselves mediators of God's recognition. They hoped that sex workers would, in turn, love God as well. Missionaries believed these transformations to occur in moments of interacting with sex workers. Additionally, the long-term, durational aspect of their relationship and the intervention of prayer (which sometimes took time to be answered) were equally important to forging these love triads.

While the sign-object-interpretant relationship is one of producing meaning, this particular love triad also produced value: missionaries believed that sex workers and missionaries provided signs of God to one another. Value, for Team Boystown, was created through semiosis, the process of making meaning. It is not an individual or even a dual process, but a "relation between two relations" on a triad (Kockelman 2006, 2): not an interaction between self and God, but multiparty relational interactions of identification and closeness. Their goal, then, was building long-term, durational relationships that the two human parties valued in themselves and believed brought them closer to God.

Missionaries' emic term for what they were doing was "building relationships." Through these relationships, they believed they were expanding and extending God's love. In order to understand the generative force of the love triads from an anthropological perspective and the ways in which they were expected to animate some interpretants and create value, I build upon Nancy Munn's concept of intersubjective spacetime. Munn argues that the value that Gawans, who lived on a small island of the coast of Papua New Guinea, saw as essential to their community vitality is intersubjective spacetime. This spacetime of self-other relationships was constituted by practices such as feeding someone, which extended or expanded human capacities and creative energy outward toward others, rather than eating alone, which confined these energies within oneself. Acts that extended intersubjective spacetime combined to build social ties with other people, some of whom lived on faraway islands. This extension of intersubjective spacetime could result in influence and even fame for the individuals that expended the energy. It could also increase the fame of the island of Gawa itself. For Munn, the spatiotemporal aspects of value creation involve the extension of an actor's action, the actor's influence in time and space through other people. Missionaries, in contrast, were interested in extending God's influence, not their own. They used themselves and sex workers as catalysts. Team Boystown missionaries were able to function as catalysts because they imagined God's fame to be spread, in part, through relational interactions.

Inspired by Munn's framework,[6] I suggest that the primary value Team Boystown saw as important to their communal vitality, and which they sought to expand through strengthening all elements of their triadic relationship with God and sex workers, was *spiritual* intersubjective spacetime. Spiritual intersubjective spacetime is a spacetime of self-other-God relations in which each party mediates the relationship between the other two. Rather than expanding one's own fame and influence in the material world, it expands that of God in the spiritual and material worlds. For Team Boystown, the immediate goals of the love triad were 1) to increase their own intimate relationships with God through their relationships with sex workers, 2) to foster sex workers' intimate relationships with God through their own prayer and actions, and 3) to pray to God to foster their relationships with sex workers.

The community that Team Boystown envisioned existed on several levels. They referred to the community they were creating in Reynosa, which included the team members of a mission in Reynosa that built a school for deaf children. These missionaries became friends with Stacy and shared her vision of what constituted a church. More broadly, I sometimes heard missionaries refer to their community as fellow "followers of Jesus," meaning the Christians they aligned themselves with, such as the members of the New Monasticism movement. Furthermore, expanding God's fame and influence had the potential to expand their community of followers of Jesus.

The expansion of spiritual intersubjective spacetime through these love triads led to nonsovereignty in two ways. First, missionaries and sex workers became entangled in each other's lives and established complex relationships that included a range of obligations. Some members of both parties described these relationships as love and friendship, and they included dependencies and conflicts. Additionally, spiritual intersubjective spacetime led to nonsovereignty because it made humans the agents of God's will instead of their own. God's desires for peoples' lives became internalized as their own, influencing their actions. While Team Boystown missionaries saw themselves as nonsovereign agents of God, they also sought to turn sex workers into agents of God's will, hoping to induce similar nonsovereignty. Because God, as the omniscient and omnipotent author of the universe, has the qualities of sovereignty, and because missionaries served as his agents or mediators, missionaries' actions included a tension between sovereignty and nonsovereignty.

The acts that, from the perspectives of missionaries, expanded spiritual intersubjective spacetime included making poor people one's neighbors (in part through building a "modern-day monastery" that missionaries also planned to live in), praying, building relationships with sex workers, learning sex workers' stories, and circulating those stories to other Christians through the Internet and face-to-face communication. These acts will be analyzed in this chapter and the next. They connected people with other people, places, and God, and they also constructed selves. In brief: they created value. A key feature of these love triads is that people could reproduce them infinitely by telling stories about love triads to other people. We will mostly examine instances of missionaries circulating stories to their Christian communities, but there were also cases of sex workers circulating these stories among themselves.

Building Relationships: Love Acts and Idioms

Love between missionaries, sex workers, and God was put into action through the circulation of material and immaterial things. Missionaries and sex workers drew upon different idioms of love, including neighborliness, friendship, romance, and kinship. The slippage between these idioms had to do with the ways in which missionaries modeled their relationships between humans upon ideas about divine love and the relationships between humans and God and Jesus.

Missionaries prayed that God would cultivate their relationships with sex workers, assuming or hoping that these relationships would expand spiritual intersubjective spacetime for both parties, increasing intimacy with God and turning them into agents of his will. Missionaries imagined that this expansion of spiritual intersubjective spacetime would transform people and change their actions.

I suggested above a reading of missionary narrations of their being called upon to work in Boystown as a nonsovereign falling in love with the imagined sex workers there, including a longing and desire to know and be known by these women. These romantic idioms sometimes slipped into sexual ones. Examining the ways in which missionary women talked about celibacy and marriage in relation to their mission work helps illuminate how they imagined sexuality and spirituality to operate triadically between a missionary, God, and another person.

Stacy said she often joked that she was "ready to marry Mexico until Ken came along." Even at her wedding in Tulsa, before she exchanged vows with Ken, her pastor joked that everyone thought Stacy was going to become the Mother Teresa of Mexico. For Stacy, "marrying Mexico" would have entailed taking a vow of celibacy, which she explained would have meant giving herself "completely to Jesus." Because she saw Jesus in "some unusual places" (like the prostitution zone), giving herself completely to Jesus would have meant giving herself completely to Mexico, to Boystown, to Aquiles (the surrounding neighborhood), and to sex workers like Eva and Rebecca. That Stacy married Ken instead of a Mexican prostitution zone and its inhabitants indicates that the two played similar mediating roles in her relationship with God.

Missionaries' conceptions of sexuality and spirituality queered the monogamous heteronormative logics of the evangelical churches they had grown up in. I was initially confused when I heard missionaries mention that Abigail and Stacy had both contemplated taking vows of celibacy: I thought they had already taken such vows. Once I finally admitted my confusion, asking, "Wait, why do you need to take an extra vow?" Ashley laughed and told me that although they were all "saving themselves for marriage,"[7] a vow of celibacy would be for life. Ashley and Stacy told me that these vows were not very popular among Christians, who usually believe that God wants people to get married (though I have since learned that others in the New Monasticism movement embrace the decision of single people to take vows of celibacy). Because missionaries conceptualized sexuality as serving sex workers, and because they imagined futures of living with and loving sex workers instead of future husbands, the love triad of Team Boystown missionaries could be argued to be queer in its departure from the normative triad of God-Husband-Wife.

Stacy conceived of sexuality as part of the social-spiritual realm for celibate people and as encompassing a nonindividuating intimate attachment and generosity toward significant others. She explained to me that when she and Abigail were considering the vow of celibacy, they were reading books by Rob Bell and Shane Claiborne. Stacy told me that Claiborne took a vow of celibacy "basically as a means to say, 'I'm not just going to connect on such a deep level with one person, but I'm going to connect with a community of people and give myself to a community, to people, to the poor and the oppressed that Jesus called me to.'" Continuing to paraphrase Claiborne, Stacy said, "We're all sexual beings. You just express it in one way or another. Even if you remain celibate until you're married, you still express your sexuality in some way, shape or form." Stacy told me that after reading these books, she was able to see herself as not suppressing her sexuality just because she planned to wait until marriage to have sex. Rather, she started to see her sexuality as an emotional component of oneself that is connected to whomever one serves. She explained that the scriptures command us to serve people, not just our spouses but one another, out of love, as the body of Christ, putting others' needs before ours. She said that she loves Ken by serving him and that they serve each other out of love, not subserviently.

Stacy still loved Boystown after her marriage. In theory, an otherwise heteronormative, physically monogamous relationship can also include the "queer" and "poly" love that I am describing. We could also think of Stacy's marriage to Ken, like those of many Christians who see God as part of their relationship, as part of a poly relationship with God (God-Stacy-Ken). But marriage eventually changed Stacy's relationship with sex workers. Using poly terminology, the love triad of God-Stacy-Ken became her primary relationship, while her love triad of God-Stacy-sex workers became a secondary one.

Jealousy did sometimes occur across triadic relationships. Rebecca would act coldly to Stacy if she did not enter la zona frequently enough. Rebecca also seemed to be jealous of Ken. She complained that Stacy never spent any time with her after she started dating him. Every time Stacy mentioned Ken's name, Rebecca made a dissatisfied face, and when Rebecca mentioned his name, she scrunched up her face and spat out the word "Ken" with disgust. In this case, jealousy appeared similar in quality to the jealousy in a romantic relationship.

Although Rebecca's jealousy surprised me at the time, in hindsight it seems prescient, as Stacy's spiritual ties and obligations to Boystown changed after she met and decided to marry Ken. Although Stacy says that Ken never told her not to go to Boystown, he "worried himself to death" while she was there. She sometimes refrained from entering Boystown in order to care for him and "protect his heart." She said,

> And so, being married to Ken, he's my number one priority. I take care of him before I take care of anybody else, you know? Boystown can be burning down, but you've got to make sure Ken is okay . . . That's what I committed myself to before God. I've committed myself to Ken in that way. To love him the way church is meant to love Christ. And he's committed to love me the way Christ loves the church.

This notion of generosity and service that Stacy defined as an aspect of sexuality permeated her relationships with sex workers. Missionaries saw themselves as serving the sex workers. Perhaps mimicking Jesus's healing of the sick, missionaries would sometimes purchase medicine for sex workers if they were ill, make them chicken soup, or take them to the doctor in addition to praying for them. Stacy sometimes brought a short-term team of doctors and several nurses to treat people in bars in Boystown and to give away medications. Once Abigail organized a week-long medical clinic outside of la zona. Abigail and a doctor went from room to room talking to people about their medical concerns. Stacy once took a pregnant sex worker to the doctor and paid for her prenatal care.

Many of the activities that constituted the intimate labor of "building relationships" were gendered and gendering. Their ways of serving sex workers were often through feminized labor. Gender was important to how missionaries conceived of and practiced their relationships and divided labor within the mission.[8] For several years, Stacy brought short-term missionary teams to Boystown to "serve" its inhabitants. She turned a crack bar into a "salon," where a hairdresser friend gave haircuts to the women. Other team members would style their hair and give them manicures and pedicures, or clean their rooms. Another team cleared the land behind María's bar of garbage and weeds, and planted a garden for her. Both short- and long-term team members would sometimes bake the women Valentine's Day cupcakes, give them flowers on Mother's Day (donated by a church in South

Carolina), or throw them small birthday celebrations or baby showers. I participated in some of these parties and deliveries of baked goods. These stereotypically feminine actions might be contrasted with those of Shane Claiborne's mission in Philadelphia, whose "relational work" included a sports league for young men. But ultimately, Claiborne and Stacy both cite Mother Teresa and Jesus as models for their mission work, so actions that would be marked as feminine in the cultural contexts of missionaries might be unmarked if compared to Christ-like acts. Since Stacy saw her service toward significant others to be a realm of sexuality, then, these could be seen as sex acts of sorts.

Furthermore, single missionaries envisioned cohabitation with sex workers rather than in a nuclear family with husbands, even if many of them did later marry men. As the modern-day monastery would be a house for representatives of all elements of the love triad (missionaries, sex workers, and God), we might say that they hoped to turn a love triad into a ménage a trois (household of three). Of course, more than three people would live in this house, but it was envisioned to include three types of entities.

Neighborliness was another primary idiom that missionaries used to describe their relationships with sex workers. According to Stacy, "we're all called to love our neighbors," and Jesus told her to make prostitutes and drug dealers her neighbors. In 2007, when several short-term teams visited Reynosa, Stacy took them on a walk around the periphery of Boystown to pray. They also set up what she jokingly referred to as Gringo Block Parties, playing games with the children of Aquiles Serdán, including soccer, jump rope, and the hokey pokey. They painted children's faces and shared juice, cookies, and grilled food with people of the neighborhood. Sometimes Team Boystown would throw parties in bars inside of the prostitution zone with a mixed group of American missionaries and (mostly) Mexican sex workers. Sometimes a member of a church congregation would pay for the food that would be served at the parties, such as chicken and tortillas. While these parties sometimes involved dancing to jukebox music in bars, they also often turned into worship services with people playing instruments, singing praise and worship songs, and praying. After the parties, the teams would pray through the night in shifts. Team Boystown planned to further materialize their neighborly relationship with sex workers by living with them in the monastery.

Missionaries used the spiritual intervention of prayer to strengthen all of the connections on the love triad. As Stacy prayed for God to enable her to forge relationships with the people of Aquiles and Boystown, she also saw any relationships with people of Boystown as being fostered by God.

In 2007, Stacy mentioned on her blog that when she first happened upon Boystown while leading a short-term team on a different project in Reynosa three years earlier, she had prayer-walked around the neighborhood asking God to do something extraordinary in Boystown, wondering if she would ever know the people who lived in those houses. She said that "God is doing something extraordinary" after she finally had the opportunity to talk to mothers in Aquiles and play with children, some of whom, she noted, were "products of Boystown" or had been conceived between sex workers and clients. These interactions between neighbors in Aquiles and missionaries were signs of God for missionaries, evidence that their prayers were working and that God's will was being fulfilled.

One of Team Boystown's main motivations was preventing the children of Aquiles from following the careers that the team (and indeed many others in Reynosa) assumed they would eventually engage in, as drug dealers and prostitutes. Missionaries hoped that the monastery would provide a space where women could be supported in giving up addictions, learning new skills, and leaving the prostitution zone. They also hoped to help prevent some of the neighborhood children from ending up in Boystown. Both Ashley and Eleanor were in part drawn to educating and playing with the children of Aquiles Serdán. Stacy and her husband planned to take some financial responsibility for Luz, to make sure that she got an education. Stacy explained that there are two purposes for building the monastery in Aquiles, two blocks away from Boystown: "Of course you want to love and care for the women and men who are working in Boystown, but really, the prevention happens with those children." She was excited that Jasmine, a little girl from the neighborhood, was going to start school the next day. She said,

> ... Imagine being nine or ten years old and growing up with a red-light district two blocks from your house. So when you're fifteen or seventeen years old and you have no skills, you can't read, you can't write, you grew up two blocks from a red-light district where some of those girls walk in and they're dressed in the clothes that you want to wear and they're buying the things that you want to be able to buy, but you'll never be able to do that because you would never be able to get a job that would pay you decently, because you have no education, it's a no-brainer what you'll choose. Of course you'll go there. Or, if you grow up watching your parents ... struggle to put food on the table for you and your family.

Stacy indicated that both poverty and a desire for consumer goods were reasons that children from Aquiles might work in prostitution, but also suggested that living so close to the prostitution zone was another important factor in making prostitution a realistic choice. She hoped that giving art classes to children would help them to imagine more creative possibilities for their lives and futures.

While missionaries and most sex workers agreed that one should try to prevent children from becoming sex workers, this is also an important site in which both groups reproduced the whore stigma. Sex workers and missionaries both rallied around the figure of the child. They valued forms of obligation cast as normative bonds between mothers and children. However, while sex workers posited their work in prostitution as motivated by maternal love and obligation, missionaries hoped and believed that God's influence would divert this love and obligation toward cohabitation with children and away from sexual labor.

Missionaries and sex workers occasionally used idioms of kinship to describe their relationships. Rebecca sometimes said that Stacy was like a sister to her. Stacy's fictive kinship relation with her "Mexican mother," Lucía, came with a number of obligations. However, as is sometimes the case with children who take care of their parents, Stacy sometimes compared Lucía to a child, such as when she left the apartment Stacy rented for her to return to drugs and Boystown.

Team Boystown, like many other New Monastics, sought to form friendships. Stacy often referred to sex workers in Boystown as her friends, and some sex workers also referred to missionaries as their friends. Stacy valued reciprocity in her relationships: she told me that she did not just want to "friend on them," or merely to be a friend to sex workers. She also wanted them to be friends to her. Thus, she shared details about her own life and struggles with them. Stacy spent a great part of six years chatting, watching *telenovelas*, and eating with the women in their rooms, listening to their stories, and praying for and with them. She would sometimes give people gifts (makeup, a blanket, a hat she had knitted herself). Sex workers also sometimes gave Stacy gifts, for example, for her birthday or Christmas. Several sex workers organized a bridal shower for Stacy before she got married. Others threw a small party in Boystown and cooked for a group of sex workers and missionaries for Valentine's Day, which in Mexico is called the *Día del Amor y la Amistad*, "Day of Love and Friendship."

Jesus Knows Your Name and Your Story: The Collection and Circulation of Sex Worker Narratives

For fifteen months, all I did was pray, and I felt like a bit of a failure. My prayers were like, "God, did you hear this this time? Because I still don't

*know the names or stories of anyone who lives inside those walls." Fifteen
months, nothin' but prayin'. I felt crazy.*
STACY

Stacy's sense of desperation from not having learned sex workers' names
and stories after fifteen months indicates that these were important signs
of God. While prayer walking around the periphery of Boystown before she
was allowed inside the walls, Stacy sometimes ran out of things to pray for
and looked for "clues" from God. One day, she passed by a house in Aquiles
with a well in front of it. She remembered the story of Jesus asking a Samaritan woman (to whom Jesus, as a Jew, would not normally be expected to
speak) for water from a well. The Samaritan woman had a reputation for being scandalous. In the biblical story, the Samaritan woman recognized that
Jesus was the Messiah when Jesus demonstrated that he knew details about
her life. When Stacy saw the well while prayer walking, she prayed that God
would provide similar moments of revealing himself to the people of Aquiles and Boystown, so that they would know "who he is." Months later, when
Stacy's house was under construction, she considered naming the monastery El Pozo, or The Well, in reference to this Bible story. She found this
story especially salient to Team Boystown's project because the woman at
the well was a "scandalous woman," Jesus revealed his prophetic powers to
her by demonstrating that he knew details about her life (how many prior
husbands she had), and the scandalous woman went on to tell people of the
town that Jesus was the Messiah. In a sense, Team Boystown tried to reenact
this scenario: they hoped to provide sex workers with the recognition that
Jesus knew their names and stories. By activating the God-missionary-sex
worker love triad, they tried to extend spiritual intersubjective spacetime in
such a way as to transform sex workers into former sex workers who would
live with their children. As Jesus knew the stories of "scandalous women,"
missionaries also sought to learn the names and stories of sex workers. But
while Jesus demonstrated knowledge of the Samaritan woman's sexually
scandalous past, missionaries sought out familial stories, which attempted
to interpellate longing maternal subjects with their questions.

Sex workers told missionaries stories of their children to justify their
work in the prostitution zone (and, as explored in previous chapters, they
also made reference to their children to justify their work to each other).
Missionaries then retold sex workers' stories, and stories about the relationships between sex workers and missionaries, to other Christians, to provide
evidence that their prayers were working. 24-7 also circulated these stories
on their website. This circulation of stories both justified the missionaries'

project and served as new signs of God for other people. Missionaries acted as mediating agents—they gave messages (sometimes through speech acts, sometimes through other actions) to sex workers of God's love. Intimacy with God was increased and God's influence was expanded, not only within love triads, but also through and beyond them as the repetition of these narratives across milieus entailed a possibility of performative efficacy, generating new love triads. Missionaries created value(s) through these circulations (signs of God, monetary value, love, and fame).

The knowledge and meta-knowledge of sex workers' names and stories were signs of God in several ways. Once Ashley and Eleanor joined Stacy's team, they would recount to me and other missionaries their experiences with meeting new "girls" and of these women sharing parts of "their stories" with them. The sex workers' stories usually involved where they were from, what brought them to Boystown, and the number and ages of their children. The missionaries would say with excitement and importance, "We met a girl named Marisa from Tabasco today, and she shared her story with us." Missionaries valued these stories and relationships as important in themselves. For Stacy and her team, learning sex workers' names and stories was an affirmation that they were supposed to be in Reynosa and evidence that each party was getting closer to God.[9] They expressed joy and excitement about these new friendship possibilities. When Stacy had not yet learned any names or stories, she saw it as the failure of signs of God to appear, which she internalized as a personal failure. It was all the more devastating because it could indicate that it was not God's will for Stacy to be in Boystown, or even that God did not exist (the missionaries admitted having doubts about the existence of God).

Learning the stories of sex workers also expanded spiritual intersubjective spacetime by strengthening missionaries' relationships with God. During my last weeks of fieldwork, I finally asked Stacy why stories and names were so important to her. She explained that she liked to think of the Bible as an incredible story written by God about humanity as well as divine faithfulness and kindness. Hearing the stories of the women of Boystown allowed her to see how God is writing the stories of individuals, which are also part of God's story of humanity. Learning the stories of others, especially her friends in Boystown, she got to know God better, seeing a different reflection of God than she could see in her own life. Even though Stacy said at other moments that her reason for seeing God there was not specifically about Boystown or Mexico, this "different reflection of God" was important. The difference between white, middle-class missionaries and "poor and forgotten" Mexican sex workers was likely a great part of what made these stories so compelling and transformative to both missionaries and their larger publics.

In addition to learning sex workers' stories, missionaries saw it as their job to complete the love triad by providing sex workers with the meta-knowledge that God knew their names and stories. They helped sex workers recognize God's love and recognition, which they hoped would be reciprocated, creating a reciprocal love relation between missionaries and God. For members of Team Boystown, "Jesus knows your name and he knows the story of your life, and he loves you" became a way to introduce themselves to sex workers. I witnessed this firsthand, heard secondhand accounts, and read missionaries' blogs with several variations of this greeting. ("God" was sometimes substituted for "Jesus.") Stacy posted a version of this phrase on her blog, noting that she shared it at a church service in a migrant shelter when two sex workers invited her to say a few words. Even when she did not feel that she had the words to express herself in a language not her own, Stacy repeated a phrase she had memorized in the language: "God knows your name, He knows the story of your life, and He loves you. From the same mouth that spoke the universe into existence, comes the whisper of your name if you'll listen."

Missionaries hoped to provide signs of God to sex workers and to inspire their recognition of God's love for them. Here is an example of Stacy describing Boystown on the 24-7 website:

> The doorways are darkened by women who have been stripped of their humanity, mere robots who are programmed to do only one thing. They don't feel anything anymore, partly because they're strung out on God-knows-what, and partly because they had to turn off their feelings in order to survive another day. But tell them Jesus loves them, and their faces change. Admittedly, some of them struggle to believe it's true but you can see that others want so badly to surrender to the pull of Jesus' love.

This blog post indicates that Stacy saw signs of God in the changing faces of the sex workers to whom she served as mediator of God's love. Her post also demonstrates that she believed prostitution to be dehumanizing, which helps explain her motivation, even though she stated that she went to Boystown simply because God told her to. These comments suggest that sex workers sell themselves rather than performing a service—beliefs that are in line with those of anti-prostitution advocates on the religious right as well as anti-prostitution feminists such as Carole Pateman and Catherine MacKinnon.

Learning sex workers' baptismal names was as important to Team Boystown as learning their stories, in part because missionaries believed their baptismal names to be the "last piece of who they are that nobody can take." When Stacy prayer-walked, she explained, she would substitute Boystown for Zion or Jerusalem in scriptures like Isaiah 62 and pray, "Because I love Boystown, I will not keep silent. Because my heart yearns for Boystown, I will not remain still." Stacy explained that the scripture talks about "how the Lord will give you a new name by his own mouth, he will change your name from desolate and forsaken to the bread of God," and that the rest of the scripture gives promises of hope and restoration. Equating a "new" name with "hope and restoration" is especially relevant because sex workers usually took on pseudonyms and kept their baptismal names a secret. Like the clients of strippers in Frank's study, sex workers revealing their names to missionaries signaled "authenticity" or "realness." But missionaries usually had to invest much more time building rapport than Frank's clients had before learning sex workers' names (Frank 2002). These names were also imbued with spiritual significance in ways that were likely not present for clients. Learning "real" names was emotionally charged for missionaries and an index of intimacy and trust. Ashley told me once, "It's a big deal when girls share their names with you." Stacy told me stories of several friends in Boystown who waited months or years before revealing their given names. One of her friends waited for two years before whispering into her ear, "Jessica is my real name," and Stacy said that she felt "the weight of how important that was."

While missionaries hoped to replace the exchange of sex and money between sex workers and clients with the reciprocal exchange of love between missionaries, sex workers, and God, this love triad was not the end goal. Missionaries hoped this loving relationship with God would motivate sex workers to live with their children, and missionaries hoped to inch toward that goal in their interactions with sex workers. When missionaries first met sex workers, they would ask them almost immediately about their children: how many they had and how old they were. I observed them, on many occasions, asking, "Do you miss them?" Sex workers usually responded in the affirmative but occasionally expressed ambivalence. Once, when Ashley and I stopped by Lola's room in June, Ashley asked, with her blue eyes wide, "Do you miss your daughter?" and Lola answered, "A little bit," and explained that she was not accustomed to being around her, and that her daughter called Lola's mother "Mom." Such responses could be read as sex workers' resistance to performing a normative role of gendered maternal longing for cohabitation, or perhaps resistance to such a personal question from a relative stranger. Because missionaries hoped that sex workers would leave Boystown and return to their families, asking them these kinds of questions was a way to incite the very emotions they inquired about, interpellating them as longing maternal subjects. By focusing upon women's relationships with children, missionaries encouraged sex workers to fulfill their gendered obligations in ways that missionaries believed to be more in line with God's desires. Asking sex workers about their family lives sometimes became a point of contention.

While some sex workers refused to perform the role of missing their children, others did seem to genuinely miss their children and long to live with them again. When Ashley and I entered Alicia's room with brownies a few days before she left Boystown, Alicia was all smiles and told us that she was incredibly happy to go home to Puebla and live with her six-month-old son. She lilted, in a joyful mixture of English and Spanish, "You should have children, it's the best thing that can happen to you, the best gift that God can give you." In these instances, sex workers and missionaries seemed to share a vision of motherhood.

Team Boystown missionaries also prayed that God would change sex workers. Sex workers often requested prayers from missionaries, and while missionaries did pray the prayers requested, they also prayed that God would reveal himself to sex workers and put the desire in their hearts to have a different career. Missionaries often talked about the desires that God placed in the hearts of sex workers to be nurses, to return to their hometowns, to "be mothers to their children" and prayed that God would continue to reveal himself to people in these ways. They also prayed that God would help drug-addicted sex workers stop using drugs.

Thus, missionaries hoped to become mediators of relationships between God and sex workers by conveying to them God's love, knowledge, and recognition, through prayer, and through trying to bring about some of the change they believed to be God's plan.

Sexual Joking

Missionaries' desires for authenticity had limits—they wanted to hear about sex workers' family lives more than they did about their work lives. The fact that I was talking to sex workers about their work lives as well as developing relationships with them that included talking about our personal lives and joking about sexual matters created tensions in my relationships with the missionaries. Scholars who have studied sexual joking in Mexico have primarily focused upon the way that homosocial relations of dominance and play are negotiated between men through *albures* (Carrillo 2002; De Genova 2005; Paz 1961). *Albures* are a multilayered game of double entendre, a call and response of sexual innuendo. Several scholars, most famously Octavio Paz, have argued that a winner and a loser emerge from this word play, with the loser being symbolically fucked by the winner. *Albures* also occur among Mexican women, although less frequently, yet this phenomenon has not been widely studied. Sexual joking was a site of both conflict and pleasure in its subversion of normative expectations of female comportment in the presence of missionaries. Jillian Hernandez has developed the concept of raunch aesthetics to refer to cultural production made by people who are seen as racially or sexually excessive (Hernandez 2014). Raunch aesthetics engages explicit sexuality and humor for the pleasure of minority audiences. While I am looking at the level of interaction instead of cultural production, raunch in this case can be seen as an interactional strategy that is a form of subtle resistance and pleasure for those marked with the whore stigma. While it is usually the less-clever man who is the butt of the joke in *albures*, there were several instances in which the missionaries were the butts of the joke, entailing resistance to missionary moralizing.

In their interactions with missionaries, sex workers without drug addictions were more likely to take on ways of speaking and conversational topics more related to their home lives, avoiding talking or joking about sex. I similarly performed a role of respectability with missionaries that I did not in almost any other area in my life. Most of the secrets that both sex workers and I kept from missionaries had to do with our sexual behavior. When I was alone with sex workers, in contrast, I joked with them in ways similar to the way I joked with most of my friends—in a raunchy, sexually explicit way.

But the more time I spent with sex workers, the more our raunchy joking started to seep into our conversations when missionaries were around. The double lives that both sex workers and I forged in relation to missionaries, in these moments, became ruptured in what gender theorist Kate Bornstein calls gender splattering (Bornstein 2013). Bornstein suggests that we all have many genders—different with one's boss than with one's father or lover. Bornstein and Caitlin Sullivan use the concept to describe situations in which we have to perform different versions of our multiply gendered selves at the same time. Gender splattering happened with greater and greater frequency when I was spending time with groups of missionaries and sex workers, and the collision of our multiply gendered selves sometimes led to laughter and occasionally to discomfort and conflict.

In May of 2009, I was having lunch with Ashley, Rebecca, and Eva in la zona. Ashley and I had just come back from Stacy's wedding in Tulsa, and we were sharing pictures and telling stories of the wedding while eating *caldo de pescado* that Eva had made for us. I said to Rebecca and Eva, "Ashley sings really beautifully!! She sang at Stacy's wedding while Eleanor played the violin and Jack played the guitar." Rebecca then asked, "And what do you play, Sarita?" I replied that I unfortunately didn't play any instruments. Eva quickly interjected, "Sarita plays the trumpet like us" and used her hands to gesture a phallic object in front of her lips. The three of us then burst into laughter, and I caught my breath to say, "Well, every once in a while." We laughed more and then it became clear that Ashley, the missionary, was not sharing our laughter but rather had a confused smile. Eva gestured toward Ashley, saying, "She doesn't understand," laughing more, and then started to chant, "Virgin! Virgin!" I stopped laughing, gender-splattered and suddenly self-conscious that not only was my sexual behavior being discussed in front of a missionary, but that she was being made fun of.

Sexual joking around missionaries often shared this pattern. At one point in the joking event, a sex worker would ask if the missionary understood what was happening and, if not, the laughter would be directed at her. While *albures* often have the outcome of a man verbally fucking another man through insult or outwitting him, in this case, it is the virginal missionary who became the butt of jokes through her presumed sexual ignorance.

The colliding of these respectable and raunchy speech-worlds caused conflicts for and with missionaries. After Eva made fun of Ashley, who was my missionary roommate, Ashley said, "I want to start going into Boystown sometimes by myself and not just with you. I don't want people to get confused and start thinking we're on the same team." At the time, this was tremendously stressful to me. I was worried about entering la zona alone because a narco who had some power in la zona had been flirting with me and trying to tempt me into his SUV with him and his bodyguard. Rebecca had recently shown us a video of a man playing a piano with his covered erect penis, and Ashley noted that "the girls" don't usually do things like this. I suspected that Ashley's concern that people might think we were on the same team was not only about me not being a Christian, but also about sex workers initiating sexual joking when I was around.

A more extended gender-splattering event occurred when several sex workers, missionaries, and I were planning a bachelorette party for Stacy. One day when the missionaries were not around, Eva said that we should get a cowboy stripper, and she gyrated her hips as if riding a horse, with a hand on her crotch while the other hand swung an imaginary lasso in the air. We all laughed and joked about going to male strip clubs together to find the best stripper. Rebecca said that at bachelorette parties for her family members, even her grandmother and mother-in-law danced with male strippers, and she said that we could ask the stripper to do dances that weren't quite as vulgar for Stacy and leave their boxers on at the end. They joked that we could get the butch dyke that Sofía was dating to wear her strap-on dildo so that they could show Stacy how to put on a condom to avoid pregnancy. Eva said that they would give Stacy sex advice and teach her how to keep her husband satisfied while she was menstruating. I was pretty excited about these party plans, which I thought would generate great data for my dissertation. I also thought it was a sweet gesture for these sex workers to practice care toward Stacy by wanting to provide her with sex education, albeit one that seemed would not center her own pleasure. But these ideas were quickly squashed by the other missionary cohost of the bachelorette party. Ashley was worried that Stacy and her fiancé would be uncomfortable with the sexualized nature of the activities and afraid it might damage the long-term relationships with sex workers that Stacy was fostering in Boystown. We ended up throwing a much tamer party than the one Eva, Rebecca, and Sofía had talked about—we ate food prepared by Eva and Sofía, gave Stacy house-related gifts, and played a game of making a toilet paper wedding dress on a partner.

One day I was sitting in a plastic chair on a street in la zona with a missionary and several sex workers and their friends who were often drunk and high. El Chilango, a gay man, kept asking a missionary, Eleanor, if she liked penis or if she was a lesbian. He made elaborate hand gestures and kept repeating his question, even though Eleanor declined to answer it. María finally yelled at him to stop. El Chilango then replied, "This is the whorehouse. The church is over there. We're in fucking Boystown." While many sex workers and I had developed the habit of suppressing our raunchiness around missionaries, Chilango's statement reminded us that we were in a space where it should be okay to talk about sex. These examples show how missionaries inspired the performance of "double lives" in which sexuality was elided and motherhood highly fetishized. Sexual joking could be read not only as perverse pleasure but also as an act of resistance to missionary moralizing.

The Social Lives of Sex Worker Narratives

Sex worker narratives took on social lives of their own through repetitions by Team Boystown missionaries, other Christians, and sex workers. Missionaries circulated sex workers' stories to other Christians. They hoped sex workers would also circulate them to other poor and forgotten people. This repetition was to extend God's influence throughout the world, thus creating value. Stacy said in her 24-7 video that her dream for Boystown was to see "teams of former drug addicts and prostitutes sent out to the nations of the world" sharing their stories of redemption, especially in places where Mexican passports were granted greater access than American ones. Sex workers with whom Team Boystown had built relationships did sometimes share aspects of their stories with other sex workers. They narrated how Stacy helped them see that God loved them, and the impact this had upon their lives.

Missionaries told stories of love triads in which missionaries' actions served as signs of God for sex workers and enabled the recognition of God's love and knowledge of their lives. These stories about the missionary-sex worker-God love triad brought about new signs of God for missionaries' Christian publics. But in being repeated, these stories were sometimes transformed. Meaning is indeterminate—created in context between all members of a speech event. A person speaking might intend one thing, but the listener's "uptake" can be different. As sex workers' stories were heard and repeated in different places, the indeterminacy of uptake led to results both expected and unexpected, including: 1) increasing spiritual intersubjective spacetime for Christian publics, 2) generating a team and support (financial and otherwise) for the mission, and 3) challenging or reproducing exoticizing ideas that foreigners (especially Americans) had about Mexicans and sex workers.

Stacy said that as she shared sex workers' stories with members of church congregations in the United States, they were able to shed some of their biases about sex workers. Before, she said, the churchgoers often conceived of sex workers as "sex-charged crazies." The stories of her friends in Boystown, she said, validated their lives and their humanity and helped Americans to feel compassion toward them. Stacy added:

> You start putting, like, names and faces on a plight of a group of people, it's a lot harder to make sweeping generalizations and to judge and to say, "No, it's so black and white." It's not. It's not at all. It's real human stories of real human struggles. Especially as people who say, "I follow Jesus." The law of Jesus is to love God and love your neighbor. You better know your neighbor's name and know their story, so you know how to love them. And so the story is very important to me. To tell the story of Jesus, and to tell the story of people who are real people, who are not forgotten.

Stacy said that sharing stories transformed "a broad spectrum of sex workers to an individual with a name and a story, and suddenly it's a little easier to muster up some compassion," which she noted was especially important in the height of the immigration debates in the United States. Abigail, who worked for the mission for deaf children, noted a similar transformation in American doctors and nurses from the United States on short-term teams providing medical services to a migrant shelter. Abigail said that at the beginning of the week, people had more conservative ideas about immigration and would say things like, "How can these people leave their children in Honduras to migrate to the US?" By the end of the week, she explained, they had allowed themselves to be changed by the stories. People who were usually against Mexican immigration to the United States were by then telling migrants that they would pray for them to make it across the border.

The website 24-7 served as a platform where Stacy could circulate sex workers' stories. The story of what Stacy was trying to accomplish in Boystown spread through emails, a blog, a well-produced video circulating on the Internet, and word of mouth. The Christians who heard this story supported Stacy financially, volunteered their labor for her cause, and prayed for her, her team, and the residents of Boystown. Stacy told me that once she established an informal relationship with 24-7 Prayer International, she was featured on a 24-7 blog and was sometimes discussed by the director. People she had never met would email her, saying, "We're praying for you in our prayer room. And we're praying for Kilo. We're praying for Lucía."

Missionaries emphasized to their Christian publics on blogs and face-to-face the transformative power of prayers in the lives of sex workers. Stacy wrote on her blog: "I'm glad to know that our prayers are seemingly being answered, little by little—Cristal is out of BT (most days), her motherly instincts are kicking in, and crack is done, if only for the time being" (July 12, 2007). Sex workers quitting drugs or leaving the prostitution zone became signs of God for missionaries. Although these attempts were often unsuccessful or short-lived, Stacy and her team saw any change as progress and the act of God by virtue of the prayers prayed by missionaries and their publics.

The circulation of the stories of sex workers, especially to missionaries' online publics, congregations in the United States, and short-term labor teams, created potentially infinite replications of new sign relationships expanding God's influence. I often witnessed Christians talking about how "moved" and "blessed" they felt at hearing about the important work that God was doing in Boystown. Stacy circulated sex workers' life stories to congregations as evidence of the validity and success of the mission. Although never measured quantitatively in terms of numbers of converts, the stories of women becoming Christians, quitting drugs, or leaving the prostitution zone served as evidence that the mission was working and reaffirmed Christians' beliefs in God's will, love, and power.

Occasionally, other Christians repeated sex workers' stories in a way that made Stacy uncomfortable with how she was given credit for helping them. Team Boystown members sometimes made reference to "helping" people, but were more likely to emphasize what God was doing—for missionaries and for sex workers—through these relationships. It was very rare that missionaries would congratulate themselves for having helped someone. Yet, through the circulation of these stories by various parties, their fame spread as much as God's. After Eleanor, Ashley, and I accompanied Sofía to her hometown when she left Boystown, an article about her experience appeared on the 24-7 Prayer website. It began with a vignette written by Eleanor:

> She opened the suitcase on the table. It was filled with photos and she began to share stories as we watched the different memories captured in faded colors. Her first communion as a little girl. Her wedding day. Her five-year-old son's cowboy-themed birthday party.
> We're in Tampico.
> The city where our friend grew up.
> We helped her move out of Boys Town and back to her family.

Another woman wrote about Eleanor "helping one woman leave behind the industry around sex and forge a new life" and asked supporters to "Please pray for the Boys Town team as they share Jesus and long to see more people free from oppression." At each subsequent repetition of this narrative across cultural milieus, some elements were lost and others gained. These missionary narratives about sex workers fetishized the gendered familial aspects of sex workers. The missionaries' narrative of Sofía emphasized her involvement in religious sacraments and motherhood, making it seem as if her work in Boystown was at the expense of these duties, whereas Sofía and many other sex workers labored in la zona precisely for their children. Lost were also the contextual factors surrounding Sofía's decision to leave. Sofía had talked about leaving for months as she was barely able to make ends meet because of reduced business in the prostitution zone and her fear of drug-related violence. But it was not until her teenage son had gone missing after becoming involved in drug cartel activity that she finally left Boystown. A complex interplay of drug violence, lack of business, and family and relationships usually factored into a woman's decision to leave the prostitution zone. Yet in the retelling of these stories, great emphasis was placed upon God as the driving force pushing sex workers to leave the prostitution zone to fulfill gendered familial obligations.

These circulations of stories of sex workers leaving prostitution heroized Team Boystown missionaries in ways that Stacy expressed discomfort with and actively tried to avoid. Stacy's blog, her involvement with 24-7, and the circulation of her story and the stories of sex workers via the Internet and word of mouth led to her becoming what her friends joked about as a "missionary celebrity." Missionaries often are granted a hero-like status in evangelical church congregations, imagined to sacrifice the comforts of American middle-class modernity to selflessly evangelize to the world's less fortunate. Stacy's fame extended far beyond her church congregation because of the publicity that 24-7 gave her. She received dozens of emails each day from people who wanted to help and inquired about visiting Boystown. Stacy took actions to curtail her celebrity status—for example, having one of her other team members speak about the mission to short-term teams. While she aimed for an expansion of the spiritual spacetime that would expand God's fame and influence, she did not feel comfortable with the expansion of her own fame. As Stacy privileged nonsovereign modes of love/ will, she might have suspected that her own fame took away from that of the true actor—God.

When Team Boystown circulated sex workers' stories, they could not always predict the uptake. White Americans experience these stories as a kind of tourism, whether they meet the workers on short-term mission teams or read or listen to sex workers' stories from the comfort of their homes or churches. Short-term teams are ways for American congregations to give youth the experience of helping the poor in another environment. Congregations get a tourist-like taste of life in a Mexican brothel by hearing the stories of Mexican sex workers told by Stacy. When I socialized with short-term teams building Stacy's house or houses for migrants, they often asked me what the most shocking thing I ever saw in the prostitution zone was. Stacy told me that she sometimes struggled with these exoticizing questions, trying to exercise patience toward those who ask them while also protecting her friends in Boystown.

Missionaries struggled with how much information to share on their blogs and in their retelling of sex worker stories. During the first few years, Stacy shared all kinds of stories, along with sex workers' work names, on her blog. When one crack cocaine–using sex worker, Angeles, also nicknamed La Politica because she was so charismatic, found stories about herself on Stacy's blog, Stacy was troubled, even though Angeles was thrilled to be mentioned on the Internet.[10] After this particular event, and gradually over the years, Stacy started to create pseudonyms and told fewer stories online.

On occasion, Team Boystown's circulations of sex workers' stories induced ideas about sex workers that the missionaries strongly opposed. When I accompanied Stacy, Ken, and some missionaries from the deaf school in a pickup truck to Monterrey for a concert, Abigail and Stacy started singing "the walls of Bo-oys town" and laughing. I asked what song they were singing, and Stacy told me the story of giving a talk about her work in Boystown at a church in South Carolina. Later, a man from the congregation emailed her a song that he claimed her stories about Boystown inspired him to write. While touched that her stories inspired him, she thought his song was inappropriate and disturbing. The man had conflated several of her stories into a single six-year-old prostitute, something that Stacy had never encountered in Boystown. Stacy quoted some of the lyrics to me:

At ten they give you reefer,
at twelve they give you crack,
but no matter what they give you
you always end up on your back

The uptake that inspired this song was unintended by the missionaries. The song created an archetypical victim to rally the public—an innocent child who is drugged and forced to work as a prostitute. I observed this combination of sympathy and exoticizing pity in some of the other missions I observed in Reynosa.

Through story-telling, the missionary-prostitute-God love triad became part of fractally larger triads as signs of God for other Christians, expanding spiritual intersubjective spacetime but sometimes also producing unintended reactions. These narratives inspired donation of financial support to the mission, sympathy for sex workers and Mexican migrants as human beings, and the reproduction of exoticizing ideas about sex workers and Mexicans.

Conclusion

Team Boystown missionaries enacted an intersubjective and relational kind of evangelism that sought to build long-term, durational relationships with "poor and forgotten" sex workers as part of a sex worker-missionary-God love triad. While missionaries saw themselves as opposed to the kinds of projects enacted by clients, there were also similarities between them. The US-Mexico border granted both mobility and economic privileges to US passport holders and rendered Mexican sex workers valuable to both parties. Team Boystown missionaries hoped to replace clients in the lives of sex workers. We could imagine that before Team Boystown arrived, sex workers were in a triadic relationship with their children and clients in which sex, money, and love circulated through parts of the triad. The missionary-sex worker-God triad was supposed to be transitional. Missionaries hoped it would eventually move sex workers to leave their profession and reside with their families, creating a Mother-Child-God triadic relationship.

As we saw in chapter 2, Stacy, like many other migrants to Reynosa, ended up leaving because of the increased drug violence in the prostitution zone, and because sounds of gunfire and explosions were keeping her baby up at night. One possible reading of this situation is that the drug war stymied possible queer futures between sex workers and missionaries. Another is that missionaries' investments in normative futures eclipsed their relationships with sex workers.

It was initially hard for me to understand Rebecca's jealousy of Stacy's husband, as I understood the love between missionaries and God vis-à-vis significant others to be limitless and of a polyamorous variety. But Rebecca's apparent fears of being replaced by Ken were warranted. Ken's discomfort about Stacy entering Boystown led to her going there less often. In the end Stacy married Ken, became pregnant, and left the prostitution zone, in great part because of her prioritizing these relationships over her relationships with sex workers. Although missionaries and some sex workers dreamed of queer futures together, these dreams never materialized in coresidency, and the queer intimacies were temporary.

CHAPTER 6

Love and Conflict in Sex Worker/
Missionary Relationships

There's a real need to be needed in Americans, and it's created like a "we need you" situation over here. The little girl Jasmine that came over and talked to us today for a long time would only come over and ask me when Americans were coming back to give her coloring books or to bring her shoes . . . and she has those things in her house, she doesn't need them, and I thought, "I don't want that to be the nature of our relationship." I'm happy to share whatever I have, that's not the issue. The issue is . . . we're both having needs met in an unhealthy kind of totally dysfunctional way. Somebody's got some nice pictures to show at home of these sweet poor little Mexican kids they helped and somebody has a stash in their room of sweet gringo treats they've been getting their whole life.
STACY WHITE

Stacy spoke of this dysfunctional relationship in an air-conditioned room on the first day I formally interviewed her. On a hot July day several months later, a member of Stacy's team named Eleanor and I found ourselves two blocks from la zona looking for friends who, it turned out, were not home. As we walked back to my car, we passed by a group of four Mexican children between the ages of about six and ten. My phone rang, and I answered it to schedule an interview with Chuck, a white American client who frequented Boystown. Meanwhile, the children were posing and smiling as Eleanor took pictures. Jasmine, the girl mentioned in the previous quote, asked me if she could see what was in my purse. Distracted by my phone conversation, I let her. Jasmine reached into my purse, grabbed a ten-dollar bill, and asked me in Spanish, "Will you give it to me?" and I shook my head no. Jasmine and I repeated this negotiation with several other items in my purse, until I finally let her have a pen in the hope that she would leave me alone. I finished my conversation with the Boystown client, and Eleanor finished taking pictures.

This exchange was an enactment of the phenomenon Stacy described: a foreign missionary taking pictures of Mexican children while the children ask for money. The geographic proximity to Reynosa's prostitution zone was what brought Eleanor, Stacy, and me to Jasmine's neighborhood, and it was within the walls of la zona where I had first met Chuck, the client with whom I was talking on the phone. There we all were, each trying to transform the border's differences into something of value—Jasmine digging dollars out of my purse, Eleanor snapping photos to show her friends outside of Mexico, Chuck looking for inexpensive sexual encounters, and me taking field notes for this vignette. While Chuck, Eleanor, Stacy, and I made our way to Boystown to meet sex workers, Stacy's mission imagined itself as existing to prevent children like Jasmine from becoming sex workers, drug users, and drug dealers.

Stacy's project relied upon the labor and financial support of short-term missions while defining itself in distinction to them. This chapter examines some of the effects of the love triad that missionaries tried to create. Stacy believed that the long-term aspect of her mission allowed her to better build relationships and an understanding of the needs of local populations. Team Boystown missionaries sought to move beyond a "dysfunctional" relationship in which Mexicans used Americans as a means for obtaining material goods and Americans used Mexicans as a means to satisfy their own desires to feel altruistic through charity. This kind of instrumentalizing runs counter to agape, the Christ-like model of unconditional love that was the ideal of their mission. Michel Callon explains that agape is a Greek term used in Christian theology to describe God's unconditional love for people; it is supposed to be the model for humans' love for each other (Callon and Law 2003). It is a selfless love that should be without aim, without means and ends, without expectation of return. Agape, however, is not a "natural state of being" for humans but rather requires effort and is difficult to achieve (Callon and Law 2003).

Team Boystown missionaries emphasized God's love and grace rather than judgment or damnation. They sought to exercise a similar selfless love and grace toward others. They explained that humans have God's grace because of Jesus's sacrifice on the cross, and they tried to achieve this agape. Stacy and her team often explicitly stated that their only job was "to love people," because that was what Jesus asked them to do, and "the rest is up to him."

While missionaries often said that loving people was the goal of their project, they hoped and expected to see other transformations to result from their actions. Three factors frequently brought tension into the picture: 1) a notion that God had a plan for peoples' lives; 2) missionaries' expectation that expanding spiritual intersubjective spacetime would help to enact God's will; and 3) their desire to enact agape, or unconditional love, but also for sex workers to love God and to stop being prostitutes. They often engaged in actions, some of which were coercive, that sought to bring about this outcome. Missionaries conceived of God as an omniscient Father who knows what is in a person's best interests and has the best plan for one's life. Missionaries' actions suggest their belief that they had a better understanding of God's plan for sex workers' lives than sex workers had. Missionaries believed that bringing about relationships between sex workers and God would help sex workers desire and embody this plan. They hoped that a spiritual intervention could change the course of a sex worker's occupational and moral career. From their perspective, the ideal outcome of this triadic relationship would be a situation in which both missionaries and prostitutes would be closer to God. In particular, prostitutes, upon realizing God's love for them, would choose other careers, return to their families, and reside with their children. Missionaries believed that if sex workers learned to hear God's voice the way that missionaries did, they would no longer engage in sex work.

The actions that were part of Team Boystown's goals of "building relationships" often combined rapport building, attending to sex workers' material needs, and gestures that straddled love and coercion. These actions were hoped and expected to expand God's love and influence. They involved a form of emotional labor, as Team Boystown sought to make the women feel their love and also God's love, even during moments of anger and ambivalence. Their emotional labor included a deep engagement and entanglement in sex workers' lives in ways that go beyond the typical missionary encounter.

This chapter argues that relationships between some sex workers and Team Boystown missionaries are characterized by interdependency and reciprocity, and that the conflicts in their relationships are primarily about love. Some conflicts resulted from tensions inherent in their beliefs and goals. The missionaries' stated goal "of loving the ones Jesus loved" and "leaving the rest up to him" strived for a Christ-like agape. The missionaries' belief, hope, and expectation was that creating love triads would result in specific kinds of transformations in sex workers and drug users. I suggest that the missionaries' project, from its inception, entailed a tension between their stated goals (to love sex workers, as God directed them) and what they hoped these goals to achieve (that sex workers would stop being sex workers and even become evangelists).

Team Boystown's relationships were haunted by the threat of becoming dysfunctional, weighed down by mutual dependencies and instrumentalizing impulses. The danger stemmed from the differential access to resources that structured the migrations of these two groups, and from the fact that the mission was set up, in part, to help the poor. The first two sections of this chapter focus on conflicts that arose in the relationships between sex workers and missionaries, first looking at conflicts originating from missionary expectations and then at conflicts resulting from sex workers' expectations. Finally, I will examine some sex workers' positive reactions to missionaries as well as some mutual transformations that resulted from their encounter. Team Boystown's love project both transcended and reified differences created by the US-Mexico border. Despite the conflicts inherent in Team Boystown's project, its actions sometimes did lead to both parties feeling closer to God.

Great Expectations: Team Boystown's Hopes for Sex Workers

In 2007 Stacy wrote on her blog about her tumultuous relationship with Cristal, a crack-using sex worker who had a young baby with her boyfriend/ pimp. In Stacy's description, Cristal was initially cold to her but warmed up after Stacy gave her gifts. Their relationship intensified after Cristal's roommate, BomBom, was murdered by clients. Stacy chronicled her relationship with Cristal in her blog, describing instances of rejection or acceptance by Cristal and her emotional reactions to these events. Her blog posts noted Cristal's "progress," which to Stacy indexed God's work. God was making changes on the days that Cristal was not using drugs; when Cristal went back to drugs, Stacy expressed frustration and a sense of failure. When Cristal became pregnant again, Stacy encouraged her to "take care of herself and her baby," by which she meant that Cristal should stop smoking crack and seek prenatal care. A high point in their relationship occurred when Stacy took Cristal for her first ultrasound and paid for it, and Cristal expressed appreciation and said that she was going to name her baby after Stacy. When I was in Reynosa, Stacy told me stories about taking Cristal to prenatal care visits, mentioning that Cristal had to borrow one of her dresses each time because she only had "work clothes." Stacy also told me that rumors circulated around Boystown that she wanted to buy or adopt Cristal's baby.

On June 8, 2007, Stacy wrote a blog post titled "Why I (of All People)

Should Not be a Missionary" that discussed an especially dramatic event on a visit to Boystown to pick up Cristal for a routine doctor's visit. Stacy wrote:

> So, just about one hour after I wrote the last post ("Dreaming of Tomorrow . . . "), I went to pick up Cristal for her next doctor's appointment. I found her, along with one of the other pregnant girls, just outside of BT [Boystown] with her crack pipe in hand, just about to smoke. She informed me that she didn't want to go to the doctor, and would I please leave her alone. I told her it was way too late for all of that, and that we should just go to the doctor because it would only take a couple of hours. This was clearly not what she wanted to do, so I reminded her that she is the only one her baby has, so she should take care of herself and her baby. Well, that really set her off and she stormed her way back to her bar.
>
> So, there I was, standing outside of BT [Boystown] having been rebuked by a pregnant prostitute, unsure of what I should do next. I got in the car and decided to go in after her. Was this inspired by the Holy Spirit? I have absolutely no idea because I didn't even stop to pray about it (reason #1 why I shouldn't be a missionary).
>
> I drove in past the police/guard station, where they always smile & wave at me and undoubtedly wonder what in the world I'm doing there. I drove around the corner, heart slightly pounding, and parked in front of the crack bar where Cristal lives. I walked inside to find her and her pregnant buddy sitting at a table. I walked over and she began yelling at me. "I know I'm the only one my baby has, so stop telling me!" I, very calmly, tried to tell her that I wasn't there to tell her that again. But I was only calm the first time I said it because she kept putting her hands over her ears (like a toddler) and yelling at me.
>
> And then it happened. I don't know what "it" was, but it happened. I got really upset. And I started crying right there in a crack bar! (reason #2 why I shouldn't be a missionary.) Her pregnant friend said to me, "why do you only help the pregnant girls?"
>
> And I started in, with a raised voice, with, "All I have ever tried to do is be your friend! Why won't you just let me be your friend? And whoever is telling you that I only help the pregnant girls is LYING to you! Go ask anyone in this place—All I want is to be your friend and help you so you can be a mom to your baby! You think I want to be a mom? Well, I don't! I just want to be your friend!"

Here we can see a conflict arising from the fact that Stacy thought of her relationship with sex workers as one of friendship. The sex workers, however, suspected instrumental intentions and framed the relationship in another common trope: that of Americans who wish to adopt or buy the babies of Mexicans. This is an example of how the asymmetrical US-Mexico relationship shaped expected circulations between citizens of the two countries. Sex workers called Stacy's intention of agape and selfless love, which she hoped to offer in the form of friendship and assistance, into question.

And after I had yelled and cried at two pregnant prostitutes in a crack bar (reasons #3–5 why I shouldn't be a missionary), we all walked away.

As I stepped outside to get in my vehicle, I saw a girl we call "La Poli" (short for *la politica*, "the politician" because she is shakin' hands & kissin' babies, even when she is strung out on all sorts of drugs). La Poli was standing there in her grandma-ish housecoat and slippers, just waiting to give me a big ol' hug with her skinny little arms. As she hugged me, I tried to act like I hadn't been crying. She whispered, "May God give you patience." And I started crying again. She had no idea what had just happened, but it didn't matter because God sent her to me in that moment. Then she began to sing, "God is here in this place. It is so beautiful that he's here. He promises to be wherever two or three are. God is here in this place." She blew me kisses while I cried, then walked away.

I drove straight to the land [that Stacy had purchased to be the refuge for sex workers], and cried and prayed and wondered if I was in the right place and should I just pack up and go home now, etc., etc. I cried for a long time.

Later that afternoon, I went to the lawyer's office, hoping to sign papers and be an official land owner in Mexico. However, in accordance with the day's activities, that did not happen. In fact, when we got there, the owner decided to raise the price of the land a bit. And the attorney informed me that we still have to wait on a few things, so I'm not totally sure of how much longer it will all take. (I have to call today to re-negotiate the price on the land.) By the time that day was over, I was ready to go to sleep.

And it all boils down to this: I just know in my gut at the end of the day that I find Jesus in BT. I don't always like it, but He strangely draws me to Himself in those distressing disguises of His—in Cristal, Nora, La Poli, all of them. Where else could I go? I wouldn't want to be anywhere else, truthfully.

Something tells me that won't be the last time I cry and yell inside those walls. I have to hope that one day, I'll see the promise of God's word be fulfilled: those who sow in tears, will reap with shouts of joy.

Lots of love from the most unlikely missionary,

[Stacy]

While this blog post narrates one of the more dramatic conflicts between missionaries and sex workers I heard about or witnessed, it serves as an example of several important dynamics in their relationship. While missionaries attempted to engage in acts of love as an end in itself, this was an event in which Stacy was explicitly evaluating and judging Cristal's behavior and trying to influence her actions. Stacy expressed frustration, anger, and sadness when the love triads between sex workers, missionaries, and God did not transform sex workers in expected ways. Both Cristal's behavior and Stacy's reaction made Stacy momentarily doubt, while crying and praying in her car, if she was "in the right place."

We can also see in this story sex workers' resistance to missionary surveillance. Stacy's judgment of Cristal's mothering of her fetus is especially salient here. Sex workers sometimes voiced frustrations surrounding missionary expectations, although their resistance usually came about in more subtle ways, if at all.[1] Cristal and her "pregnant buddy" resisted through refusal of doctor's visits, smoking crack, and yelling. By not following Stacy's instructions, sex workers like Cristal asserted their right to make their own choices.

Rumors and stories of Americans buying or adopting the babies of sex workers, especially those with crack addictions, were widespread in Boystown. Stacy had no intention of adopting Cristal's baby, but she did write on her blog about how her life was going to change after its birth. Some members of a short-term team even gave Stacy a baby shower so that she would have the necessary items to help Cristal take care of her baby. Thus, though Cristal's accusations did not reflect Stacy's plans or intentions, there was a way in which Stacy's team members and perhaps even Stacy herself imagined Stacy as a coparent to the baby. Furthermore, Stacy seemed to imagine herself in a parenting role toward Cristal herself. Although missionaries did not instrumentalize sex workers in exactly the way that sex workers feared, they were nevertheless instrumentalized in the sense of showing the missionary signs of God and the efficacy of her actions.

Sex workers continued to circulate rumors of Stacy's baby-purchasing after Cristal's baby was born. Cristal also continued to resist Stacy's intended acts of friendship and help. In July, after Cristal had given birth, a mutual friend told Stacy that Cristal was now living outside of Boystown, that she had quit using crack so that she could breastfeed, and that she looked fatter (indexing her decreased drug use). When Stacy ran into Cristal again one day and told her she looked forward to meeting the baby, Cristal replied, "You'll NEVER meet her." Later, in July, Stacy wrote,

While I'm sad I haven't seen the baby yet, I'm glad to know that our prayers are seemingly being answered, little by little—Cristal is out of BT (most days), her motherly instincts are kicking in, and crack is done, if only for the time being.

Blog posts like these reveal a great deal of ambivalence on the part of missionaries. While Stacy found evidence of God's work, Cristal's blatant rejection of her efforts made her call into question whether or not she was enacting God's will. Stacy's emotional reaction is indicative of a relationship much more tumultuous and intense than could be fostered by short-term missionary projects.

La Poli's actions served as a salve to Stacy's reaction. Stacy even suggested that La Poli was a sign of God—sent by him to comfort Stacy. La Poli's expression of warmth and joy toward Stacy was much more typical of the reactions that I observed of sex workers to Team Boystown's project.

Pressuring Women to Leave Boystown

Missionaries wanted sex workers to leave the prostitution zone and saw giving this message as an act of care. Sex workers sometimes interpreted these actions as support and help and sometimes as unwanted pressure, coercion, and meddling. Many sex workers wanted to leave prostitution, and many drug-addicted women wished for sobriety. Sex workers might have sometimes talked about wanting to leave the prostitution zone because they knew this was what missionaries wanted to hear. But most sex workers had plenty of reasons of their own to want to leave la zona.

Missionaries believed sex workers' anticipated dates of leaving Boystown to operate on a timeline linked to the spiritual world. To missionaries, sex workers leaving la zona were part of God's plan, which they would be able to enact once they were spiritually open to fulfilling God's desires for their lives. However, most sex workers operated in a timeline related to their imagined accumulation of money. Sex workers without addictions and without pimps usually planned to leave la zona after reaching their goal of saving money, a goal rarely met. Boystown, for these sex workers, had been imbued with hopes of economic success that were seldom fulfilled.

Missionaries engaged in a number of attempts to get sex workers to stop using drugs, to leave the prostitution zone, or to feel compelled to take on cohabitation with children or in some other way to "be good mothers." In addition to asking questions about their children, missionaries also asked questions about what sex workers' dreams were for the future. Stacy wrote in her blog that after a few conversations with a sex worker she had just met, she asked the woman if she ever thought about leaving Boystown and asked if she had a dream for her life. Stacy wrote that she was excited but also afraid to ask such loaded questions because she worried that she might jeopardize the friendship she was building. Another woman told Stacy her dream was to open a hair salon. Cubana hoped to open a restaurant with her son. Eva wished to buy a piece of land and a house to live in with her family. Rebecca desired to become a nurse. Once missionaries learned these dreams, they would often bring them up to sex workers when trying to motivate them to leave or to agree on a departure date. Sex workers would often set a date for leaving, often in conjunction with Stacy or Ashley. Yet, as the date approached, the sex worker would break the news that the date would be postponed to the missionary, who was usually disappointed and sad. As most sex workers left la zona to visit their families for about a month in December and January, this was often the time tentatively scheduled to leave for good. Rebecca shared a plan with missionaries to return to Puebla to go to nursing school at the end of 2008. Stacy wrote on her blog on November 13, 2008, about visiting Rebecca with a gift that some of Stacy's friends in Tulsa put together: a backpack full of new shoes, a stethoscope, and notebooks. She wrote on her blog that Rebecca listened to her own heart with the stethoscope and started crying. Stacy wrote:

> Then she told me that she had bad news—that she is actually coming back after Christmas to work a little longer. She said she needs to buy a car, and she will start school in August. After much protesting on my part, I could see that she was determined to buy this car. Realizing that my new task is to focus on August, I had to pull myself together. I did tell her, however, that if July rolls around and she's still here, I am breaking up friends with her. I won't speak to her anymore, I told her. She kind of smiled because she knew that it wouldn't be possible for me to stop talking to her. I told her to keep her stethoscope where she can see it, to remind her of the dreams God has placed in her heart to be a nurse.

Through this blog post, we can see how missionary actions in relation to sex workers leaving la zona could be read as both support and pressure. Although it is unclear whether Stacy's threat was delivered seriously, as a bluff, or completely in jest, the threat of "breaking up friends" is somewhat coercive. Stacy's gift to Rebecca is also a materialization of the hopes and prayers of many Christians for Rebecca as she sees it each day. While I believe it was gifted with intentions of love and friendship, it certainly was not a "free gift." It entails an expectation that Rebecca would leave la zona in order to use these items—a further obligation on the part of Rebecca.

Once they had closer relationships with sex workers, Team Boystown missionaries often put pressure on sex workers to leave la zona. For example, Stacy frequently told a story of a very ill ninety-year-old woman named Josephina who had lived in Boystown for fifty years. When Stacy met her, Josephina was unable to walk, her room smelled bad, and her diapers were not regularly changed. After a good deal of research, Stacy found a nursing home in a nearby town that was willing to take her. But the day that the nursing home was scheduled to pick her up, Josephina died in Boystown. Stacy sometimes shared this story with her sex worker friends, warning them that they would end up this way if they didn't leave la zona. I heard her recount to other missionaries what she told Rebecca: "If you do not find a way to get out, you are going to end up just like Josephina. You're going to live the rest of your days here and you're going to die alone, and nobody is going to find you for days after you die."

Stacy's desire that Lucía, her self-proclaimed "Mexican mother," would leave Boystown resulted in several conflicts. The mother/daughter kinship relation here is especially interesting given that Stacy cared for Lucía and nagged her about what she should do—activities more likely to be taken on by mothers toward daughters than by daughters toward mothers. Lucía had been addicted to crack cocaine and alcohol for many years, including the first several years that Stacy knew her. Stacy explained to me that she found Lucía sleeping in an outdoor makeshift tent in Boystown, joking that she was living at the "hotel four winds." She asked herself what she would do in that case if Lucía were her own mother. Taking on the obligation entailed in the fictive kinship relationship, Stacy rented an apartment for Lucía outside of la zona, and some of her friends helped her to furnish it. She explained her frustration when Lucía "marched herself back to Boystown" a week later and started using drugs again. Stacy noted that part of the reason why Lucía had difficulty staying away from Boystown was because her relations there were "like family." Stacy got into a fight with Lucía about this. She later took flowers to Lucía for Mother's Day, and Lucía refused the flowers, which made Stacy feel sad and hurt. When she told me the story several years after the event, Stacy indicated that she had been somewhat naive and had made many mistakes in her relationship with Lucía, emphasizing how much grace Lucía showed to her despite her actions. Years later, after Lucía had stopped drugs and was caring for her granddaughter, she wanted Stacy to rent her another apartment.

These conflicts, which sometimes led to feelings of frustration by missionaries or sex workers and sometimes led to fights, came about in great part due to tensions about love. On the one hand, missionaries believed that love should be an end in itself. On the other hand, their beliefs and desires indicated their expectation that particular kinds of results emerge from their actions. Stacy's blog post from May 11, 2007, is a good example of the ambivalence that she often expressed. She wrote about her fight with Lucía after Lucía left the apartment she rented for her and moved back into Boystown to use drugs, and she also told of another sex worker who returned to Boystown and drugs. She described her frustrations with "people who constantly choose their addictions over freedom" and her realization that "no matter how much you love someone, you can never force them to make good choices." This quote from her blog demonstrates the way in which the means/end love conflict created contradictory feelings and expectations for Stacy:

> I have heard myself say a thousand times that I didn't come to BT to shut it down or "get people saved." I simply came to love the ones Jesus loves; the changing of lives part is up to Him. I'm constantly forgetting what it is that Jesus has asked of me in there, which is to love people, to love Him in His most distressing disguises. And this journey is working something in me as much as it's working something in the lives of people who live in BT.

Making qualitative judgments thus brought disappointment and sometimes doubt about whether the missionary was enacting God's will and plan for her life. Stacy kept trying to embrace agape. Perhaps this constant forgetting that she was not sent to Boystown to "get people saved" was built into Team Boystown's missionary project. When she failed to see results from her actions, she read this stasis as both a personal failure and a failure to see signs of God. Missionaries found it difficult to "just love people" without pressuring them to change or evaluating their actions.

Conflicts Originating from Sex Workers' Expectations

When Lucía was living with her granddaughter, Luz, at a Christian migrant shelter, she became very concerned that a supposed lesbian who was sharing living quarters with them might molest Luz in her sleep. Lucía talked to me about her concerns, which made me nervous, because I wondered if she thought that all lesbians molested children. Lucía emphatically expressed her desperation to move out of the migrant shelter. On the day of Estrella's suicide in Boystown and the next day during the funeral, when we were all mourning with the family, Lucía repeatedly approached Stacy and Ashley trying to convince them to pay for an apartment for her. Lucía invited herself to ride in our car with Ashley, Stacy, Eva, and me from the funeral service to the gravesite. She was still angry with Stacy for not having answered her phone calls or rented her an apartment yet, and she was angry with Ashley and me for not answering our phones or putting pressure on Stacy. Lucía told us that she had poems for all of us, but that she would not give them to us because she was upset with us. Ashley gave Lucía a photograph of all of us at Stacy's wedding while we were in the car. Lucía said, "I'm giving you your poem, because you were good and gave me a photo." Eva replied, "Oh, you see how it is? She only wants to give you something if you give her something first."

In this vignette, we can see the kinds of pressures that sex workers placed upon missionaries for economic support. Lucía felt especially entitled to Stacy's help because of the kinship obligation as her "Mexican mother." I witnessed many instances in which Lucía, who had recovered from crack addiction, or practicing crack users asked Stacy for money and other items. Lucía would call Stacy repeatedly to ask for money. Missionaries often gave her money for whatever she claimed to be desperate for at the time. I gave her money for laundry soap and food. Ashley and I gave Lucía money to pay for her granddaughter's school after she called Stacy repeatedly and could not get an answer. Missionaries, who tried to buy people medicine or food when they could, sometimes encountered complications when negotiating the economic aspects of their relationships with people in la zona. Stacy mentioned to me that someone was always desperate for something in Boystown. She added that many of these people, especially those with drug addictions, didn't know how to set proper boundaries in their own lives, so she tried not to feel guilty even when they pressured her, but it was difficult. Stacy told me that many people would say to her, "I'm desperate for you to come here," and she recognized that they were sometimes manipulative. This sense of desperation was sometimes directed toward material goods and sometimes toward time and intimacy.

The fictive kinship relation between Lucía and Stacy was a source of jealousy and conflict. Sex workers accused Lucía and other drug users of instrumentalizing their relationships with Stacy. Eva also sometimes gave gifts to missionaries and made food for them, but she criticized Lucía's demand for something in exchange for a poem. Perhaps what was being debated here was the temporality of the gift exchange. While both Eva and Lucía expected certain reciprocity in their relationships with missionaries, Lucía demanded an immediate exchange, while Eva suggested that this transactional immediacy rendered the relationship instrumental. Furthermore, sex workers were jealous of the attention Lucía received and saw her as taking advantage of Stacy by expecting her to give money.

I observed several occasions in which these dynamics resulted in conflicts or confrontations. This happened, for example, when Stacy and I planned to have a pasta lunch with Eva and Rebecca in Eva's room. After some chitchat, Rebecca's tone became serious, and she told Stacy that she needed to put Ashley in line. Rebecca reported to Stacy that Lucía kept mentioning she had been promised a rented apartment from either Stacy or Ashley. Rebecca said, "Lucía and people like her are *abusiva*, and they only want to be your friend if you give them something. They aren't your friend just for the sake of friendship. If you are going to rent her an apartment or give her a room in the house you are building, you should let us live there too. We could bring our families here and they could work for you." Eva added, "My daughters are good at selling things."

Rebecca told Stacy that she needed to make Lucía work if she was going to live at the monastery, and Stacy agreed that Lucía would need to work to earn her keep. Rebecca and Eva then started to brainstorm aloud with Stacy about what kind of work they could do for the mission. Eva suggested that perhaps she could take care of sick people and give injections. Holding her little plastic basket of condoms, lubricant, and wet wipes (many sex workers kept such baskets on or near their beds), Eva started joking about how she would have sex with people for money and give the money to the poor. We all laughed.

While Eva made some jokes, Rebecca frequently changed her tone, warning that Lucía was *abusiva*, asking Stacy and her friends for things and then selling them. Eva agreed and said, "When you all give us bags of little shampoos and things, me and Rebecca, we use them or give them to our families back home. Lucía and *ellos* [they, the drug users] sell them, they even sell them to us, and we get a good price, of course, but then they just take the money and buy alcohol and crack. So you think you are doing something good, but you are just feeding their vice. It would be better if you gave those things to us."

Rebecca said that Lucía and the other drug users worked in la zona at a time when gringos brought a lot of money, so they grew accustomed to asking for and being given money. She said, "We Mexicans often have the problem that we think that all gringos are rich, but it's not true." Stacy agreed and then repeated a variation of the same statement that opened the introduction to this chapter. She told Eva and Rebecca that gringos are also to blame for this because missionaries come for a week and give people a lot of things they don't need. Stacy said that then gringos feel like they did a good thing because they gave stuff away, while Mexicans think that gringos are just there to give gifts.

This vignette sheds light upon several important dynamics in the relationships between sex workers and missionaries. Stacy's monastery was seen as a potential source of security for sex workers and was also a site of conflict and jealousy. Rebecca's theory about why Lucía and others expect money from gringos was in line with Stacy's comments about the dysfunctional relationship between Mexicans and Americans. There was mutual knowledge on the part of sex workers and missionaries of the expected circulations between citizens of the two countries. Furthermore, we can see that some missionaries and some sex workers hoped to avoid instrumentalizing their relationships and wanted to believe that they were not merely transactional. In speaking of *ellos*, Eva and Rebecca, both non-drug-using sex workers, referred disparagingly to the drug- and alcohol-using sex workers to establish themselves as more genuine friends. However, Eva and Rebecca, by saying that Stacy should give shampoo samples to them instead of to drug users and should let them live with her instead of Lucía, also sought to benefit materially from their friendship with Stacy. They argued that they were more entitled to these material benefits than people who transformed charity or gifts into vice. Eva and Rebecca also called into question the real effects of missionary work—questioning their value if sex workers transformed their acts of generosity into vice rather than the reproduction of a family.

Both Eva and Rebecca had been worried about Lucía's relationship with Stacy long before I witnessed this confrontation. Five months earlier, Eva had told me that Stacy had "a lot of patience" and that once Stacy finished constructing her house, "all of the crazies would want to live there." It took me a few months to realize that when non-drug-using sex workers referred to the "crazies" (*locos*), they were talking about drug users, who they said *andan locos* (go around being crazy) in reference to being intoxicated. Rebecca had been angry with Ashley for several months because she did not like the way Ashley handled Lucía's requests. Rebecca ignored Ashley and would not look her in the eye for several weeks. Meanwhile, she was much nicer to me, calling me "Sarita," touching my hand and making eye contact, directing everything she said to me and completely ignoring Ashley when we visited her room. When I was with Rebecca and Stacy, she usually directed this attention to Stacy and ignored me.

Rebecca would act coldly to Stacy if she did not enter la zona for a couple of weeks. When I was at Stacy's house, I'd hear Rebecca call her repeatedly for twenty-minute blocks of time if Stacy did not answer the phone. Stacy complained about this to me, and Rebecca told me on several occasions, "Stacy doesn't answer her phone unless I call her at six a.m. when she's still asleep, so that's when I call her." I heard stories from other sex workers about Rebecca excluding other sex workers from a dinner party at Stacy's house because she wanted time alone with Stacy. Rebecca's conflict with other sex workers about closeness in relation to Stacy was so extreme that she refused to attend Stacy's bachelorette party that Ashley, Sofía, and I organized.

These examples demonstrate the ways in which rivalries between sex workers were relevant to, and enacted through, relationships with missionaries. Stacy was involved in triadic relationships between God and several sex workers, and these examples indicate jealousy across triads. I never witnessed sex workers engaging in conflicts due to competition over clients, but I did occasionally hear these stories. I did witness sex workers competing for Stacy's friendship, time, affection, and gifts. For example, when Stacy and I took brownies to Boystown, Rebecca tried to convince her to give all of them to her instead of handing them out to other sex workers. Some of the sex workers pressured Stacy and other missionaries about the frequency of their visits to la zona. Stacy said that once, when she did not visit la zona for two weeks because she was sick, several people were upset with her. These pressures made Stacy feel stressed and overwhelmed.

Abigail also experienced forms of nonsovereingty in relation to her obligations to sex workers. When she entered la zona both with Stacy and alone in 2006 and organized for doctors to do medical clinics in la zona, she became close to a woman named Silvia, who asked Abigail for money to pay off her pimp so that she could return to her mother in Tampico. After Abigail helped her to return home, Silvia called Abigail repeatedly and threatened to use crack again or commit suicide if she did not visit her in Tampico. Silvia's threats were effective, and Abigail visited. Abigail realized that Silvia was manipulative, unstable, and perhaps dangerous—Silvia's mother told her she had tried to kill her in the middle of the night, and Silvia refused to take Abigail to the bus station to return to Reynosa. In retrospect, Abigail talks about her naivete in this situation and how difficult it was to navigate how much to try to help people or to get involved with their lives. It's an example of the kinds of pressures sex workers put upon missionaries and how missionaries' intertwined lives with sex workers entangled them in a web of obligations, sometimes affecting their lives in ways that they could not control.

Reciprocity, Transformations, Friendship, and Hope

While the majority of this chapter has been devoted to conflicts, I witnessed much more approval than disapproval of Stacy's project from sex workers. They thought it was morally good to help the poor and sought potential material, social, and spiritual benefits from relationships with missionaries. This section examines sex workers' positive responses to Team Boystown, their support of the project, and the transformations that sex workers claimed were achieved from their encounters with missionaries.

On an especially hot day in May during the midst of the swine flu outbreak, when there was even less traffic than usual in Boystown, Eva, Sofía, and I sat on a log outside Eva's room to chat and enjoy the breeze. We saw two men selling popsicles out of carts, one wearing a medical mask due to the swine flu outbreak and the other joking about selling anti-influenza popsicles. We bought some. While we ate our mango-and-chile-flavored popsicles, a woman named Rosa approached us. Although I had never met her before, I gathered from her appearance and behavior that she was addicted to crack cocaine. Rosa was thin, with a weathered face, a black eye, and yellowish-brown stubs for front teeth. She was carrying a cellular phone that she frantically explained had dropped in the toilet. Eva helped her to take the chip and battery out of the phone and told her to put all of the pieces on a television or refrigerator to dry. Rosa said it would be better to put it on Eva's television instead, because it would get stolen in Rosa's room. Eva tried to resist, but Rosa insisted. Eva asked her if she washed the phone after taking it out of the toilet, and Rosa replied, "No, but the toilet is clean."

Eva and Sofía then looked at each other wide-eyed and started laughing, both amused and disgusted. Rosa ignored them and asked me if I spoke English or Spanish. After I told her that I spoke both, Rosa switched to English, possibly as a way to exclude Eva and Rebecca. She asked them who I was, and Eva said, "*una hermana*," implying that I was a missionary. Rosa asked me, "Do you know Stacy?" I said yes, and added that Stacy was my friend. Rosa smiled brightly and jumped up and down, asking me to send Stacy her best wishes. I told her that Stacy had just gotten married, and she said that this made her very happy and asked me to send along her congratulations. Rosa said,

Stacy helped me a lot. When I met her, I was a drug addict, and . . . well, I still am, but now just a little bit, not a lot. But I used to be REALLY skinny! And now I'm fat. [Stacy] taught me that God loved me, and now I'm fat like a samurai!

Rosa punctuated her exclamation with a fighting samurai gesture.

Non-drug-using sex workers sometimes tried to help drug-using ones, but at other times made them the butt of jokes. More significantly, since Eva told Rosa that I was a missionary and she knew that I was Stacy's friend, these factors were likely to have influenced her response. I was so often in Boystown with missionaries that it is possible much of what I observed and was told was influenced by my association with them, even when I explicitly told people that I was an anthropologist and neither a Christian nor a missionary. However, it is generally impossible to determine whether or not what is being told is "genuine" or "authentic." Sex workers' claims that Stacy has brought them closer to God are analytically interesting in either case.

This vignette demonstrates the kind of unfolding love triad that Stacy and her team explicitly hoped to create. Rosa suggested that Stacy's pronouncement of God's love for her was a sign of that love. She claimed that Stacy inspired a recognition of that love, as well as a material transformation in body fat. In some cases, missionary practices were believed to produce transformations in drug-using sex workers, and this expansion of spirituality was seen to influence the actions of those who used drugs less frequently and became fatter. It is impossible for me to know whether or not sex workers like Rosa were actually using drugs less frequently and getting fatter. But her claim of fatness brought about by God's love via Stacy's mediation indicates that she either believed missionaries were transforming sex workers, or at least felt compelled to validate the work of missionaries in this way.

I often heard stories like Rosa's that pointed to the moment of Stacy telling them that God loved them as a moment of transformation. Angeles, or La Politica, another crack-using sex worker, also told me that after Stacy taught her that God loved her, she had mostly retired from sex work, except for servicing a few important clients. La Poli said she was now primarily cutting hair and doing odd jobs for a living.

The following blog post shows evidence of some of the mutual appreciation and love in relationships between missionaries and sex workers, and is also a case in which the love triad was claimed to be successfully transformative. On her blog on November 13, 2008, Stacy described some of her frustrations in Boystown and her feelings of failure. She then described running into a "strikingly beautiful" woman named "Sally" in Boystown whom she had known for two and a half years (at this point she used pseudonyms to protect the privacy of the women). Stacy recounted that when she met Sally, she told her the same thing that she tells all the girls, "Jesus knows your name, the story of your life, and he loves you," and said that Sally cried. Sally shared this story with other sex workers while introducing Stacy. Stacy wrote:

> Today I sat down with Sally to catch up, and the most unexpected things came out of her mouth. She reminded me of our first conversation: "Do you remember when you told me that Jesus loves me? [Stacy], those words have impacted the rest of my life." She went on to tell me she has decided to leave BT, to go home to be a mom to her 9-year old daughter. "I am leaving this place, to live my life for God." As if that wasn't big enough, she began to share words that sounded like poetry to me: "[Stacy], don't give up hope; don't give up faith. Keep telling the girls that Jesus loves them. I'm leaving now, and many others will leave, too. You have been so patient; you have been our friend, you throw birthday parties for us. You have made many sacrifices with your life. When we sacrifice for God, there are beautiful consequences. My life is a beautiful consequence." Needless to say, this left me in tears. I told Sally that her words today have impacted my life, just like my words impacted hers. I was amazed in that moment as I realized that no one else on this whole planet can encourage me the way my friends in BT can. Their words of "keep going" and "yes, it matters" carry more weight than anyone else's words.

According to Stacy, the interactional moment in which her words became an index of God's recognition and love was a turning point for Sally. The result was everything the missionaries hoped and expected: a recognition of God's love, an ensuing relationship with God, leaving Boystown, and cohabitation with a child. Furthermore, the fact that this story is shared on Stacy's blog demonstrates to her Christian publics that not only their efforts of prayer but also Stacy's efforts of building relationships had led to some kind of transformation. Stacy would never pat herself on the back in this way, but would thank God as the sovereign force underlying all of this transformation.

This blog post also shows evidence of reciprocity between sex workers and missionaries. Both pointed to the power of the words of the other. They mediated God's love and recognition for each other. Stacy's statement that encouragement by people in Boystown "carries more weight" than encouragement by others was backed by my observation of Stacy and other missionaries. While I saw Team Boystown members receive positive responses from other Christians about the "important work" they were doing in Reynosa, they usually downplayed these compliments, and I never saw them repeating these messages to other people. However, when sex workers voiced approval of their projects or claimed to have experienced changes as a result of their actions, missionaries seemed deeply moved and were more likely to retell these stories both on their blogs and in face-to-face interaction.

As with Rosa, I saw many people's faces soften as they opened up to me after I mentioned that I was a friend of Stacy's. I noticed that when sex workers and other adults and children of Boystown saw Stacy, their faces lit up, and they ran to greet her with a big hug and kiss on the cheek.

Sex workers used missionaries as saint- or priest-like intermediaries, whom they asked to say prayers to God on their behalf. Sex workers, former sex workers, and other people with whom the missionaries came into contact frequently requested prayers: for their financial situations, health, and the health of their loved ones, as well as for the strength from God to resist drugs and alcohol. On the day of Estrella's suicide, María begged Stacy to pray that her daughter would "go with God." Some sex workers seemed to believe in the transformative capacities of missionary prayers. Sofía told me that she thanked missionaries for their prayers and for sending her a Psalm that she prayed when her son was missing. When her son returned to her alive,[2] one of her friends who was also missing a son asked Sofía to share the Psalm with her, because the prayer clearly worked. Missionaries granted these prayer requests, but infused them with their desires. For example, Stacy and her team, along with praying the requested prayers, would also pray that God would enact his will upon the sex workers, soften their hearts, and show them his dreams for their lives. When I was mistaken for a missionary, I was also asked to pray for people. When two missionaries and I accompanied Sofía to Tampico as she left Boystown, I asked Ashley why we were getting so many prayer requests from Sofía's family, and she replied,

> People always ask me and Stacy to pray for them and I think they believe that because we're white and American and missionaries, God hears our prayers more. People always tell Stacy to pray for them and she always tells them, "I will, but why don't you pray too? God will hear your prayers, too," and they're like, "Eh, I don't know."

I am not sure to what extent missionaries' whiteness and Americanness made Mexicans believe that God would be more receptive to their prayers, but what is missing from Ashley's statement is the way in which this tension surrounding prayer is symptomatic of a general difference between Catholic and evangelical theologies. Most of the people with whom Team Boystown works in Mexico are Catholic, and Catholics pray through intermediaries (saints) or ask priests to say prayers for them. Evangelical Christians, on the other hand, seek to develop a personal relationship with Christ, and direct prayer is an important part of that relationship. Although Team Boystown missionaries did not explicitly attempt to convert the people they met from Catholicism to Protestantism, their wish that people would feel comfortable praying directly to God expressed the tenets of their particular faith. Missionaries did not want to remain mediators, but rather hoped that "building relationships" would lead sex workers to pursue intimate relationships with God and talk to him directly. It was as though they hoped or imagined that they would temporarily replace not only clients but also saints until God took both of their places. Although the missionaries' commitment to the people of Boystown was meant to be long-term, their mediating role in the love triangle with individual sex workers was meant to be transitional.

Although different understandings about prayer may have been symptoms of different theologies, I rarely observed conflicts. Boystown's residents were generally open to a wide variety of spiritual and religious practices and beliefs, and did not see them as mutually exclusive. Many of the sex workers in Boystown identified as Catholic, prayed to Catholic Saints as well as la Santa Muerte, believed in *brujería* (witchcraft), attended local evangelical sermons to obtain free food or clothing, and entertained the idea of joining Stacy's monastery and becoming *hermanas*. Eva, for example, told me that she was raised Catholic until her parents converted to Pentecostalism. She sometimes prayed to God and sometimes to the saints. When she was sick, she would sometimes go to a doctor and sometimes to a *curandera*, a traditional healer that often uses a mix of indigenous medicinal practices and Catholic rituals to address spiritual, medical, psychological, and social problems. Eva lit candles, prayed, and gave tributes to la Santa Muerte after a *curandera* in Oaxaca healed her from a terribly painful health condition that made the skin on her body look like elephant skin. She also told me that she might one day become a *hermana* and live on Stacy's land, but she noted that she would never stop praying to la Santa Muerte or lighting a candle for her, because la Santa Muerte had healed her in the past and she feared what might happen if she were to stop praying. I met a few sex workers who saw rigid boundaries between these practices, like Lola, who did not believe in God but only in la Santa Muerte; Rebecca, who was critical of la Santa Muerte and identified as Catholic; and Lucía, who was an avid evangelical convert. However, most residents of Boystown, like Eva, were open to any spiritual practices that would bring results.

Thus, some sex workers indicated that their relations with missionaries and God lead to subjective, spiritual, and material transformations in their lives. These cases did not always represent the full kind of transformation that missionaries hoped for and expected. Some of these women still lived in Boystown and used drugs and (even if less frequently) sold sex. But these sex workers did express a knowledge that God loved them, which was part of the message that Team Boystown hoped to deliver, and missionaries pointed to small transformations that they linked to this knowledge of love.

Sex workers were generally supportive of Stacy and her team becoming their neighbors. Although they did see potential material benefits, some sex workers and others in the neighborhood were also excited about the possibility of spending more time with Team Boystown members. Beyond potential material benefits, they also enjoyed the company of missionaries and reaped social and spiritual benefits from their relationships.

Whenever I talked to sex workers about the construction of Stacy's house, they expressed excitement about the possibility. Stacy wrote on her blog that several sex workers told her, "We want to be here to break the first rock, and we want to cut ribbon, too. You know this already, but we support you and what you want to do here." Several sex workers and drug dealers, migrants staying in a nearby migrant shelter, and pastors from different US cities attended the groundbreaking of the land as construction started.

Furthermore, sex workers and other people in the neighborhood saw Stacy's desire to be their neighbor as a sign of missionaries' acceptance, love, and investment in the people of the neighborhood and of la zona. Lucía would laugh about how Stacy talked proudly about building her house in Aquiles "as if it were a luxurious neighborhood!" Aquiles was one of the most stigmatized neighborhoods in Reynosa, one that middle- and upper-class locals would often emphasize never having been to. Señor Corona, an elderly man who lived across the street from Stacy's land (but not in the prostitution zone), told me on many occasions how happy he was that Stacy was building her house across from his, because she was making the neighborhood more beautiful. He also expressed how happy he was to be surrounded by so many young Americans, whom he thought of as his "friends and neighbors," and that he was excited to learn more English from them and to teach them Spanish. Señor Corona told me that after his son died, he would probably have killed himself if it weren't for all of his American friends who spent time talking to him. Stacy and her friends made him feel loved. Several missionaries lived with Señor Corona for a few months, fixing up his house, and others fed him regularly. A couple of missionaries and I made him a birthday cake one day and ate it with him in his house while he showed us old pictures and told us about his life.

As we saw in chapter 5, missionaries received from their relationships with sex workers a closer relationship to God, the satisfaction of having helped someone, social capital in Christian circles that sometimes led to celebrity, and financial support for their mission. Team Boystown members said that they saw Jesus more in the "drug addicts and prostitutes" in la zona than in any other aspects of their lives, and much more than in their home churches, where they saw a good deal of hypocrisy. Stacy told me over brunch at her house one day that she was not in Boystown and Reynosa because her heart is overflowing with love, but rather because she "sees Jesus there." They often talked about friendships with sex workers in ways that indicated a great deal of investment, emotion, and obligation.

While the vignette about being "rebuked by a pregnant prostitute" described a moment in which some sex workers questioned their friendship with missionaries, it is also important to note the ways in which other sex workers often reciprocated missionaries' friendly acts. Eva sometimes cooked for Stacy, Ashley, Eleanor, and me on the small hot plate in her room. María also fed us occasionally. Stacy told stories in her blog of sex workers giving her presents, and I was with Rebecca and Eva once as they bought Stacy a talking toy parrot for her birthday. Sofía, Ashley, and I organized a bachelorette party for Stacy before her wedding and invited sex workers and missionaries to the party. Several sex workers spent hours cooking before the party, and everyone bought her gifts, despite the fact that money was very hard to come by with fewer clients in la zona. Sofía told me later that it was important to her to be able to throw a bachelorette party for Stacy, because Stacy had thrown so many parties for women in Boystown, and it was a rare opportunity to show her friend how much she cared about her.

One benefit that some sex workers derived from relationships with missionaries was a feeling of trust and intimacy and the ability to talk about aspects of their lives that they often did not feel comfortable discussing with their colleagues. As described in chapter 3, many sex workers felt morally obligated to protect their families from their work, which entailed not divulging information that could be used against family members, a necessary part of the double life strategy they employed. I observed that sex workers were more likely to share details of their family situations and some of their problems to outsiders like missionaries and anthropologists than they were to their coworkers. They sometimes explicitly asked us not to share details about their family lives and problems with other sex workers.

When I visited Reynosa in December 2011 with Stacy, two and a half years after I had left, Eva cried and said she was very lonely, because she did not have anyone to talk with about her problems. She said that she didn't trust other sex workers enough to talk about these issues, and she could not talk to her children either because she had to be strong for them. When Team Boystown made the decision to leave Reynosa, I flew in from Chicago to accompany Ashley and Eleanor in having a meal with Eva and Rebecca to say goodbye. Everyone cried, and there was great sadness. Not only were sex workers disappointed that Team Boystown would not become their neighbors and that they would not have the possibility of living in the monastery, but all parties expressed sadness that they would not be able to spend time together and be part of each other's daily lives.

Although "love" is difficult to measure, based upon my observations of interactions between sex workers and missionaries as well as my conversations with members of each group, I can say that some sex workers and some missionaries shared feelings of mutual affection, care, and sympathy toward one another. I often enough heard them describe their relations as ones of love and friendship. They used the verb *querer*, which is reserved for more familial love, friendship love, and a less intense form of romantic love (*amar* is the more serious "in love" verb). Sex workers and missionaries often cried together, usually in relation to a sex worker's story of hardship. Sex workers' and missionaries' faces softened and lit up when they would greet each other with a big hug and a kiss on the cheek. They were eager to hear news of each other and expressed deep concern when there was bad news and joy at good news. One of the missionaries, Ashley, was so touched by her time in Boystown and so saddened when Stacy and her husband decided to abort the mission that she has been trying to put together a team to take back to Reynosa since she returned to Tulsa in 2011 to work as a barista. While some sex workers questioned whether their relations with missionaries were friendships, others insisted on them being friendships. In these cases, I witnessed reciprocal acts of friendship as well as evidence of trust, intimacy, and care between missionaries and sex workers.

Conclusion

The concern that Stacy expressed at the beginning of this chapter about the "dysfunctional" transactions between Americans and Mexicans in the short-term mission encounter was one that was resisted by both sex workers and missionaries and that continued to haunt their relationships. One can read the dynamic between sex workers and missionaries in Boystown as in some ways reproducing this transaction between Americans exchanging "sweet gringo treats" for artifacts and stories of exotic poverty and a feel-good sense of having helped the poor. Yet many of the conflicts examined in this chapter originated in sex workers' and missionaries' worries about these kinds of instrumentality. These concerns were mutual. The missionaries and the sex workers had similar conflicts, concerned as they were about using their relationship as a means for something else. For sex workers, this "something else" was usually material, and sex workers surveilled each other's interactions with missionaries and accused each other of instrumentalizing them. Sex workers sometimes put great pressure on missionaries to visit them in Boystown, to buy them things, or to give them money. Missionaries, in turn, did not want their relationships with sex workers to be instrumentalized for their own self-making projects to make them feel good for having "helped" someone. However, they did seem to feel good when they witnessed what they read as improvements in sex workers' lives (such as quitting drugs or leaving the prostitution zone), and they had self-doubts when sex workers' behavior was not changing. Missionaries struggled between "just loving people," a model of Christ-like agape, and judgments about the behavior of sex workers linked to hope for outcomes. Missionaries saw themselves as catalysts of God's wishes for sex workers, resulting in subjective, spiritual, and material transformations that would turn them into nurses and hair dressers. These expectations of sex workers' transformations led to conflicts between missionaries and sex workers. Missionaries placed pressure on sex workers to leave Boystown, conform to their ideals of motherhood, or quit using drugs, and the sex workers sometimes resisted this pressure.

Many of the conflicts in their relationship were tied to the way in which the US-Mexico relationship created certain kinds of expected circulations or exchanges between citizens of the two countries. The difference created by the geopolitical US-Mexico border enabled and propelled Team Boystown's project and was valuable to their mission. This difference was also something Team Boystown missionaries sought to minimize through establishing relationships with sex workers. The border allowed both parties to get something of value from the other. Sex workers received things from missionaries such as medicine, gifts, and small amounts of money, and some hoped that their relationships with missionaries might materialize in a place to live. They also received emotional support, intimacy, and friendship, as well as prayers. Missionaries got to feel good about themselves, were treated as heroes in their congregations, and their lives were enriched. Furthermore, relationships between sex workers and missionaries sometimes made both parties feel closer to God, and this divine access was in part mediated by the difference created by the border. Sex workers did not materially benefit from Team Boystown in ways that were long-term or sustainable. However, insofar as the goal was to make "prostitutes" their neighbors and love them, Team Boystown was successful, at least temporarily. Some sex workers said they believed that God loved them after they were told so by missionaries, and some pointed to changes in their lives that they attributed to missionary love or prayers, such as leaving la zona, quitting drugs or using them less frequently, or returning to live with their children. All Team Boystown missionaries and some sex workers indicated feeling closer to God as the result of their relationships. In addition to mediating each other's relationships with God, some sex workers and missionaries valued their relationships with each other.

Ultimately, the complex and dramatic relations between Team Boystown missionaries and several sex workers reveal a deeply intertwined intimacy that would likely not have been possible in short-term mission encounters. Despite concerns and accusations of instrumentality on both sides, I argue that their relationships were characterized by interdependency and often reciprocity. These relations included enabling, transformative, and disabling elements. This may have been possible because of the distinctly intersubjective and relational nature of Team Boystown's project, which focused on long-term, durational relationships and engagement in each other's lives. This engagement led to strong attachments between some missionaries and sex workers, relationships that were described in terms of love, friendship, and kinship. They also contained dramas, jealousies, and conflicts, as most close-knit human relationships do.

Conclusion

"Vice is ending because God is mad. No clients come to visit us. We are completely alone."

Eva said this to Lucía and me in March 2009 as the three of us stood in her doorway gazing upon the empty streets of la zona. Her comments suggest a feeling of isolation stemming from the abandonment by clients, by God, and perhaps by the state. Missionaries and an anthropologist would eventually leave her, too. Eva and Lucía both suggested that the paucity of clients in Boystown was caused by God's anger toward sexual sin. In Boystown, both prostitution and drug use were considered "vices." While God was apparently ending the "vice" of prostitution, drug organizations that catered to the "vice" of drugs were gaining power inside and outside of the prostitution zone. Casting the blame for social ills on vice resonates with neoliberalism's tendency to blame individuals for their fates while ignoring the social forces that shape them. Eva's words suggest that God's anger was directed toward people like *her*, one of the many instances in which sex workers grappled with the deeply gendered politics of blame. If Eva suggests that God's anger was sparked by the sale of sex for money, does this imply that Reynosa's narco violence was evidence of his wrath, a way to punish sexual sin? I doubt that Eva would make this argument, yet her comments reflect an internalization of the whore stigma.

This was only one of the many instances in which people blamed the most powerless for social problems. Reynosa, like many border cities, has seen radical changes in the past decades. It has grown substantially due to the influx of internal migrants who work at maquiladoras. It has also become militarized, and inundated by drugs and run by drug traffickers. In Reynosa, while nearly everyone was afraid of being killed by narcos, and people of every class whispered rumors about narcos, everyone frequently and loudly complained about veracruzanos and Central Americans. The coexistence with, and prominent discursive rise of, the social other of the veracruzano during an era of increased drug violence indicates how gossip served as a racialized outlet for social anxieties. If the drug industry and the maquiladora industries were fueling the economies of border cities, then why did locals blame veracruzanos—maquiladora workers and other migrants—for the city's problems? Perhaps this scapegoating happened because locals were afraid to openly criticize drug cartels. It also allowed them to blame moral and "cultural" problems on nonlocals and distance themselves from the "backstage" produced by prostitution, drug trafficking, and the maquiladora industry. For the Reynosa bourgeoisie, poor brown women engaging in transactional sex were even more marked with the whore stigma than registered sex workers because they were "not public women" and thus not regulated the way sex workers were. Anxiety placed upon nonlocal bodies, bodies that indexed ties to other geographical spaces and that were moved to the border by global capital, called attention away from violence and sources of anxiety that were more locally grounded. These were also the bodies most likely to be found in mass graves.

Ideologies of value reaffirmed the power dynamics concerning the image of the narco and that of the whore/migrant: while narcos were feared, respected, and thought of as near-celebrities, internal migrants marked with the whore stigma were thought to bring cultural ruin to the city. Local elites' anxiety surrounding working-class women and men in Reynosa, while seemingly evidence of regional rivalry, was in fact a way to distance themselves from racialized indigeneity as well as posit Reynosa as a metropole. In this case, a fractalization served to erase the racialized elements and to frame the critique as a regional one.

In Reynosa, as in many diverse contexts around the world, the whore stigma and other forms of judgment against racialized, gender-deviant, and poor people also create different kinds of value. For example, Donald Trump's 2016 presidential campaign drew upon moral panic surrounding Mexicans as criminals, rapists, and "bad hombres." These discourses created value by propping up white supremacy, justifying forms of economic domination and violence, and creating profit in the form of private detention facilities, border walls, and all of the lucrative aspects of the war on drugs. What got erased from these discussions was the way in which the United States has strengthened Mexican drug cartels and taken part in actions that have widened the wealth gap in Mexico. The United States has played an important role in helping to create violence and instability in Mexico and Central America, profiting from it, and placing blame on the other side of the border. The association of Mexicans with violence and criminality creates profit for some, while migrants die in the desert and in drug wars.

The whore stigma and other forms of racialized judgment also created value for a variety of people in Reynosa. Drug organizations profited from sex workers' weekly fees and used them as protesters against the Mexican military. When I asked Eva why the drug organization forced sex workers to march on the front lines, she said, "Because we shouldn't be here. We shouldn't be doing this." Even though sex workers' actions were legal, they understood them to be morally ambiguous in a way that allowed drug organizations to capitalize on the whore stigma. Missionaries' projects created value through the whore stigma through stories of Jesus granting redemption to sex workers. These stories also countered the whore stigma by making sex workers seem more human to outsiders. The whore stigma was racialized through the categories of veracruzana and *padrotera*, which also created value for those who employed it against others. For sex workers, the violence of the whore stigma was in tension with the potential economic benefit of using the border to create value. The only benefit that some sex workers received from the whore stigma was the relative boost in status of putting others down. Many of these parties also relied upon sex workers' obligations as mothers. Both sex workers and missionaries reproduced the whore stigma in their investment of the normative bond between mother and child and their fear that children would one day become sex workers.

Eva's comments about the end of vice point more directly to three sources of agency or blame: sex workers (supposedly the source of vice), God himself (the agent), and the drug organizations that emptied the streets of Boystown. The projects of sex workers and missionaries were intertwined in complex ways with multiple sovereigns. The actions undertaken by state actors and drug organizations sometimes enabled their projects and sometimes hindered them. While sex workers and missionaries imagined God to be more powerful than either state actors or narcos, drug organizations had the capacity to cut short their projects, as well as their lives. Battles for sovereignty between state and nonstate actors during the drug war also influenced ideas of personal sovereignty. People who might have previously understood themselves as autonomous agents in control of their destinies were forced to reevaluate this idea in relation to fear of drug violence. Drug cartels shaped subjectivity in Reynosa not only for those less empowered, like sex workers and Central American migrants, but also for all kinds of people, including American missionaries and sex tourists, who were historically empowered to feel relatively safe in border cities. Both American missionaries and sex tourists not only were afraid of drug-related violence but also relied upon contacts with cartel members to securely go about their projects. Missionaries and sex workers had some sort of relations with drug cartels because they worked in cartel territory. Some also had intimate ties and friendships with them. When Stacy befriended a drug dealer/pimp in la zona, she saw this as a sign of God, and this friendship would lead the way to many more contacts in Boystown. According to this logic, God could work through members of the same drug organization that was terrorizing the local population.

The US-Mexico border creates difference that can be transformed into different kinds of value. This book has shown how the capacity to create such value factored into rendering a Mexican border city a destination for migrants' projects. Reynosa turned from a site of hope to a site of fear for many of its migrants. After the December 2007 flooding of Reynosa with soldiers, locals experienced a heightened sense of insecurity and threat of violence which I observed in my fieldwork from August 2008 to August 2009. The threat intensified further during the six months after I left Reynosa in August 2009, because two cartels that had worked together in Reynosa (the Gulf Cartel and the Zetas) split and battled over territory. While I was in Reynosa, the city was more associated with drug trafficking than many other cities in the region. Young men who traveled to nearby cities said that others often thought they were narcos. When I was in Reynosa, sex workers also felt that they had the option of returning to their places of origin to feel safer. But in the months and years that followed, many of their own hometowns began to resemble Reynosa.

While drug cartels had already been embedded in border cities for some time, the militarization of the border strengthened the power of drug trafficking organizations in relation to Reynosa's residents. The intensification of the power of drug organizations following militarization blurred these lines of differentiation in ways that made many migrants' projects untenable. While earning money through the trafficking of drugs, which was one part of the "vice" economy and the economy in general in Reynosa, cartels increasingly became embedded in every aspect of social and economic life. The Central American migrant might have been the inverse of the narco, rumored to be killed by narcos and then thrown into a mass grave. Central Americans might have been the subjects on which cartels tested their techniques of domination. Eventually, the differences that separated Mexicans from Central Americans and US passport holders became less clear as more and more people worried they would become corpses dumped into mass graves. All actions were interpreted as cartel actions, at least judging by the rumors that circulated. The intensification of cartel power led to the breakdown of prior ways of thinking about intimacy, agency, and value.

This, in turn, shaped the projects, businesses, and subjectivities of Reynosa residents. The economic projects of drug organizations and the projects of state actors with various forms of involvement with cartels shaped the ability for both missionaries and sex workers to create value from the difference of the US-Mexico border. These changes in Reynosa had direct effects on the projects of a number of residents of and visitors to Reynosa. The thwarted flow of tourists into Reynosa made the projects of those who depended upon the tourist economy, including sex workers, more difficult. Once narcos became the key actors in Reynosa, the forms of difference that were previously used toward value-making projects became blurred. The projects that brought migrants to Reynosa—creating value through fostering intimate ties—became unsustainable. Most of the sex workers who migrated to Reynosa did so because they could make more money there than in their places of origin. This was far more tenable when there were American tourists spending dollars and Mexican clients spending pesos. Years later, many sex workers in Boystown were barely able to pay their bills because there were so few clients, and so they left.

Stories were a means through which border residents spread intimacy and terror and created value, and these stories were often circulated beyond Reynosa. A variety of border residents shared stories about drug violence. Sex workers shared rumors about themselves and their children being sold in parts or wholes to Americans, demonstrating anxieties about the value and the fate of their bodies in relation to US capital and drug trafficking organizations. They also circulated narratives about one another to posit themselves as better mothers. Missionaries collected and circulated stories of sex workers and God that they spread throughout the English-speaking world. These stories created different kinds of value—they bolstered the power of drug organizations, allowed some sex workers to gain respectability, and helped missionaries feel closer to God.

For johns, missionaries, and sex workers alike, getting a little piece of the value produced by the difference the border creates became much more difficult. In this case, the local manifestation of the intensified power of drug cartels in a border city not only generated anxiety but also made the moral, intimate, and economic projects of people in Reynosa much more difficult to achieve. Although the soldiers and federal police sent by President Calderón likely impacted the business of the drug cartels, cartels made sure that Reynosa's residents would pay the price for the drug war. Militarization not only worsened violence throughout Mexico but also perhaps strengthened drug organizations as they wove fear into the nation's social fabric.

Team Boystown members moved back to Tulsa and South Africa. Stacy and her husband now have three children and do not plan to live in Reynosa. She works as a real estate agent. When Stacy left Reynosa, she gave her property along with the building that was to be her "modern-day monastery" to another mission project that helped build it. That organization has converted the property into a school for the deaf. While Ashley would have liked to continue Stacy's project and realize God's dream for a monastery there, it was not possible, as the mission that owns the property did not believe it to be tenable to have a transitional house for drug addicts and sex workers occupy the same space as a school for the deaf. Ashley is working as a barista in Tulsa and is active with a 24-7 community there, hoping to create another team to continue the project in Reynosa. She hopes to return with a program for drug and alcohol addiction in la zona and in Aquiles Serdán. She has also since gotten married and had a child, and she visits Reynosa every few years. Eleanor has contemplated other mission projects working with sex workers but stated that she will not return to live in Reynosa.

Months after both they and I had left Reynosa, I met up with Sofía and Rebecca separately in Mexico City. They were no longer working in prostitution, and both emphasized that what they missed the most about Reynosa was the money they earned there. As Rebecca and I walked through the streets of Mexico City, she entered almost every shop we passed, browsing through clothing and jewelry, pointing out all of the things that she liked and looking at the prices. She said that remembering Reynosa saddened her as she no longer had money. But she seemed to have lost the hope that she had invested in Reynosa's prostitution zone to transform her sexual labor into profit that could then be transformed into commodities and more durable forms of value like property or a business. Just as for missionaries, for her Reynosa was no longer a place that held the possibility of the kinds of project that had once taken her there.

Lucía remains free of drugs and continues taking care of her granddaughter, Luz, whom I remain in contact with through social media. She sometimes writes to me with news of Lucía or reports on gun battles near or inside of la zona. Luz is very vocal about her queerness on social media, and I wonder how Lucía is taking the news. I am newly in touch with Cubana, who has been sober since 2011. She managed to spend a month in Cuba, and is now living in Mexico City and working at a restaurant.

Eva is the only sex worker without a drug addiction that I know of who continued to live in la zona for many years after the missionaries left. She had managed to save some money she hoped to use to buy a plot of land and build a house. In 2010 she was diagnosed with uterine cancer and had to use the money to get a hysterectomy. She didn't work for months after that, and she told me she only survived because some older men who were frequent clients continued giving her food and small amounts of money. This was one of several periods in Eva's life in which clients took care of her when she was sick. Because of other health complications, Eva retired from sex work but continued to live in her room in Boystown and sell drinks at a bar inside la zona. She eventually became manager of the bar and was in charge of collecting rent from several rooms for the owners of a particular block of la zona.

During my reunion with them after we had all left Reynosa, Eva and Sofía talked about God and prayer much more often than they had in the past. This may have been the influence of the missionaries, or perhaps an effect of their increasingly dire situation as the violence of the drug war intensified. Both times that Sofía's son was missing, she said that she prayed for his return. When I reunited with Eva in 2011, she told me that one sex worker had recently had her fingers chopped off and another's daughter was delivered to her mother chopped up in small pieces. She told me of a friend of hers who, along with her husband and children, was dissolved in a barrel of acid. She also told me of witnessing dead bodies splayed all over the city, full of blood, and said it was like living in a war zone, like the one she escaped during the Civil War in El Salvador in the 1980s. I asked Eva if she thought there was anything that could be done to improve the security in Mexico. She told me that she didn't think so, and that all we could do was pray that God would keep her safe.

God didn't keep Eva safe. Eva now has twelve grandchildren, a number that startled me because in 2009 she was very worried about having a new mouth to feed. She is sick and her medicine is expensive. Eva finally left la zona in January 2018, but not of her own choice: she was kidnapped in the middle of the night from her room by people associated with a drug organization. Eva was blindfolded for a week without food or water, and she was threatened, humiliated, and interrogated. She was finally thrown on the side of the road. She was able to borrow money from friends to get to her daughter in central Mexico. Eva lost all of the phone numbers in the phone she left behind when kidnapped, but her daughter was able to get in contact with several missionaries and with me through social media. She can no longer work in la zona because she is afraid of being killed if she goes back. Missionaries and I raised money to help her during this difficult time. Many of my friends and family members pitched in. Eva had planned to cross the border to work as a live-in housecleaner on the US side of the border, but she has abandoned that plan on learning that the smuggling fee has doubled.

Eva's kidnapping was part of a larger set of conflicts surrounding Reynosa's prostitution zone. Her kidnappers claimed that the bar where she was working was trafficking women, and they interrogated her about her role in this while physically abusing her. She swore to them that she did not traffic women. Eva told me that the part of la zona she worked in was shut down because it was illegally owned by the mayor of Reynosa. I found newspaper articles from news sources outside of Reynosa reporting that the husband of Reynosa's current mayor was a co-owner of that block of bars and rooms. An investigative reporter who lives in Mexico City brought attention to the case, implicating the mayor in sex trafficking, sex slavery, child prostitution, and ties with a drug organization. The mayor took to Twitter to try to clear her husband's reputation.

This Mexico City–based journalist also appealed to the respectability politics of his fellow Mexican audience by highlighting an international audience and international participants in the sex industry in his report. The journalist cited footage from the documentary film *Whore's Glory*, made by an Austrian filmmaker, to support his argument that women were trafficked. He and other journalists referred to American clients visiting la zona, and many articles called la zona Disneylandia. He denounced corruption in la zona, emphasizing US participation in the Mexican border brothel while highlighting Mexican corruption and vice.

While this reporter might have meant to help sex workers, he actually made their lives more difficult. Another example of actions that claim to help sex workers are the US house bills that became law in the United States in April 2018—the Stop Enabling Sex Traffickers Act (SESTA) and Allow States and Victims to Fight Online Sex Trafficking Act (FOSTA). These laws have put sex workers at risk by shutting down online spaces where they formerly found and screened clients. Laws like this make sex work more dangerous and increase risks of violence and death. Governmental and nongovernmental organizations, the religious right, and radical feminists unite in creating a moral panic surrounding prostitution that materializes in legislation which makes sex workers' lives more difficult and dangerous. In rumors, news stories, and firsthand accounts a variety of people, including many who claim to help them, blame the most vulnerable populations for larger social problems.

My findings offer further evidence for the value of an ethnographic approach to understanding hostile situations like drug war zones, where freedom of the press is compromised and survey data or brief interviews would not yield the textured data and analysis of long-term research. My analysis contributes to a growing body of literature demonstrating how the most vulnerable populations suffer the consequences of "wars" against drugs, crime, or terrorism, and showing how these wars are waged on those who are poor, racially marked, and violating gender norms.

La zona fostered both violence and safety for sex workers, and relations both enabling and disabling. Boystown allowed sex workers to be the object of surveillance of state actors, drug organizations, and foreign missionaries who all claimed to be acting with the well-being of sex workers in mind. Moreover, these parties leveraged sex workers' gendered obligations as sex workers and as mothers. Sex workers were made visible by the architectural structure of la zona. It also allowed them to judge each other's behavior. The spatial features of la zona also increased sex workers' vulnerability to drug organizations. The enclosed walls trapped them inside, and an apparatus was in place to collect money from them. However, because they knew people there who might defend them if necessary, a security apparatus was in place in part for their protection, and they would not be harassed by the police for practicing prostitution there, sex workers preferred working inside rather than outside of la zona.

La zona fostered surveillance and vulnerability as well as their queer intimacies with one another, with clients, with members of drug organizations, and with missionaries. Some of these relations were described as family-like, some involved sex, and some involved coercion, love, and obligation. Borders are thought of as having two sides, but this book has shown some of the many relationships that constitute the border by focusing upon groupings of three.

In the time and place of extreme inequality and violence that this book examines, love and obligation fueled the projects of migrants to border cities. Most of these migrants then entered into new relations of love and obligation in Reynosa, some of which endured after they left it. Love and violence are no more dichotomous than the border itself. The whore stigma is often used to justify the murder of sex workers and other "disreputable" women. But it is reproduced, as well as contested, by people who love sex workers, including other sex workers and missionaries. And while mine is not an in-depth study of narcos, one could suspect that many of the people enacting violence are also propelled by love and obligation. Love and intimacy are not complete others to obligation, stigma, violence, and coercion. They are often tied up in the same relationships. There are important reasons for criticizing the actions of missionaries who seek to change racial and economic others. I hope that this book has shown that to only paint sex workers as victims to missionaries, at least in this case, would be to overlook many of the other complicated dynamics that occur, including friendship and love. In some cases, both missionaries and sex workers claimed that the other helped them to feel closer to God. My ethnography suggests a conceptualization of love that is nonsovereign, and full of obligations; people who loved each other often also put immense pressure upon each other and shaped each other's lives in ways they could not control. Love in Reynosa's drug war was forged in context of stark inequalities and violence, and it often contained coercion, but it often gave people connection, comfort, and hope. I suspect the dynamics of love examined herein are not unique to la zona, though, and there is more to learn by centering love in other complicated times and places.

Notes

Introduction

1. In the interest of the privacy and security of my interlocutors, all names have been changed, with the exception of two people who asked me to use their given names.

2. A local *cronista* who had written books on the history of Reynosa had referred to prostitution as "el vicio" in an interview with me. The book is peppered with instances in which sex workers and former sex workers referred to prostitution, drug use, and excessive alcoholism as "vicio." There is historical evidence of other activities being referred to as vices in Mexico—namely, gambling (Garza 2007, 34), male homosexuality (Nesvig 2000), masturbation (Nesvig 2000), and political corruption (Lomnitz 2000). Vice is a term sometimes used by the Catholic Church and in legal documents.

3. The label "cisgender," as opposed to "transgender," describes people "who have a match between the gender they were assigned at birth, their bodies, and their personal identity" (Schilt and Westbrook 2009, 461). Trans and gender-nonconforming sex workers were not allowed to work in la zona and worked a few blocks away on Aldama Street. Local men engaged in transphobic discourses about how it was easy to be "tricked by *travestis*" who passed for, and were often more beautiful than, cis women. In the remainder of this book, the terms "women" and "men" denote cis women and men unless otherwise stated.

4. The study's participants almost never distinguished between Gulf Cartel members and Zetas during the time of my fieldwork (and thus in the examples included in this book). They are more likely to make such distinctions now, because the two groups have made efforts to differentiate themselves since splitting up.

5. Stacy explained that prayer walking, which is referred to as praying "on site within sight," is most prevalent in places that are not open to evangelism.

6. The term "Team Boystown" was first used jokingly by the missionaries but later came to be used seriously. Missionaries referred to the group as "the team" or "our team," but I refer to them as "Team Boystown" for clarity and continuity.

7. Border-crossing journeys in such places are more dangerous due to great stretches of desert and extended heat exposure. Between the beginning of the

Southwest Border Strategy in 1994 and 2005, the number of migrants found dead on the border doubled (Government Accountability Office 2006). The increasing power of drug organizations over major migration routes made these journeys even more dangerous.

8. Neoliberal ideologies assert that individual freedoms should be liberated through strong private property rights, free trade, and free markets. These ideas have also underpinned policies that richer countries coerced poorer countries to implement under economic duress. In the early 1980s, many formerly colonized countries owed more than $700 billion to European, US, and Japanese banks. Due to a worldwide recession, they were unable to pay back their debts. Economists in Washington, DC, came up with a solution: give these countries new loans (from the World Bank and the International Monetary Fund) so that they could keep paying their debts. But these loans came with conditions called structural adjustment— the borrowing countries were required to enact policies that supposedly made their economies more efficient. Some of these conditions included reducing or removing trade barriers, removing restrictions on foreign investment in industrial production and financial services, as well as privatizing some state-owned industries. These policies facilitated US and international corporations' access to low-cost labor, tax breaks, and virtually duty-free crossing of goods with little regulation.

9. Neo-Marxists like James J. Biles explain that the surge in informal employment is "a livelihood strategy that allows house-holds to cope with the vagaries of neoliberalized labor markets in which work is poorly remunerated and precarious, rather than scarce" (Biles 2008, 552).

10. While southern Mexicans were discriminated against in border cities, Central American migrants lived in constant fear. Due to their extralegal status, Central American migrants were more vulnerable to abuse by policemen and drug organizations during their journeys across the southern border, throughout Mexico, and in northern border cities (Kovic and Kelly 2006).

11. Under Calderón, the number of murders documented by the Mexican statistics agency INEGI rose from 8,867 in 2007 to 27,213 in 2011 (Molzahn, Rios, and Shirk 2013, 1).

12. Calderón's war included investigating the police force in Reynosa, taking their guns away for nineteen days, and forcing policemen to provide voice samples to compare with recordings of threats made over police radio (Roig-Franzia 2008). This led to finger pointing; a Reynosa police chief claimed that the military investigation of the police force was futile, and that corruption and collusion could instead be found in the state police, federal police, and military (Roig-Franzia 2008). Twelve signs accusing government officials of protecting rival cartels were hung in public places in Reynosa and other border cities in August 2008 containing messages such as, "Mr. Calderón, if you want to stop crime, start with your corrupt cabinet" (Taylor 2008).

13. My conception of value has been influenced by Nancy Munn's theorization of value as that which a group sees as essential to their community vitality and seeks to expand or extend through action (Munn 1986). Munn's conception of value is especially useful because it attends to not only the social forms that represent value but also the human actions that materialize value. Furthermore, Munn draws attention to practices through which humans "construct their social world, and simultaneously their own selves and modes of being in the world" (7). Munn's theory

of value allows me to attend to the social, material, and intersubjective aspects of value—focusing upon the way that people represent the importance of their actions to themselves, actions that invest time and energy in both objects and relations. David Graeber notes that Munn's conceptualization of value as "the way people represent the importance of their own actions to themselves" allows for an analysis transcending the gift/commodity dichotomy. This is because it accounts for the human investment in the production and maintenance of both objects and social relations (Graeber 2001, 45).

14. For example, Georg Simmel argued that prostitution led to the "mutual degradation" of all parties involved, linking the "essence of prostitution" to the "nature of money itself" and arguing that both led to indifference and the lack of attachment (1978 [1900]), 414; see also 1971).

15. Viviana Zelizer argues that prostitution is suspect in many situations, in part because it is often assumed that monetary transactions and intimate relationships are not only separate but also mutually corrupting. Zelizer argues that the intermingling of intimate relationships and monetary transactions, far from being limited to cases that are generally considered to be prostitution, are actually widespread (Zelizer 2000). Susan Gal's semiotic analysis helps us to see that this division between the intimate and economic is linked to the distinction between public and private, which are both coconstituting cultural categories and indexical signs that can be used to categorize nearly anything and employed as tools for arguments about the social world (Gal 2002).

16. Arlie Hochschild conceptualized emotional labor to explain how certain jobs require workers to induce or suppress feelings in order to give the appearance of having the correct feelings for a particular job or to induce the correct feelings in other people (Hochschild 2003 [1983]). While Hochschild conducted research among flight attendants and bill collectors for Delta Airlines, she noted that many other jobs sometimes require emotional labor, such as those of nannies, secretaries, prostitutes, and nurses. While she reserved the term "emotional labor" for situations in which this work is sold for a wage (and has exchange value), she used the terms "emotion work" and "emotion management" to refer to "private" situations in which these acts have use-value (7).

17. The base price for sex, one hundred pesos (about $8 US), covered penetration in the missionary position. If the client wanted a sex worker to remove her clothes or wanted additional sexual positions or sex acts, he had to negotiate extra fees beforehand. This pricing system is common in other parts of Mexico. If a client was paying in dollars, they would usually be charged ten dollars as the base price.

18. Laws against pimping and brothel keeping can be used against sex workers' family members who might live off of their wages or with sex workers who share living arrangements. The criminalization of third parties leads to the prosecution of sex workers and their friends and family members, limits sex workers' access to housing, and compromises the safety of sex workers (NSWP Global Network of Sex Worker Projects 2016).

19. In Mexico City, between 1863 and 1926 women who regularly had sex with more than one partner (presumably whether or not they charged for sex) were required to "have their photographs taken, give their names and addresses to sanitary authorities, and undergo periodic gynecological examinations to check for signs of syphilis or other contagious genital afflictions" (Bliss 2001, 15). The conflation of sex

workers and women with multiple sexual partners is not specific to the US-Mexico border or to Mexico.

20. The concept of intersectionality was developed by black feminists in the United States who found that black women suffered from particular kinds of oppression and discrimination that were addressed by neither race nor gender-based rights movements. Although they did not use the term "intersectionality," the Combahee River Collective stated in 1977 that "the major systems of oppression are interlocking" in reference to "racial, sexual, heterosexual, and class oppression" (1986). Legal scholar Kimberlé Crenshaw (1989) coined the term to show how black women were subject to employment discrimination in ways that exceeded the legal definitions of both race and sex. Since Crenshaw, the term has expanded to look at many axes of oppression.

21. A former Chihuahua state public prosecutor, Arturo Gonzalez Rascon, exemplified this when he told the newspaper *El Diario* in February 1999, "Women who have a night life, go out late and come into contact with drinkers are at risk. It's hard to go out on the street when it's raining and not get wet" (Grinberg 2004).

22. Even victims' families were harassed by and implicated in the supposed sexual deviance of their daughters. Wright provides accounts of activists and victims' families being heckled, receiving death threats, and almost being beaten with baseball bats. Mothers of disappeared women were called whores and told that their daughters were whores (Wright 2004, 378).

23. As Eng, Halberstam, and Muñoz (2005) paraphrase Warner, "Attention to those hegemonic social structures by which certain subjects are rendered 'normal' and 'natural' through the production of 'perverse' and 'pathological' others, Warner insists, rejects a 'minoritizing logic of toleration or simple political interest-representation in favor of a more thorough resistance to regimes of the normal'" (2005, 3).

24. Patty Kelly's *Lydia's Open Door* examines a *zona de tolerancia* similar in structure to the one in Reynosa. Kelly frames the zona in Tuxla, Chiapas, in the context of government efforts to present a "modern" Mexico through notions of social control and hygiene by regulating the sexual behavior of poor women who engage in sex work, which stigmatizes them. Some of the dynamics described in Kelly's ethnography are similar to those in Reynosa—in terms of the spatial layout of the prostitution zone, the reasons for which women entered the sex industry, and the challenges they incurred in negotiating their stigmatized labor with obligations to family members and to each other. Reynosa's prostitution zone nevertheless differs from the one in Chiapas in that it has a much longer history and reflects some of the particularities of its location on the US-Mexico border, namely the overwhelming presence of drug organizations as well as drugs, and of Americans who cross the border, including missionaries.

25. Collier and Yanagisako state, "Although it is apparent that heterosexual intercourse, pregnancy, and parturition are involved in human reproduction, it is also apparent that producing humans entails more than this" (1987, 31). They argue that gender and kinship are relevant to not only the production of people but also the production of things.

26. Weiner argues that "the reproduction of social relations is never automatic, but demands work, resources, energy, and the kind of attention that continually

drains resources from more purely political endeavors," and that kinship is "a decisive marker and maker of value" (Weiner 1992, 4).

27. Evelyn Brooks Higginbotham coined the term "the politics of respectability" (1993) to describe how low-income black women in the Baptist church fought for civil rights in part through showing the world that they were worthy of respect by exhibiting qualities of cleanliness, sexual purity, and temperance. But an unintended consequence of holding themselves to these standards was leaving out people who could not uphold them. While showing it was not Higginbotham's original intention, scholars and activists have emphasized the political dangers of respectability politics. Cathy Cohen argued in the 1990s that people like drug users, HIV-positive people, and sex workers were ignored by black leaders who sought respectability at the expense of the most marginalized (Cohen 1999). The term is now primarily used to emphasize how people both in dominant and marginalized groups alike police marginalized people by the norms of the dominant group. These norms might include manners of dress, speech, and sexual behavior.

28. The concept of transactional sex has been used in African studies (Hunter 2002; Cole 2004) to describe relationships that involve material and sexual exchanges. The concept was developed in part to distance conversations from prostitution's stigmatized nature because Africans were already racialized and stigmatized (Cole and Thomas 2009, 9). Researchers in public health and epidemiology tend to employ the term to encompass all kinds of sex-for-something transactions, including money. Here I use the term "transactional sex" to distinguish it from the relations that people categorize as prostitution. Emily Wentzell (2014) uses the framework to analyze relationships in central Mexico between older men using erectile dysfunction drugs and their *amiguitas*, who are often single mothers for whom they buy gifts and provide financial support in exchange for sex and companionship.

29. For several reasons, it is important not to reproduce this idea of victimhood. First, many sex workers would disagree that they are victims. Second, discourses of sex worker victimhood underlie paternalistic policies that limit their capacities to migrate and work safely and legally under the guise of "protecting" them. Finally, as Anne McClintock argues, people who are categorically assumed to be victims are more likely to be victimized (1992).

30. Patchen Markell argues that "the desire for sovereignty is impossible to fulfill, because it is itself rooted in a misrecognition of the basic conditions of human activity" (2003, 22). Anthropologist Danilyn Rutherford similarly states that "to dream of sovereignty is to dream of overcoming one's dependence on others," which she calls an impossible dream (Rutherford 2012, 21). Anthropologist Holly Wardlow's theorization of "positive" and "negative" agency also does important work toward conceptualizing agency outside of the liberal framework (Wardlow 2006). Sharon Krause theorizes nonsovereign agency as "socially distributed agency" (2015) and Lauren Berlant has written about "lateral agency" (2011a). Berlant's discussion of the nonsovereignty of love, specifically, and of social relationships, more generally, inform my ideas (Berlant and Hardt 2011; Berlant 2011b). Most political theorists have built upon the works of Hannah Arendt to theorize nonsovereign agency (Markell 2003; Zerilli 2005; Krause 2015), but most anthropologists and cultural theorists begin with different sources.

31. While Catholic missionaries have been in Mexico since the time of the

Spanish invasion, Protestantism was not tolerated until 1857 (Baldwin 1990, 3), and the non-Catholic minority has remained relatively small. There has been a Protestant presence in Mexico since the late nineteenth century (Bastian 1990; Baldwin 1990; Bowen 1996, cited in Cahn 2005, 3), but self-identified evangelicals were fewer than 2 percent of the Mexican population until 1980, when they reached 3.3 percent; they had grown to 7 percent by 2000 (Cahn 2003, location 92). Evangelicals in Mexico have been less involved in political struggles than have proponents of Liberation theology, a progressive wing of Catholicism (for a study investigating some of the reasons why evangelicals have been less involved in politics, see Bonicelli 1993). Liberation theology was born in 1968 in a meeting of Latin American bishops in Colombia (Norget 1997, 101). A movement for the "church of the poor" steeped in Catholic ideologies, Marxism, and socialism, it empowered poor people to fight for their own liberation (Norget 1997, 101). Team Boystown missionaries, while seeing their project as concerned with "social justice," were not actively involved in political struggles. While their project was political in the sense that they sought to create a different kind of social world, they built personal relationships with and through sex workers and God rather than through transforming society.

32. Stacy read books by and attended talks of Shane Claiborne, a pioneer in the New Monasticism movement and the founder of The Simple Way, a Christian intentional community in Philadelphia that lives among and publicly advocates for the poor and homeless.

33. In *Punk Monk: The New Monasticism and the Ancient Art of Breathing*, Andy Freeman and Pete Greig, who are founding members of 24-7 and friends of Stacy's, advocate prayer and monasticism as revolutionary. Stacy's project is described in the book as an example of the "danger" and transformative power of prayer, because she prayed to God to send someone to Boystown and the "someone" he sent was herself, changing her life as well as those of the residents of Boystown.

34. 24-7 Prayer started with a student-led prayer vigil in 1999 in Chichester, England. Participants who set up institutions connected to the 24-7 Network can either create Prayer Rooms, physical spaces reserved for continuous or regular intervals of prayer, often in shifts; or Boiler Rooms, which are "missional communities inspired by ancient Celtic monasticism" focusing upon prayer, mission, and justice.

35. Stacy later became more officially affiliated with 24-7, and she and her team members were featured on the 24-7 website. In fact, the affiliation extended to the bureaucratic: when Stacy filed paperwork in Reynosa to start a nonprofit organization and buy the land for the house, 24-7 Prayer Mexico was used as the name of her organization.

36. Unlike Stacy's project, which is atypically fluid and flexible, the mission for deaf children had a board of directors. They mixed the goals of evangelism with providing a service needed by the poor. None of the missionaries I interviewed felt that the deaf were especially their calling, but they saw a "need" because deaf students in Mexico were educated with hearing students and without special instruction, resulting in their often finishing school without the ability to read, write, or communicate.

37. While there is plenty of evidence of conflict between Catholics and Protestants in Latin America, my observations in Reynosa were much closer to the findings of Peter S. Cahn (2003), whose research focuses upon the relationships between peacefully coexisting evangelicals and Catholics in Tzintzuntzan, Michoacán. Cahn demonstrates that this peaceful coexistence was possible in part because Protestant

congregations accepted their followers' participation in political and ceremonial events to honor Catholic saints, contribute financially to local fiestas, and keep up ritual *compadrazgo* relationships. Cahn notes that the followers were often more tolerant than clergymen or pastors, and it is possible that if I would have conducted research on religious leaders, I would have seen more conflict than I did.

Chapter 1: *Dinero Fácil*

1. The concept of a moral economy was first developed to describe why peasants rebelled against practices that violated their norms about moral, proper, or just economic behavior (Thompson 1971; Scott 1976). The concept has been used primarily to analyze premarket societies, in contrast to "political economies" that are found in market societies (Booth 1994). This was a way that some analysts found to avoid imposing homo economicus upon premarket societies and describing "economic" behavior in situations where the "economy" was socially embedded. My argument does not rely upon a division between premarket and market societies, and in my ethnographic example, no such rebellions occurred. I follow Booth's suggestion that "all economies, including the near-to-pervasive-market economies, are moral economies, embedded in the (ethical) framework of their communities" (Booth 1994, 662).

2. While drug trafficking was not the focus of my research, I collected some data about it because of the important role it played in the daily lives of the people I observed and interviewed in Reynosa. Due to the sensitive and potentially dangerous nature of investigating drug trafficking, and because it was not the main focus of my research, my data is limited. Thus, any arguments I make about the drug industry are preliminary hypotheses that could be explored with future research.

3. Julie Chu's (2010) use of Goffman's concept of the moral career, which she uses to analyze the politics surrounding the expected mobilities of two kinds of subjects—"model overseas Chinese" and "peasants"—was influential to my analysis.

4. This genital contact, according to firsthand accounts, is only sometimes penetrative.

5. As these analysts point out in different ways, the invocation of sexualizing and racializing ideologies is often intimately tied to the political and economic contexts in which they circulate. For example, Stoler demonstrates that in several colonial contexts, concerns about protecting white women from "primitive" colonial men "intensified during real and perceived crises of control—provoked by threats to the internal cohesion of the European communities or by infringements on its borders" (Stoler 1997, 21).

6. Sociologist Erving Goffman used theater metaphors to make a point about how people present certain versions of themselves to the world versus what they do in private or try to hide—he called these the "front stage" and "back stage" (Goffman 1959).

7. I was always surprised that people spoke so freely of their hatred of Mexican Americans to me. People often asked me about my racial/ethnic background, and I always told them that I identify as Mexican American although I have a white father, and that Spanish was my mother's first language, but she did not teach it to me so I had to learn it in school. They never seemed to place me in the same category as

the Mexican Americans they disliked, although I was never sure if it was because of my education, my skin color, my accent in Spanish, which probably marks me as a non-native speaker, or the fact that I was born in San Antonio (a city that people in northern Mexico thought was beautiful).

8. Yen Le Espiritu found a similar phenomenon among Filipino migrants to the United States (Espiritu 2001). Espiritu argues that the construction of white women as sexually immoral and Filipinas as virtuous and chaste allowed Filipino migrants in the United States to resist racism by constructing themselves as morally superior to the dominant group. The kinds of racism that Espiritu describes this response to are parallel in some ways to those in the US-Mexico case, including racist and anti-immigrant discourses surrounding migrants and the association of Filipinas with prostitution (because of the sex industry catered toward US servicemen in the Philippines).

9. Schein notes that while notions of "the Other" imply a binary, "any given subject position can include relations to *more than one other*" and that the "significant other" can shift in different moments and contexts (1994, 450). Her analysis focuses upon Chinese identity in relation to white Westerners and rural and minority "internal others" who were seen as both more traditional and more backward in relation to elite Chinese.

10. Pablo Vila documents similar regional rivalries in Ciudad Juárez and El Paso (Vila 2000). For example, Vila describes that *chilango*, a term for residents of Mexico City that can be derogatory in certain contexts, is applied in Juárez not only to people from Mexico City but also at times to any person from the south (Vila 2000). According to Vila, southerners are generally seen as poor and lazy, while *chilangos* are also claimed to be clever, rude, and arrogant. Negative feelings toward *chilangos* reached an apex after the 1985 Mexico City earthquake when many displaced people from the city migrated north. Northerners felt "invaded," and bumper stickers appeared that stated, "If you are a patriot, kill a Chilango" (43).

11. Wright explains that in Juárez, a maquiladora manager told her that Mexican workers had to be given uniforms because without them the office had looked like one of the cantinas in the red-light district. Other managers made references to girls perhaps having second jobs at the bars (Wright 1998).

12. Similarly, someone from Juárez told Pablo Vila, "I get very mad . . . and I always . . . I don't know if all those who live here, who were born here, think, 'If I were a ruler, I'd stop all the arrival of people [from the interior of Mexico] here' . . . I mean control it . . . do it almost in the same manner as the United States is doing it, make a kind of border . . . now, I don't think like that, but for a long time, I blamed all the people that were coming here because of what they generated, like all those houses made out of cardboard . . . and it gets me very angry seeing so many people living without homes; I get angry seeing so much trash in my town and my house, and I blamed the people coming from other parts of Mexico, I would say, 'If they would not come, they would not dirty me . . .'" (Vila 2000, 35–36). Others that Vila interviewed associated migrants with crime, saying, "People really do go over there [to the US] to work! But those who can't make it, well they stay here and break the law, right?" (Vila 2000, 37).

13. Castañeda et al. also found similar statements in their interviews of female commercial sex workers in Mexico City (1996). Castañeda et al. argue that when sex workers refer to their work as a "necessary evil," this is a way for them to "res-

cue their work" because they perceive the double standard that allows male sexuality to be linked to "enjoyment, pleasure, and carnality" and link the sexuality of the "good woman" with "procreation and affection, instead of with desire" (Castañeda et al. 1996, 235).

14. Similarly, a sex worker interviewed by Castañeda et al. also said, "Thanks to us, there isn't so much rape" (1996, 236).

15. Chu also examines how the imagined mobility or stasis of different categories of persons was a part of their moral careers. She demonstrates how the state household registration system in China that classified certain subjects outside of rural areas as "peasants" not only officially limited their mobility but also shaped the expected kinds of mobilities of these subjects in ways that were sometimes naturalized as ontology. Chu demonstrates how conflicting ideas about moral careers were part of a "politics of destination" as people reiterated or contested the imagined trajectory of particular subjects from "fateful pasts" to their present and "future destinations" (Chu 2010, 96).

16. I have not been able to find other research or reports backing this claim about drug use to stay awake for twenty-four-hour shifts, but several newspaper reports have also mentioned cartels running their own rehabilitation centers (from which they forcibly recruit cartel members).

Chapter 2: Rumors of Violence and Feelings of Vulnerability

1. According to Campbell (2009, 23), a cartel uses bribes to gain loyalty from the military commander or head of federal police in a district. After loyalty has been purchased, soldiers and officers are used to protect storage facilities or drug lords. Furthermore, many members of drug organizations have ties to high-ranking politicians and officials in the government and military.

2. Michael Taussig (1984, 464) notes that a culture of terror is in part constituted "in the coils of rumor, gossip, story and chit-chat."

3. Scholars of language in context would argue that this is the case with most utterances and gestures (Silverstein 1993; Hall 1999). Austin suggests that perhaps all utterances are performative, to some degree.

4. Lauren Berlant (2011) argues that the present is always first experienced at the level of affect.

5. I believed most of the narco-stories discussed in this book and, given my difficulty discerning between when my fear was paranoid and when it was reasonable, my avoidance of assessing the truth-value of the narratives I analyze is perhaps even more crucial.

6. Some gun battles occurred between military and drug organizations and others between rival groups. Experts have suggested that Calderón's strategy of arresting kingpins fomented succession wars within major cartels and the splintering of groups, intensifying violence on the ground (Guerrero Gutiérrez 2011; Molzahn, Rios, and Shirk 2013).

7. In May 2010, 55 bodies of migrants were found in abandoned mines outside Mexico City; in July 2010, 51 corpses of migrants were found outside Monterrey (Ramsey 2011). In August 2010, 72 migrant corpses full of bullets were found in San Fernando, a town ninety miles south of Reynosa that was controlled by Zetas

(Associated Press 2011). In April 2011, 145 bodies were found in mass graves. Mexican authorities arrested 16 police officers and 17 Zetas in connection with the graves (Wilkinson 2011).

8. I have since found newspaper articles speculating that these were "narco-protests" (Lacey 2009).

9. Historically, the PRI political party used similar tactics to rig elections, offering poor people money or food and a ride in exchange for a vote (Lettieri 2014).

10. In February 2009, the US State Department advised Americans to avoid places associated with drugs and prostitution; by 2010 these advisories became more generalized warnings to avoid whole cities and states in Mexico when several Americans were killed.

Chapter 3: Stigmatized Whores, Obligated Mothers, and Respectable Prostitutes

1. *"La revición [sic] medica de las mujeres es una obligación no es un capricho yo me preocupo por tus hijos. Atentamente, Depto. de Sanidad."*

2. *"A veces nosotras, como mamas, tenemos la culpa."*

3. *"Lo que faltaba fue mi tiempo."*

4. Castañeda et al. (1996) discuss a double bind that sex workers in Mexico City face in relation to their roles as both prostitutes and mothers. Their analysis focuses upon the "social schizophrenia" that they argue characterize these women's lives. I will not make use of this term.

5. *Nadie sabe como es Liliana Margarita López Cabrera. Es la otra parte de la Cubana. Liliana es elegante, culta, respetuosa, humilde y sencilla. Es mucho mas para el que quiera es una gran amiga, la que estará pendiente de ti siempre. Liliana mantiene una tristeza tan grande dentro de ella que no permite que nadie a su alrededor viva su tristeza.*

6. She told me she had been there for thirty-two years, but a later version of her memoir states that she arrived in Reynosa in 1989.

7. Several other studies of sex workers have cited consumerism as a reason for sex work. Patty Kelly, for example, mentions that the ability to buy consumer goods is one of the reasons that sex workers in Chiapas continue to work (2008). When I was in la zona, women rarely discussed their ability to buy clothing, jewelry, and other items, but instead focused upon supporting their families, probably because that was part of how they defined themselves as respectable sex workers. However, subsequent conversations I have had with women who have left la zona suggest that spending power was also part of what kept them working.

8. Lola told me that she earned two hundred dollars an hour in Las Vegas, but she also started working when she was thirteen. Eva had worked as a *cuidadora* at clandestine brothels in Texas, where she said that each client paid sixty dollars and each sex worker got to keep half the amount. She was paid three hundred to four hundred dollars a week as a *cuidadora*, which she says was good money, but dangerous (because these brothels would sometimes be robbed by thieves or raided by the police) and boring (because one has to stay inside of the house working from 10 a.m. to 10 p.m.).

9. Patty Kelly found in la zona Galáctica in Tuxla, Chiapas, that only a dozen

out of 140 sex workers had pimps (Kelly 2008, 131), and Yasmina Katsulis reported that it was very rare for sex workers in Tijuana to have pimps (Katsulis 2009, 42).

10. Kelly also notes that because many of the women brought by pimps come from Puebla, the word *poblana* (which can be an adjective or noun to describe a person or thing from Puebla) in some cases became synonymous with the word "pimped" (Kelly 2008, 232).

11. Montiel Torres notes that while pimps started off pimping women from their own communities, they gradually started to recruit from other communities so as to avoid conflict in their towns (Montiel Torres 2009, 96–97).

12. My Mexican American grandparents got married in a very similar way in a small town in central Texas in the 1950s.

13. While Frida did not mention this, it is also very likely that Alejandro's house was large and extravagant, which would serve as further evidence that he was a pimp.

14. Other ethnographic accounts have confirmed that the pimp's mother often cares for children. Luísa María Calderón also notes that sometimes the pimp's first partner/prostitute looks after the children and takes on more of the household labor (Calderón 2001, cited in Montiel Torres 2009).

Chapter 4: "Sometimes We, as Mothers, Are to Blame"

1. Stacy told me that Ana (Lucía's daughter) has the timid demeanor that some say is attributed to internalized shame felt by "children of la zona." Stacy explained, "People have told them all their lives they're bastards. They're like street kids but not confident in the way that street kids usually are."

2. Chilango was also a drug addict and alcoholic. He has since died.

3. *"procreada por una pareja que de alguna manera estuvieron [sic] ligados [sic] con el ejercicio del oficio más antiguo del mundo."*

4. *"Yo pienso q en primer lugar no debo de vivir aqui (Z.R.). 'Me agovio' y en Segundo debo de conocer gente nueva convivir con gente normal q me haga sentir bien aunque si me pongo a reflexionar Tendría que desaserme de los personas q hasta ahora conozco."*

5. Luz's father was in jail for charges of rape because Ana was underage when Luz was conceived.

6. At the time I conducted fieldwork, the rule against children in Boystown was more strongly enforced, and there was even a sign prohibiting children at the entrance. When I would go to the prostitution zone with Lucía and her granddaughter, Luz, to visit Luz's mother, Luz had to stay at the entrance with the security guards.

7. In Mexican Spanish, *educada* is generally used to refer less to formal education and more to how well-mannered, polite, and "cultured" a person is.

Chapter 5: The Love Triad between
Sex Workers, Missionaries, and God

1. I do not believe that either Stacy or David tried specifically to recruit white people. But, based upon my observations, these are the people who joined them.

2. I use Nancy Munn's conception of value as that which a group sees as essential to their community vitality and seeks to expand or extend through action.

3. The baby, Olive, was sometimes referred to as a member of Team Boystown, but since she only lived in Reynosa for a couple of weeks and was an infant at the time, I do not count her as an official team member.

4. The now-defunct Kerista Commune invented the term "compersion."

5. Kockelman explains: "A sign stands for its object on one hand (a) and its interpretant on the other (b) in such a way as to bring the latter into a relation to the former (c) *corresponding* to its own relation to the former (a)" (Kockelman 2006, 81).

6. Munn's theoretical framework was deeply influenced by the ethnographic data she interpreted (Munn 1986), and there are limits to applying her framework to other ethnographic examples. However, I hope that an application of some of her concepts to my ethnographic data helps to demonstrate how missionaries create value through their actions. There are several important differences between my analysis and Munn's, including: 1) Among the Gawans, it is fame of people and of Gawa that are extended. In this case it is God's influence and fame that are to be expanded, not the fame of individuals. However, the fame of individuals was sometimes expanded. 2) The realm in which value transformation occurs is different. Among the missionaries, the scope of outward extension begins (and continues) into the spiritual realm. 3) Munn examines value in Gawa as functioning primarily dialectically, in terms of positive and negative transformations, while the missionary projects I observed and analyzed were primarily defined by positive value transformations.

7. Most of the missionaries I talked to about sex in Reynosa believed that God wanted them to abstain from all sexual contact until marriage. However, they emphasized God's grace in the case that this was not achieved.

8. In Team Boystown, for example, it was men who oversaw the construction work, while it was women who were focused upon "building relationships" with female sex workers (they also built relationships with some men inside and outside of la zona, mostly drug addicts). When I was living with missionaries, "the boys" tended to fix problems with our cars and apartments, while we baked them cakes for their birthdays. We ate many meals communally, and it was usually the job of "the boys" to grill meat, while female missionaries and I made salads and desserts. On several occasions, I saw female missionaries eating less meat, because they said that "the boys" needed it after a hard day of physical labor.

9. Stacy and her team members also shared their own stories with sex workers.

10. In my experience, the sex workers who used crack cocaine were much less concerned with keeping their names and identities a secret. In fact, when I interviewed her, Angeles asked me if I would put the interview on the Internet, and when I told her that I would not, she expressed disappointment.

Chapter 6: Love and Conflict in Sex Worker/Missionary Relationships

1. In most of my observations in both Reynosa and Mexico City, resistance in face-to-face interaction, especially when the interaction is marked by a class inequality, takes place in very subtle ways that usually involve the avoidance of telling

a person something it is perceived they do not want to hear, or of saying that something will happen later (*ahorita*, in a little while) or tomorrow, instead of indicating the improbability or impossibility of the action that is being discussed.

2. This is the same son who is now believed to be dead, but his body has not been found.

Bibliography

Aguilar, Rubén, and Jorge G. Castañeda. 2009. *El narco: la guerra fallida*. México, D.F.: Punto de Lectura.

Agustín, Laura María. 2007. *Sex at the Margins: Migration, Labour Markets and the Rescue Industry*. London and New York: Zed Books.

Ahmed, Sara. 2010. *The Promise of Happiness*. Durham, NC: Duke University Press.

Aizura, Aren Z. 2014. "Trans Feminine Value, Racialized Others and the Limits of Necropolitics." In *Queer Necropolitics*, edited by Jin Haritaworn, Adi Kuntsman, and Silvia Posocco, 129–148. New York: Routledge.

Alvarez, Maribel. 2003. "Made in Mexico: Souvenirs, Artisans, Shoppers, and the Meaning of Other 'Border-Type Things.'" PhD diss., University of Arizona.

Anapol, Deborah M. 1997. *Polyamory: The New Love without Limits: Secrets of Sustainable Intimate Relationships*. San Rafael, CA: IntiNet Resource Center.

Anderson, Ben. 2009. "Affective Atmospheres." *Emotion, Space and Society* 2 (2): 77–81.

Anderson, Joan B., and James Gerber. 2008. *Fifty Years of Change on the US-Mexico Border: Growth, Development, and Quality of Life*. Austin: University of Texas Press.

Andreas, Peter. 1995. "Free Market Reform and Drug Market Prohibition: US Policies at Cross-Purposes in Latin America." *Third World Quarterly* 16 (1): 75–87.

———. 1996. "US: Mexico: Open Markets, Closed Border." *Foreign Policy* no. 103: 51–69.

Anzaldúa, Gloria. 1987. *Borderlands/La Frontera: The New Mestiza*. San Francisco: Spinsters/Aunt Lute.

Associated Press. 2011. "Seventy-Two Bodies at Burial Site as Mexicans Seek Missing." April 8, 2011.

Austin, J. L. 1962. *How to Do Things with Words*. Cambridge: Harvard University Press.

Ayuntamiento Reynosa. 2005. Plan Municipal de Desarollo 2005-2007. reynosa.gob.mx/plan_municipal/plandedesarollo.pdf. Accessed August 24, 2008.

Bakewell, Elizabeth. 2010. *Madre: Perilous Journeys with a Spanish Noun*. New York: W. W. Norton & Co.

Baldwin, Deborah J. 1990. *Protestants and the Mexican Revolution: Missionaries, Ministers, and Social Change*. Urbana: University of Illinois Press.

Bashkow, Ira. 2006. *The Meaning of Whitemen: Race and Modernity in the Orokaiva Cultural World*. Chicago: University of Chicago Press.

Bastian, Jean Pierre, and Comisión de Estudios de Historia de la Iglesia en Latinoamérica. 1990. *Protestantes, liberales y francmasones: sociedades de ideas y modernidad en América Latina, siglo XIX*. Mexico: Comisión de Estudios de Historia de la Iglesia en América Latina: Fondo de Cultura Económica.

Bateson, Gregory, Don D. Jackson, Jay Haley, and John Weakland. 1956. "Toward a Theory of Schizophrenia." *Behavioral Science* 1 (4): 251–264.

Bennett, Herman L. 2009. *Colonial Blackness: A History of Afro-Mexico*. Bloomington: Indiana University Press.

Berlant, Lauren. 2008. "Thinking about Feeling Historical." *Emotion, Space and Society* 1 (1): 4–9.

———. 2011a. *Cruel Optimism*. Durham, NC: Duke University Press.

———. 2011b. "A Properly Political Concept of Love: Three Approaches in Ten Pages." *Cultural Anthropology* 26 (4): 683–691.

Berlant, Lauren, and Michael Hardt. 2011. "No One Is Sovereign in Love: A Conversation between Lauren Berlant and Michael Hardt." Interview by Heather Davis and Paige Sarlin. No More Potlucks. nomorepotlucks.org/site/no-one-is-sover eign-in-love-a-conversation-between-lauren-berlant-and-michael-hardt.

Bernstein, Elizabeth. 2007. *Temporarily Yours: Intimacy, Authenticity, and the Commerce of Sex*. Chicago: University of Chicago Press.

———. 2010. "Militarized Humanitarianism Meets Carceral Feminism: The Politics of Sex, Rights, and Freedom in Contemporary Antitrafficking Campaigns." *Signs* 36 (1): 45–71.

Bielo, James S. 2011. *Emerging Evangelicals: Faith, Modernity, and the Desire for Authenticity*. New York: New York University Press.

Biles, James J. 2008. "Informal Work and Livelihoods in Mexico: Getting By or Getting Ahead?" *Professional Geographer* 60 (4): 541–555.

Bliss, Katherine Elaine. 2001. *Compromised Positions: Prostitution, Public Health, and Gender Politics in Revolutionary Mexico City*. University Park: Pennsylvania State University Press.

Boellstorff, Tom. 2007. *A Coincidence of Desires: Anthropology, Queer Studies, Indonesia*. Durham, NC: Duke University Press.

Bonicelli, Paul J. 1993. "Serpent-Doves and Sons of Thunder in Mexico: Comparing the Politics of Latin American Evangelicals." PhD diss., University of Tennessee.

Booth, William James. 1994. "On the Idea of the Moral Economy." *American Political Science Review* 88 (3): 653–667.

Bornstein, Kate. 2013. *My New Gender Workbook: A Step-by-Step Guide to Achieving World Peace Through Gender Anarchy and Sex Positivity*. New York: Routledge.

Bowen, Kurt. 1996. *Evangelism and Apostasy the Evolution and Impact of Evangelicals in Modern Mexico*. Montreal: McGill-Queen's University Press.

Brennan, Denise. 2004. *What's Love Got to Do with It? Transnational Desires and Sex Tourism in the Dominican Republic*. Durham, NC: Duke University Press.

———. 2014. *Life Interrupted: Trafficking into Forced Labor in the United States*. Durham, NC: Duke University Press.

Briggs, Laura. 2002. *Reproducing Empire: Race, Sex, Science, and US Imperialism in Puerto Rico*. Berkeley: University of California Press.

Broughton, Chad. 2008. "Migration as Engendered Practice: Mexican Men, Masculinity, and Northward Migration." *Gender and Society* 22 (5): 568–589.

Butt, Leslie. 2005. "'Lipstick Girls' and 'Fallen Women': AIDS and Conspiratorial Thinking in Papua, Indonesia." *Cultural Anthropology* 20 (3): 412–441.

Cahn, Peter S. 2003. *All Religions Are Good in Tzintzuntzan: Evangelicals in Catholic Mexico.* Austin: University of Texas Press.

———. 2005. "A Standoffish Priest and Sticky Catholics: Questioning the Religious Marketplace in Tzintzuntzan, Mexico." *Journal of Latin American Anthropology* 10 (1): 1–26.

Calderón, Luisa María. 2001. "Parejas de Prostitutas-proxenetas y Roles de Pareja en una Comunidad Rural," ponencia presentada en la Mesa: Nuevos programas y cambios en salud reproductiva de la población mexicana. IV Reunión del SODEME, México.

Callon, Michel, and John Law. 2003. "On Qualculation, Agency and Otherness." Centre for Science Studies, Lancaster University. lancaster.ac.uk/fass/resources /sociology-online-papers/papers/callon-law-qualculation-agency-otherness.pdf.

Campbell, Howard. 2008. "Female Drug Smugglers on the US-Mexico Border: Gender, Crime, and Empowerment." *Anthropological Quarterly* 81 (1): 233–267.

———. 2009. *Drug War Zone: Frontline Dispatches from the Streets of El Paso and Juárez.* Austin: University of Texas Press.

———. 2014. "Narco-Propaganda in the Mexican 'Drug War': An Anthropological Perspective." *Latin American Perspectives* 41 (2): 60–77.

Campbell, Howard, and Tobin Hansen. 2014. "Is Narco-Violence in Mexico Terrorism?" *BLAR Bulletin of Latin American Research* 33 (2): 158–173.

Carrillo, Héctor. 2002. *The Night Is Young: Sexuality in Mexico in the Time of AIDS.* Chicago: University of Chicago Press.

Castañeda, Xochitl, Victor Ortiz, Betania Allen, Cecilia Garcia, and Mauricio Hernandez-Avila. 1996. "Sex Masks: The Double Life of Female Commercial Sex Workers in Mexico City." *Culture, Medicine and Psychiatry* 20 (2): 229.

Castillo, Debra A., María Gudelia Rangel Gómez, and Bonnie Delgado. 1999. "Border Lives: Prostitute Women in Tijuana." *Signs* 24 (2): 387–422.

Cattelino, Jessica R. 2008. *High Stakes: Florida Seminole Gaming and Sovereignty.* Durham, NC: Duke University Press.

Chapkis, W. 1997. *Live Sex Acts: Women Performing Erotic Labor.* New York: Routledge.

Cheng, Sealing. 2010. *On the Move for Love: Migrant Entertainers and the US Military in South Korea.* Philadelphia: University of Pennsylvania Press.

Chu, Julie Y. 2010. *Cosmologies of Credit: Transnational Mobility and the Politics of Destination in China.* Durham, NC: Duke University Press.

Cohen, Cathy J. 1997. "Punks, Bulldaggers, and Welfare Queens: The Radical Potential of Queer Politics?" *GLQ* 3 (4): 437–465.

———. 1999. *The Boundaries of Blackness: AIDS and the Breakdown of Black Politics.* Chicago: University of Chicago Press.

Cole, Jennifer. 2004. "Fresh Contact in Tamatave, Madagascar: Sex, Money, and Intergenerational Transformation." *American Ethnologist* 31 (4): 573–588.

Cole, Jennifer, and Lynn M. Thomas. 2009. *Love in Africa.* Chicago: University of Chicago Press.

Collier, Jane Fishburne, and Sylvia Junko Yanagisako. 1987. *Gender and Kinship: Essays toward a Unified Analysis*. Stanford, CA: Stanford University Press.

Comaroff, Jean, and John L. Comaroff. 2001. *Millennial Capitalism and the Culture of Neoliberalism*. Durham, NC: Duke University Press.

Combahee River Collective. 1986. *The Combahee River Collective Statement: Black Feminist Organizing in the Seventies and Eighties*. Albany, NY: Kitchen Table: Women of Color Press.

Cornyn, John. 2010. "Cornyn Says Spillover Violence in Texas Is Real and Escalating." PolitiFact Texas. March 17. politifact.com/texas/statements/2010/mar/27 /john-cornyn/cornyn-says-spillover-violence-texas-real-and-esca.

Crenshaw, Kimberlé. 1989. "Demarginalizing the Intersection of Race and Sex: A Black Feminist Critique of Antidiscrimination Doctrine, Feminist Theory and Antiracist Politics." *University of Chicago Legal Forum* 1989 (1): 139–168.

Crónica de Hoy. 2009. "Tres horas de balacera entre militares y sicarios en Reynosa." February 18. cronica.com.mx/notas/2009/415512.html.

Cruz, Ariane. 2016. *The Color of Kink: Black Women, BDSM, and Pornography*. New York: New York University Press.

Cruz Carretero, Sagrario del Carmen. 1989. "Identidad en una comunidad afromestiza del Centro de Veracruz; La población de Mata Clara." PhD diss., Universidad de la Américas, Puebla.

Curtis, James R., and Daniel D. Arreola. 1991. "Zonas de Tolerancia on the Northern Mexican Border." *Geographical Review* 81 (3): 333–346.

Davis, Angela. 2001 [1983]. *Women, Race and Class*. London: Women's Press.

De Beauvoir, Simone. 1953. *The Second Sex*. New York: Knopf.

De Genova, Nicholas. 2005. *Working the Boundaries: Race, Space, and "Illegality" in Mexican Chicago*. Durham, NC: Duke University Press.

De León, Jason. 2015. *Land of Open Graves: Living and Dying on the Migrant Trail*. Berkeley: University of California Press.

De Meis, Carla. 2002. "House and Street: Narratives of Identity in a Liminal Space among Prostitutes in Brazil." *Ethos* 30 (1–2): 3–24.

Derrida, Jacques. 1982. *Margins of Philosophy*. Translated by Alan Bass. Chicago: University of Chicago Press.

Dewey, Susan. 2011. *Neon Wasteland on Love, Motherhood, and Sex Work in a Rust Belt Town*. Berkeley: University of California Press.

Diaz-Cayeros, Alberto, Beatriz Magaloni, Aila Matanock, and Vidal Romero. 2011. "Living in Fear: Mapping the Social Embeddedness of Drug Gangs and Violence in Mexico." SSRN Scholarly Paper ID 1963836. Rochester, NY: Social Science Research Network.

Di Leonardo, Micaela. 1987. "The Female World of Cards and Holidays: Women, Families, and the Work of Kinship." *Signs* 12 (3): 440–453.

———. 1997. "White Lies, Black Myths: Rape, Race and the Black 'Underclass.'" In *The Gender/Sexuality Reader: Culture, History, Political Economy*, edited by Roger N. Lancaster and Micaela di Leonardo, 53–70. New York: Routledge.

Du Bois, W. E. B. 1903. *The Souls of Black Folk*. New York: Bantam Classic.

Ehrenreich, Barbara, and Arlie Russell Hochschild, eds. 2003. *Global Woman: Nannies, Maids and Sex Workers in the New Economy*. London: Granta.

Elisha, Omri. 2008. "Moral Ambitions of Grace: The Paradox of Compassion and Accountability in Evangelical Faith-Based Activism." *Cultural Anthropology* 23 (1): 154–189.

Eng, David L., Judith Halberstam, and José Esteban Muñoz, eds. 2005. "What's Queer about Queer Studies Now?" Special issue. *Social Text* 23 (3–4). Durham, NC: Duke University Press.

"En la pobreza, 47.4% de población en México." 2009. *El Economista*, June 19. elecono mista.com.mx/notas-online/politica/2009/07/19/pobreza-474-poblacion-mexico.

Erfani, Julie A. 1995. *The Paradox of the Mexican State: Rereading Sovereignty from Independence to NAFTA.* Boulder, CO: L. Rienner.

Espiritu, Yen Le. 2001. "'We Don't Sleep around like White Girls Do': Family, Culture, and Gender in Filipina American Lives." *Signs: Journal of Women in Culture and Society* 26, no. 2 (Winter 2001): 415–440.

Estrada, Luis. 2010. *El infierno.* Mexico: Bandidos Films: Distrimax, S.A. de C.V.

Fenster, Mark. 1999. *Conspiracy Theories: Secrecy and Power in American Culture.* Minneapolis: University of Minnesota Press.

Foster, Robert John. 2008. *Coca-Globalization: Following Soft Drinks from New York to New Guinea.* New York: Palgrave Macmillan.

Foucault, Michel. 1978. *The History of Sexuality.* New York: Pantheon Books.

———. 1995. *Discipline and Punish: The Birth of the Prison.* New York: Vintage Books.

Frank, Katherine. 2002. *G-strings and Sympathy: Strip Club Regulars and Male Desire.* Durham, NC: Duke University Press.

Freeman, Andy, and Pete Greig. 2007. *Punk Monk: New Monasticism and the Ancient Art of Breathing.* Ventura: Regal Books.

Freeman, Elizabeth. 2010. *Time Binds: Queer Temporalities, Queer Histories.* Durham, NC: Duke University Press.

"From Tulsa to Boystown: Walking the Streets with Kelly Greene." 2016. 24-7 Prayer International. January 16. 24-7prayer.com/blog/691/from-tulsa-to-boys-town -walking-the-streets-with-kelly-greene.

Gal, Susan. 2002. "A Semiotics of the Public/Private Distinction." *Differences: A Journal of Feminist Cultural Studies* 13 (1): 77–95.

Gamburd, Michele Ruth. 2000. *The Kitchen Spoon's Handle: Transnationalism and Sri Lanka's Migrant Housemaids.* Ithaca, NY: Cornell University Press.

Garza, James Alex. 2007. *The Imagined Underworld: Sex, Crime, and Vice in Porfirian Mexico City.* Lincoln: University of Nebraska Press.

Gilman, Sander. 1985. "Black Bodies, White Bodies: Toward an Iconography of Female Sexuality in Late 19th-century Art, Medicine, and Literature." *Critical Inquiry* 12 (1): 204–242.

Goffman, Erving. 1959. *The Presentation of Self in Everyday Life.* Garden City, NY: Doubleday.

———. 1961. *Asylums: Essays on the Social Situation of Mental Patients and Other Inmates.* Garden City, NY: Anchor Books.

———. 1963. *Stigma: Notes on the Management of Spoiled Identity.* Englewood Cliffs, NJ: Prentice-Hall.

Gould, Deborah B. 2009. *Moving Politics: Emotion and ACT UP's Fight Against AIDS.* Chicago: University of Chicago Press.

Government Accountability Office. 2006. "Illegal Immigration: Border-Crossing Deaths Have Doubled since 1995; Border Patrol's Efforts to Prevent Deaths Have Not Been Fully Evaluated. Report to the Honorable Bill Frist, Majority Leader, U.S. Senate."

Graeber, David. 2001. *Toward an Anthropological Theory of Value: The False Coin of Our Own Dreams*. New York: Palgrave.

Grant, Melissa Gira. 2014. *Playing the Whore: The Work of Sex Work*. London and New York: Verso Books.

Gregory, Chris A. 1982. *Gifts and Commodities*. London: Academic Press.

Griffith, David. 2009. "The Moral Economy of Tobacco." *American Anthropologist* 111 (4): 432–442.

Grinberg, Emanuella. 2004. "In Juarez Murders, Progress but Few Answers." April 9. cnn.com/2004/LAW/04/09/juarez.

Guerrero Gutiérrez, Eduardo. 2010. "Security, Drugs, and Violence in Mexico: A Survey." San Miguel de Allende: Sixth Annual North American Forum.

Guy, Donna J. 1991. *Sex and Danger in Buenos Aires: Prostitution, Family, and Nation in Argentina*. Lincoln: University of Nebraska Press.

Halberstam, Judith. 2005. *In a Queer Time and Place: Transgender Bodies, Subcultural Lives*. New York: New York University Press.

Hall, Kira. 1999. "Performativity." *Journal of Linguistic Anthropology* 9 (1–2): 184–187.

Hannem, Stacey, and Chris Bruckert. 2017. "'I'm Not a Pimp, but I Play One on TV': The Moral Career and Identity Negotiations of Third Parties in the Sex Industry." *Deviant Behavior* 38 (7): 824–836.

Hernandez, Jillian. 2014. "Carnal Teachings: Raunch Aesthetics as Queer Feminist Pedagogies in Yo! Majesty's Hip Hop Practice." *Women & Performance* 24 (1): 88–106.

Hartigan, John. 2005. *Odd Tribes: Toward a Cultural Analysis of White People*. Durham, NC: Duke University Press.

Herrmann, Gretchen M. 2015. "Valuing Affect: The Centrality of Emotion, Memory, and Identity in Garage Sale Exchange." *Anthropology of Consciousness* 26 (2): 170–181.

Heslop, Andrew. 2011. "Mexico, Pakistan Most Deadly Places for Journalists in 2010—WAN-IFRA." January 14. World Association of Newspapers and News Publishers. wan-ifra.org/articles/2011/01/14/mexico-pakistan-most-deadly-places-for-journalists-in-2010.

Heuertz, Christopher L. 2008. *Simple Spirituality: Learning to See God in a Broken World*. Downers Grove, IL: IVP Books.

Heyman, Josiah. 2004. "Ports of Entry as Nodes in the World System." *Identities: Global Studies in Power and Culture* 11 (3): 303–327.

Higginbotham, Evelyn Brooks. 1993. *Righteous Discontent: The Women's Movement in the Black Baptist Church, 1880–1920*. Cambridge, MA: Harvard University Press.

Hill Collins, Patricia. 2004. *Black Sexual Politics: African Americans, Gender, and the New Racism*. New York: Routledge.

Hirsch, Jennifer S., and Holly Wardlow, eds. 2006. *Modern Loves: The Anthropology of Romantic Courtship and Companionate Marriage*. Ann Arbor: University of Michigan Press.

Hoang, Kimberly Kay, and Rhacel Salazar Parreñas, eds. 2014. *Human Trafficking Reconsidered: Rethinking the Problem, Envisioning New Solutions*. New York: International Debate Education Association.

Hochschild, Arlie Russell. 2003 [1983]. *The Managed Heart: Commercialization of Human Feeling*. Berkeley: University of California Press.

hooks, bell. 1992. *Black Looks: Race and Representation*. Boston: South End Press.

Hoskins, Janet. 2002. "Predatory Voyeurs: Tourists and 'Tribal Violence' in Remote Indonesia." *American Ethnologist* 29 (4): 797–828.

Hunter, M. 2002. "The Materiality of Everyday Sex: Thinking Beyond 'Prostitution.'" *African Studies* 61 (1): 99–120.

Irvine, Judith T., and Susan Gal. 2000. "Language Ideology and Linguistic Differentiation." In *Regimes of Language: Ideologies, Polities, and Identities*, edited by Paul V. Kroskrity, 35–84. Santa Fe, NM: School of American Research Press.

Katsulis, Yasmina. 2009. *Sex Work and the City: The Social Geography of Health and Safety in Tijuana, Mexico*. Austin: University of Texas Press.

Keeley, Brian L. 1999. "Of Conspiracy Theories." *Journal of Philosophy* 96 (3): 109–126.

Kelly, Patty. 2008. *Lydia's Open Door: Inside Mexico's Most Modern Brothel*. Berkeley: University of California Press.

Kempadoo, Kamala, Jyoti Sanghera, and Bandana Pattanaik, eds. 2012. *Trafficking and Prostitution Reconsidered: New Perspectives on Migration, Sex Work, and Human Rights*. Boulder, CO: Paradigm.

Kirsch, Stuart. 2002. "Rumour and Other Narratives of Political Violence in West Papua." *Critique of Anthropology* 22 (1): 53–79.

Knobloch, Erin D. 2016. *Testimonio del Abismo: The Figuring and Disfiguring Effects of Trauma, Drugs, and Autobiography*. Master's thesis, University of Texas Rio Grande Valley.

Kockelman, P. 2006. "A Semiotic Ontology of the Commodity." *Journal of Linguistic Anthropology* 16 (1): 76–102.

Kovic, Christine, and Patty Kelly. 2006. "Fronteras seguras, cuerpos vulnerables: Migración y género en la frontera sur." *Debate Feminista* 33: 69–83.

Krause, Sharon R. 2015. *Freedom beyond Sovereignty: Reconstructing Liberal Individualism*. Chicago: University of Chicago Press.

Kulick, Don. 1998. *Travesti: Sex, Gender, and Culture among Brazilian Transgendered Prostitutes*. Chicago: University of Chicago Press.

Lacey, Marc. 2010. "Small Bomb Is Thrown at U.S. Post in Mexico." *New York Times*. April 11. nytimes.com/2010/04/11/world/americas/11mexico.html.

Lettieri, Michael. 2014. "Wheels of Government: The Alianza de Camioneros and the Political Culture of PRI Rule, 1929–1981.'" PhD diss., University of California San Diego.

Livingston, Jessica. 2004. "Murder in Juárez: Gender, Sexual Violence, and the Global Assembly Line." *Frontiers: A Journal of Women Studies* 25 (1): 59–76.

Lomnitz, Claudio, ed. 2000. "Vicios públicos, virtudes privadas—la corrupción en México." Mexico City: Centro de Investigaciones y Estudios Superiores en Antropología Social (CIESAS); Grupo Editorial Miguel Ángel Porrúa.

———. 2001. *Deep Mexico, Silent Mexico: An Anthropology of Nationalism*. Minneapolis: University of Minnesota Press.

López Díaz, Benito. 2008. "EnLineaDirecta.info—Registra Estancamiento La Planificación Familiar." July 13. enlineadirecta.info/index.php?option=view&article =59722.

Low, Setha M. 2016. *Spatializing Culture: The Ethnography of Space and Place*. New York: Routledge.

Luna, Sarah. 2005. "Ciudad Juárez, Reconsidered: Violence and the Problem of the Whore on the US/Mexico Border." Master's thesis, University of Chicago.

———. 2018. "Affective Atmospheres of Terror on the Mexico-US Border: Rumors of Violence in Reynosa's Prostitution Zone." *Cultural Anthropology* 33 (1): 58–84.

Lutz, Catherine A., and Jane L. Collins. 1998. *Reading National Geographic*. Chicago: University of Chicago Press.

Machado, Daisy L. 2003. *Of Borders and Margins: Hispanic Disciples in Texas, 1888–1945*. Oxford, UK: Oxford University Press.

———. 2006. "Women and Religion in the Borderlands." In *Encyclopedia of Women and Religion in North America*, edited by R. S. Keller, R. Radford Ruether, and M. Cantlon, 1134–1140. Bloomington: Indiana University Press.

Magaña, Rocio. 2011. "Dead Bodies: The Deadly Display of Mexican Border Politics." In *A Companion to the Anthropology of the Body and Embodiment*, edited by Frances E. Mascia-Lees, 157–171. Oxford: Wiley-Blackwell.

Malinowski, Bronislaw. 1962 [1929]. *The Sexual Life of Savages in North-western Melanesia: An Ethnographic Account of Courtship, Marriage, and Family Life Among the Natives of the Trobriand Islands, British New Guinea*. New York: Harcourt, Brace and World.

Manuel Meza, José. 2008. "Vivir de la 'maquila' un reto monumental." *Contralinea Tamaulipas*. tamaulipas.contralinea.com.mx/archivo/2008/julio/htm/vivir -de-maquila.htm.

Markell, Patchen. 2003. *Bound by Recognition*. Princeton, NJ: Princeton University Press.

Martínez Maranto, Alfredo. 1994. "Dios pinta como quiere: Identidad y cultura en un pueblo afromestizo de Veracruz." In *Presencia Africana en México*, edited by Luz María Martínez Montiel, 525–573. México D.F.: Consejo Nacional para la Cultura y las Artes.

Masquelier, Adeline. 2000. "Of Headhunters and Cannibals: Migrancy, Labor, and Consumption in the Mawri Imagination." *Cultural Anthropology* 15 (1): 84–126.

Mauss, Marcel. 1967. *The Gift: Forms and Functions of Exchange in Archaic Societies*. New York: Norton.

McClintock, Anne. 1992. "Screwing the System: Sexwork, Race, and the Law." *boundary 2* 19 (2): 70–95.

McDonald, James H. 1995. "NAFTA and the Milking of Dairy Farmers in Central Mexico." *Culture and Agriculture* 15 (51–52): 13–18.

———. 2005. "The Narcoeconomy and Small-town, Rural Mexico." *Human Organization: Journal of the Society for Applied Anthropology* 64 (2): 115–125.

Meiu, George Paul. 2015. "'Beach-Boy Elders' and 'Young Big-Men': Subverting the Temporalities of Ageing in Kenya's Ethno-Erotic Economies." *Ethnos* 80 (4): 472–496.

———. 2017. *Ethno-erotic Economies: Sexuality, Money, and Belonging in Kenya*. Chicago: University of Chicago Press.

Milenio. 2010. "Turismo Cayó 40% Este Año, Dice Director Estatal de Promoción." milenio.com/cdb/doc/noticias2011/d9733f1d182257206a2cdeac4ffofe06.

Miller-Young, Mireille. 2015. *A Taste for Brown Sugar: Black Women in Pornography*. Durham, NC: Duke University Press.

Mitchell, Gregory Carter. 2016. *Tourist Attractions: Performing Race and Masculinity in Brazil's Sexual Economy*. Chicago: University of Chicago Press.

Moll, Rob. 2005. "The New Monasticism." September 25. *Christianity Today*. christianitytoday.com/ct/2005/september/16.38.html.

Molzahn, Cory, Viridiana Rios, and David A. Shirk. 2013. "Drug Violence in Mexico: Data and Analysis through 2012." Special report, Justice in Mexico Project. San Diego, CA: Trans-Border Institute. justiceinmexico.org/drug-violence-in-mexico-data-and-analysis-through-2012.

Montiel Torres, Óscar. 2009. "Trata de Personas: Padrotes, Iniciación y Modus Opernadi." Master's thesis, Instituto Nacional de las Mujeres.

Mora, Anthony P. 2011. *Border Dilemmas: Racial and National Uncertainties in New Mexico, 1848–1912*. Durham, NC: Duke University Press.

Muehlmann, Shaylih. 2013. *When I Wear My Alligator Boots: Narco-Culture in the US-Mexico Borderlands*. Berkeley: University of California Press.

Munn, Nancy D. 1986. *The Fame of Gawa: A Symbolic Study of Value Transformation in a Massim (Papua New Guinea) Society*. Cambridge, UK: Cambridge University Press.

Navaro-Yashin, Yael. 2002. *Faces of the State: Secularism and Public Life in Turkey*. Princeton, NJ: Princeton University Press.

Nesvig, Martin. 2000. "The Lure of the Perverse: Moral Negotiation of Pederasty in Porfirian Mexico." *Mexican Studies/Estudios Mexicanos Mexican Studies/Estudios Mexicanos* 16 (1): 1–37.

Norget, Kristin. 1997. "The Politics of Liberation: The Popular Church, Indigenous Theology, and Grassroots Mobilization in Oaxaca, Mexico." *Latin American Perspectives* 24 (5): 96–127.

NSWP (Global Network of Sex Worker Projects). 2016. Policy Brief: The Decriminalization of Third Parties. nswp.org/resource/policy-brief-the-decriminalisation-third-Parties.

Olivo, Antonio. 2008. "Calderon Pledges to Boost Economy." *Chicago Tribune*. February 13. articles.chicagotribune.com/2008-02-13/news/0802120689_1_mexican-president-felipe-calderon-us-mexico-border-mexican-schools.

Osborn, James. 2008. "Mexico: Drug War Means an Early Night in Reynosa." *McAllen (TX) Monitor*. February 9. mapinc.org/drugnews/v08/n161/a01.html?397.

Padilla, Mark B., Jennifer S. Hirsch, Miguel Muñoz-Laboy, Robert E. Sember, and Richard G. Parker. 2007. *Love and Globalization: Transformations of Intimacy in the Contemporary World*. Nashville, TN: Vanderbilt University Press.

Parreñas, Rhacel Salazar. 2001. *Servants of Globalization: Women, Migration and Domestic Work*. Stanford, CA: Stanford University Press.

Passel, Jeffrey, and D'Vera Cohn. 2009. "Mexican Immigrants: How Many Come? How Many Leave?" Pew Research Center: Hispanic Trends. July 22. pewhispanic.org/2009/07/22/mexican-immigrants-how-many-come-how-many-leave.

Paz, Octavio. 1961. *The Labyrinth of Solitude: Life and Thought in Mexico*. Translated by Lysander Kemp. New York: Grove Press.

Pérez Arellano, Raymundo. 2013. "Testimony #1: 'We Got Out of Tamaulipas Alive.'"

Dissident Blog. March 9. dissidentblog.org/en/articles/testimony-1-we-got-out
-tamaulipas-alive.

Pheterson, Gail. 1986. *The Whore Stigma: Female Dishonor and Male Unworthiness.*
The Hague: Ministerie van Sociale Zaken en Werkgelegenheid.

Polanyi, Karl. 1957. *The Great Transformation.* Boston: Beacon Press.

Povinelli, Elizabeth A. 1997. "Sex Acts and Sovereignty: Race and Sexuality in the
Construction of the Australian Nation." In *The Gender/Sexuality Reader: Cul-
ture, History, Political Economy,* edited by Roger N. Lancaster and Micaela di
Leonardo, 513–530. New York: Routledge.

Priest, Robert J., and Brian M. Howell. 2013. "Introduction: Theme Issue on Short-
Term Missions." *Missiology: An International Review* 41 (2): 124–129.

"Publica Diario Oficial salarios mínimos para 2008." 2007. *El Universal.* December 27. eluniversal.com.mx/notas/470546.html.

Ramirez, Antonio. 2009. "Sin Opciones: Cansada de la vida, adolescente se cuelga."
La Tarde de Reynosa. June 11.

Ramsey, Geoffrey. 2011. "Video: 'Highway of Death' Runs Past Mass Graves in
Northern Mexico." In Sight: Organized Crime in the Americas. April 13. web
.archive.org/web/20120305141108/http://insightcrime.org/insight-latest-news
/item/773-video-highway-of-death-runs-past-mass-graves-in-northern-mexico.

"Repudian abusos por operativos en Reynosa, Tamaulipas." 2008. *Proceso.* January 31. proceso.com.mx/?p=196410.

Restall, Matthew. 2009. *The Black Middle: Africans, Mayas, and Spaniards in Colonial Yucatan.* Stanford, CA: Stanford University Press.

Richard, Analiese, and Daromir Rudnyckyj. 2009. "Economies of Affect." *Journal of
the Royal Anthropological Institute* 15 (1): 57–77.

Rivers-Moore, Megan. 2016. *Gringo Gulch: Sex, Tourism, and Social Mobility in
Costa Rica.* Chicago: University of Chicago Press.

Roig-Franzia, Manuel. 2008. "Drug Cartels' Reign of Terror on Border." *Seattle
Times.* March 22. seattletimes.com/nation-world/drug-cartels-reign-of-terror-on
-border/.

Rossiaud, Jacques. 1988. *Medieval Prostitution.* New York: Blackwell.

Rubin, Gayle. 1975. "The Traffic in Women: Notes on the 'Political Economy' of Sex."
In *Toward an Anthropology of Women,* edited by Rayna R. Reiter, 157–210. New
York: Monthly Review Press.

Rutherford, Danilyn. 2012. *Laughing at Leviathan: Sovereignty and Audience in
West Papua.* Chicago: University of Chicago Press.

Ryan, Johnny. 2008. "World's Finest Mexico Jokes." Cartoon. *Vice* 15 (6). The Mexican Issue.

Sahlins, Marshall. 1974. *Stone Age Economics.* London: Tavistock Publications.

Sánchez, Martín, David Carrizales, Carlos Camacho, and Raymundo León. 2007.
"Asesinan en Río Bravo a ex eiputado y 5 acompañantes." *La Jornada.* November 30. jornada.unam.mx/2007/11/30/index.php?section=politica&article=022n2
pol.

Sandoval, Chela. 2000. *Methodology of the Oppressed.* Minneapolis: University of
Minnesota Press.

Schein, Louisa. 1994. The Consumption of Color and the Politics of White Skin in
Post-Mao China. *Social Text* 41 (Winter 1994): 14–35.

Schilt, Kristen, and Laurel Westbrook. 2009. "Doing Gender, Doing Heteronormativity: 'Gender Normals,' Transgender People, and the Social Maintenance of Heterosexuality." *Gender and Society* 23 (4): 440–464.

Schneider, Rachel. 2018. "A Web of Subversive Friends: New Monasticism in the United States and South Africa." *Religions* 9 (6): 184.

Scott, James C. 1976. *The Moral Economy of the Peasant: Rebellion and Subsistence in Southeast Asia.* New Haven, CT: Yale University Press.

Shimizu, Celine Parreñas. 2007. *The Hypersexuality of Race: Performing Asian/American Women on Screen and Scene.* Durham, NC: Duke University Press.

Silverstein, Michael. 1993. "Metapragmatic Discourse and Metapragmatic Function." In *Reflexive Language: Reported Speech and Metapragmatics*, edited by John Arthur Lucy, 9–32. New York: Cambridge University Press.

Simmel, Georg. 1971. *On Individuality and Social Forms; Selected Writings.* Chicago: University of Chicago Press.

———. 1978 [1900]. *The Philosophy of Money.* London and Boston: Routledge and Kegan Paul.

Snorton, C. Riley, and Jin Haritaworn. 2013. "Trans Necropolitics: A Transnational Reflection on Violence, Death, and the Trans of Color Afterlife." In *The Transgender Studies Reader 2*, edited by Susan Stryker and Aren Z. Aizura, 66–76. London: Routledge.

Somerville, Siobhan. 1994. "Scientific Racism and the Emergence of the Homosexual Body." *Journal of the History of Sexuality* 5 (2): 243–266.

Stevenson, Mark. 2010. "8 Reporters Kidnapped in Reynosa, Press Group Says." *Brownsville (TX) Herald.* March 11. brownsvilleherald.com/article_94d19cc5-eef7-5972-aec5-34716e18f581.html.

Stewart, Kathleen. 1999. "Conspiracy Theory's Worlds." In *Paranoia within Reason: A Casebook on Conspiracy as Explanation*, edited by George E. Marcus, 13–19. Chicago: University of Chicago Press.

———. 2007. *Ordinary Affects.* Durham, NC: Duke University Press.

Stoler, Ann Laura. 1997. "Carnal Knowledge and Imperial Power: Gender, Race, and Morality in Colonial Asia." In *The Gender/Sexuality Reader: Culture, History, Political Economy*, edited by Roger N. Lancaster and Micaela di Leonardo, 13–36. New York: Routledge.

Storistic.blogspot.com. "The Mythical Donkey Show." 2003. February 7. storistic .blogspot.com/2012/02/mythical-donkey-show.html.

Stout, Noelle M. 2014. *After Love: Queer Intimacy and Erotic Economies in Post-Soviet Cuba.* Durham, NC: Duke University Press.

Strathern, Marilyn. 1988. *The Gender of the Gift: Problems with Women and Problems with Society in Melanesia.* Berkeley: University of California Press.

Sue, Christina. 2010. "Racial Ideologies, Racial-Group Boundaries, and Racial Identity in Veracruz, Mexico." *Latin American and Caribbean Ethnic Studies* 5 (3): 273–299.

———. 2013. *Land of the Cosmic Race: Race Mixture, Racism, and Blackness in Mexico.* New York: Oxford University Press.

Taniguchi, Hanako. 2011. "Veracruz y Estado de México, las entidades con el mayor aumento de pobres." CNN. August 1. expansion.mx/nacional/2011/08/01/veracruz-y-estado-de-mexico-las-entidades-con-el-mayor-numero-de-pobres.

Taussig, Michael. 1984. "Culture of Terror—Space of Death. Roger Casement's Putumayo Report and the Explanation of Torture." *Comparative Studies in Society and History* 26 (3): 467–497.

———. 1986. *Shamanism, Colonialism, and the Wild Man: A Study in Terror and Healing.* Chicago: University of Chicago Press.

Taylor, Jared. 2008. "Days after Mexican President Denounces Crime, Banners Accuse Administration of Corruption." *McAllen (TX) Monitor.* August 29.

Thompson, E. P. 1971. "The Moral Economy of the English Crowd in the Eighteenth Century." *Past and Present* no. 50: 76–136.

Torres, Alberto. 2011. "Choferes eluden la 'vía de la muerte.'" *El Universal.* April 13. archivo.eluniversal.com.mx/nacion/184735.html.

Vila, Pablo. 2000. *Crossing Borders, Reinforcing Borders: Social Categories, Metaphors, and Narrative Identities on the US-Mexico Frontier.* Austin: University of Texas Press.

Villagran, Lauren. 2011. "Mexico Suffers Stiff Income Inequality, Despite Improvement." *Smart Planet.* December 7. smartplanet.com/blog/global-observer/mexico-suffers-stiff-income-inequality-despite-improvement/1007.

Vite Pérez, Miguel Ángel. 2014. "Reflexiones sobre la violencia y vulnerabilidad en México." *Espiral (Guadalajara)* 21 (61): 227–258.

Wardlow, Holly. 2006. *Wayward Women: Sexuality and Agency in a New Guinea Society.* Berkeley: University of California Press.

Warner, Michael, ed., for Social Text Collective. 1993. *Fear of a Queer Planet: Queer Politics and Social Theory.* Minneapolis: University of Minnesota Press.

Weiner, Annette B. 1992. *Inalienable Possessions: The Paradox of Keeping-While-Giving.* Berkeley: University of California Press.

Weitzer, Ronald, Sheldon X. Zhang, Anthony Marcus, Amber Horning, Ric Curtis, Jo Sanson, and Efram Thompson. 2014. "Conflict and Agency among Sex Workers and Pimps: A Closer Look at Domestic Minor Sex Trafficking." *Annals of the American Academy of Political and Social Science* 653 (1): 225–246.

Wentzell, Emily. 2014. "'I Help Her, She Helps Me': Mexican Men Performing Masculinity through Transactional Sex." *Sexualities* 17 (7): 856–871.

White, Luise. 1997. "The Traffic in Heads: Bodies, Borders and the Articulation of Regional Histories." *Journal of South Asian Studies* 23 (2) 325–338.

Whittaker, Matt. 2006. "Labor of Love?" *McAllen (TX) Monitor.* April 17.

Wilkinson, Tracy. 2011. "Mexico Mass Graves: Body Count from Mass Graves Reaches 145." *Los Angeles Times.* April 15. latimes.com/world/la-xpm-2011-apr-15-la-fg-mexico-bodies-20110416-story.html.

Wright, Melissa W. 1998. "Maquiladora Mestizas and a Feminist Border Politics: Revisiting Anzaldúa." *Hypatia* 13 (3): 114–131.

———. 1999. "The Dialectics of Still Life: Murder, Women, and Maquiladoras." *Public Culture: Bulletin of the Project for Transnational Cultural Studies* 11 (3): 453.

———. 2004. "From Protests to Politics: Sex Work, Women's Worth, and Ciudad Juárez Modernity." *Annals of the Association of American Geographers* 94 (2): 369–386.

———. 2011. "Necropolitics, Narcopolitics, and Femicide: Gendered Violence on the Mexico U.S. Border." *Signs* 36 (3): 707–731.

Yeh, Rihan. 2012. "Two Publics in a Mexican Border City." *Cultural Anthropology* 27 (4): 713–734.

————. 2018. *Passing: Two Publics in a Mexican Border City.* Chicago: University of Chicago Press.

Zelizer, Viviana A. 1994. *The Social Meaning of Money.* New York: Basic Books.

————. 2000. "The Purchase of Intimacy." *Law and Social Inquiry* 25 (3): 817–848.

Zerilli, Linda M. G. 2005. *Feminism and the Abyss of Freedom.* Chicago: University of Chicago Press.

Zheng, Tiantian. 2009. *Red Lights: The Lives of Sex Workers in Postsocialist China.* Minneapolis: University of Minnesota Press.

Index

escalation of violence, 3, 9–10, 70, 198–199; impact on la zona, overview, 202–204; protests against military, coerced, 80–81, 197. *See also* death and violence, fear of

mission (Team Boystown): affiliations, 24–25; donations and support, 140, 168, 171; inception of, 4–5; missionaries as mediators of prayer, 125, 155–160, 185–192; outcomes and followup, 199–202; success narratives, 185–192. *See also* goals of Boystown mission; missionaries, short-term; missionary/sex worker/God triadic relationship

missionaries, short-term: benefits of mission successes, 191–194; borderland history of, 23; departure from Reynosa, 83–84, 192; inspiration and compulsion to work, 142–143, 154, 167; modern movements, 23–25; projects in Boystown, 4–5, 127, 152–153

missionary/sex worker/God triadic relationship: characterization of, 168–169; idiomatic concepts and acts of love, 149–155; nonsovereignty in, 149; sex worker narratives, and missionaries' goals, 155–160, 163–168; success narratives, 185–192

mistresses, prostitutes as, 57–58

Mitchell, Gregory, 20

mobility, importance of, 34–35, 51, 63, 82, 104, 140

monastery project by "Team Boystown," 5, 83, 142, 154

Montiel Torres, Óscar, 104–105, 106

moral careers: concept overview, 42; drug trade, characterization of, 63–67; of drug-using sex workers, 119–121; drug workers and sex workers, gendered valuation of, 59–63, 68; and normalization of death, 17, 45, 65–67; of *padroteras*, 112, 116. *See also* respectability, moral hierarchies of

moral economies: border situation overview, 16, 41–43, 68; "easy money" stigma of Boystown sex

workers, 52–59; of la zona, 123, 129, 132–135; in Reynosa, 11. *See also* respectability, moral hierarchies of

moral hierarchies. *See* respectability, moral hierarchies of

moral individualism, 145

moral/material care double bind, 94–96, 100

moral panic around prostitution, 21, 202

motherhood, obligations of: double lives, negotiating, 91, 96–100; dynamics of, examples, 89–91; failures of and drug/alcohol addiction, 63, 100, 117, 121–130, 130–135; material/moral care double bind, 94–96, 100; and pimps' motivations for fathering children, 107, 114; respectable mother/prostitute dichotomy, 91–94, 166; single mother perspective, 18; and social hierarchy of sex workers, 18, 19, 117–118; and triadic relationships, 155, 169. *See also* children of la zona; familial obligations

motivations of sex workers, 2–3, 30, 94, 102, 116, 214n7

Moynihan, Daniel Patrick, 118

Muehlmann, Shaylih, 2, 62

Munn, Nancy, 148, 206–207n13, 216n2

murders: drug trade related, 9–10, 64, 79, 198–199, 201; femicides in Ciudad Juárez, 17, 30–31, 45, 67; and normalization of death, 17, 45, 65–67. *See also* death and violence, fear of

names, given vs. alias. *See* alias identities and double life challenges

narcocorridos (ballads heroizing drug traffickers), 61, 73–74

narcoeconomy and effects of neoliberalism, 8

narcos. *See* drug trade

nationalism/national identity (Mexican) and border cities, 43, 45–46

"necessary evil": border industries, 43–44; drug trade as, 60–63; prostitution as, 19, 53, 56–60; vice as, 68